Changing Meat Cultures

Changing Meat Cultures

Food Practices, Global Capitalism, and the Consumption of Animals

Edited by
Arve Hansen and Karen Lykke Syse

ROWMAN & LITTLEFIELD
Lanham • Boulder • New York • London

Published by Rowman & Littlefield
An imprint of The Rowman & Littlefield Publishing Group, Inc.
4501 Forbes Boulevard, Suite 200, Lanham, Maryland 20706
www.rowman.com

86-90 Paul Street, London EC2A 4NE

British Library Cataloguing in Publication Information Available

Library of Congress Cataloging-in-Publication Data Available

ISBN 978-1-5381-4265-3 (cloth)
ISBN 978-1-5381-6427-3 (pbk.)
ISBN 978-1-5381-4266-0 (electronic)

Contents

List of Figures and Table

FIGURES

TABLE

Chapter 1

New Meat Engagements

Cultures, Geographies, Economies

Arve Hansen and Karen Lykke Syse

Within the last two generations, meat consumption has changed dramatically across the world. Not only do we eat more meat, we eat different meats than we used to (see Milford et al. 2019). During the second half of the 1900s, these changes were at first fairly subtle and not particularly culturally invasive or dramatic. In many countries, they were perhaps associated with a general growth in affluence, a change to the better, a change to a new day and age in which penny-pinching and hard times were exchanged with more material comfort. This was not a novelty in itself; in most countries, meat consumption has been a sign of social status, and a high level of meat consumption has generally signaled the social distinction of the meat eater. Three decades ago, the sociologist Nick Fiddes (1991, 13) wrote that "time and again, in different contexts, cultures, social groups, and periods of history, meat is supreme," tying the income bracket directly to the amount of animal products people included in their diets. This causality does not necessarily hold true today. First of all, cutting back on meat consumption can equally be an elite activity. We have long known this from countries like India—home to more than a sixth of the global population—where vegetarianism is firmly embedded in many food practices and has a strong hold among elites. But over the recent decades various versions of meat reduction has become increasingly common also in a range of affluent societies (see Mylan 2018; Ruby 2012). Second, global feed trade and the industrialization of animal killing have made meat more affordable to much larger segments of a rapidly growing global population. In many ways, although still in highly unequal ways, what used to be an elite activity has been democratized.

Although meat consumption has been on a steady rise globally, it is very unevenly spread, and the poorest countries in the world eat little of it compared to the wealthiest. Among the most meat-intense diets, the average U.S.

citizen eats 101.1 kilos of meat every year. By comparison, the average person in Africa's most populous country, Nigeria, eats 3.5 kilos of meat every year while the average person in India only eats 4.4 kilos of meat (OECD 2021). Although meat consumption on average and to some extent tends to increase with affluence, the relationship between meat consumption and income is not clear-cut, and there are large variations between countries at similar income levels (Mathijs 2015; see also Hansen 2018). Furthermore, while some of the richest countries in recent years have seen a slight decrease in per capita meat consumption, many middle-income countries have seen dramatic increases. Most of the increase in global meat consumption now takes place in the Global South, but again the trend is unevenly spread. While African countries with some exceptions tend to have low per capita meat consumption levels, many Latin American countries have seen surging meat consumption, and India is the exception more than the rule if we look at recent trends in Asia (OECD 2021). China's meat boom and all its complex local and global consequences is most notable, as discussed in several chapters in this volume (see also Schneider 2017, 2019). In sum, daily consumption of meat used to be confined to rich countries, but has over the past 50 years become a global phenomenon.

Although in highly uneven ways, meat has moved from the periphery to the center of human diets, a process Tony Weis (2013) has conceptualized as "meatification." Questioning the democratization of meat consumption is not a task we wish to instigate, however, our culinary cultural response to the possibilities that democratization has enabled is ripe for discussion. The changes have been intense, immersive, and changed the way we eat, buy, kill, and keep animals (Bjørkdahl and Syse 2013, 2021; Patchirat 2013; Syse and Bjørkdahl 2021). In short, meat cultures have changed. As the authors in this volume will explore, meat cultures are heterogeneous. Nevertheless, there are some general traits concerning what and how we eat that we can use as a baseline. Brillat-Savarin (1848) was perhaps the first in Western food discourse that explored foods' distinguishing qualities. Pierre Bourdieu (1984) later focused both on distinctions and its connected social practices and found that what we eat shapes, and is shaped by, our identity, our social belonging, and our cultural standing. Claude Lévi-Strauss (1970) argued that the preparation of food constitutes a kind of language that explains a society's structure, using the various forms of transformations of food from nature to culture as a starting point. The anthropologist Mary Douglas (1975) emphasized the role of food within "small scale social relations" rather than in grand structures. The list could go on, but the point is to show that in analyzing meat cultures, we are indebted to a rich tradition of social and cultural inquiry that has disentangled the complexity of food and its pivotal position in society.

Food is deeply cultural, and so is meat. Annie Potts (2016) sees meat culture as the lived expression of the violent ideology labeled by psychologist Melanie Joy as "carnism," an invisible belief system that naturalizes the consumption of (certain types of) animals. Potts furthermore defines and specifies meat culture as the "shared beliefs about, perspectives on, and experiences of meat," developed through "representations and discourses, practices and behaviours, diets and tastes" (Potts 2016, 20). She highlights that meat culture is dynamic and context-specific, and this is also our point of departure. Yet meat cultures vary to such an extent that we prefer using the plural form. While acknowledging the subjectivity and individual suffering of nonhuman animals, we are also particularly interested in understanding how these animals become part of industrialized meat cultures. As the contributions in this book investigate, these meat cultures shape and are shaped by the expansion of global capitalism, particularly through the globalization of industrialized animal killing and standardization of meat products embedded in this expansion. But the contributions also show that industrial meat cultures may produce potentials for radical change away from the contemporary factory farms. The mass suffering embedded in this model produces reactions from consumers and new opportunities for producers, and alternative ways of eating and producing meat and meat replacements may bring about revolutionary changes.

CHANGING MEAT CULTURES

The general increase in wealth and thus food options in high- and middle-income countries has driven our food practices in a particular direction. Although we can decide whether we would like to eat fish, meat, cereals, or vegetables, and prepare these foods using inspiration from a global cuisine, the numbers tell us that we more often than before tend to opt for meat. Meat has entered the center stage, and particularly two kinds of meat: pork and chicken. Our starting point is that these decisions are an expression of the social practices and material contexts where they take place, including the complex systems involved in producing, distributing and selling the food we eat. The increasing dominance of capitalist relations in food production and provision around the world has led to particular outcomes. While the encounters between global capitalism and local meat cultures generally create hybrid food cultures, they have an increasing reliance on industrial scaled animal slaughter in common.

The idea of this book came from observing the different expressions of these processes from different perspectives and in highly different contexts. If we start in Vietnam, a middle-income country and "emerging economy" in Southeast Asia where one of the editors has lived during several periods, meat was until quite recently a relatively rare treat. Many Vietnamese people remember a time when meat was something mainly consumed on special occasions. Compare that to the bourgeoning meat markets in the streets of contemporary Vietnamese cities, or the supermarket shelves full of fresh and frozen meat and processed meat products. Or to the rich servings of meat in the most affordable of street food meals, or to the fried chicken at KFC, or to the many new steak houses, or to the generous plates of meat at barbeques at the many different local or Korean-inspired restaurants. In just a few decades Vietnamese food practices changed from almost meatless to often meat-intense. The many delicacies that have made Vietnamese food famous around the world tend to all have meat in them. These changes did not happen by chance. They have taken place alongside large-scale economic and social transformations in the country, and are the result of both planned and unplanned development processes. Until quite recently, Vietnam was a very poor country suffering from severe food insecurity, the outcome of French and U.S. imperialism and a largely unsuccessful socialist planned economy. Since the 1980s, however, the Leninist-capitalist hybrid model embraced by the ruling Communist Party has resulted in Vietnam becoming one of the world's biggest "development success stories" (see London 2020). Agriculture has been at the center of these changes, including a rapidly expanding meat industry. But so has trade agreements, which see cheap, frozen meat arriving in large quantities from other countries, often from the other side of the globe. At the same time, food practices have changed. For example, it has become common for the urban middle classes to eat out several times a day, and they have a wealth of options, ranging from street food to high-end restaurants. Gradually, but rapidly, meat, and especially pork, has become a normal part of most meals. Also the consumption of, chicken is increasingly normalised, as cheap, frozen chicken, produced by the rapidly upscaling domestic meat industry or imported from industrial systems elsewhere, make it to most corners of the country. The meatification of Vietnamese diets has both happened through new culinary imports and, most importantly, through the gradual meat intensification of "traditional" dishes and practices (Hansen 2018).

Jump back to the late 1970s to Norway, where the editors of this volume live. In the supermarket meat counters, rotisseries appeared—a smoking hot cupboard filled with golden roast chickens, dripping juices and fat, swirling around until they were cooked, detached from their hooks, and placed under a hot lamp, steaming fragrances to entice customers to put this ready-cooked, easily accessible, and totally new food stuff into their trolley. The smell of roast chicken became the smell of grocery shopping. Chicken went from being a rare foodstuff to becoming one of the most common foods served in Norway, and the only food Norwegians eat more of is pork (Helsedirektoratet

2017). This is due to a general increase in wealth in Norwegian society, but has also been enabled by global feed imports. These same imports have allowed a massive growth in pork production. Pork is cheap, plentiful, served throughout the year, throughout the week most every day. It has an important role in the fast-food market; ham is placed on pizzas, bacon covers chargrilled burgers, and hot dogs made of pork are sold in every Norwegian petrol station. It is a family summer staple in the shape of pork sausages, chops and filets on the barbeque, and as hams and cured meats at breakfast tables. Its consumption has been heavily promoted by the equivalent to the Norwegian meat lobby, The Marketing Board for Meat and Eggs. Today it is also added to foods that used to be culturally significant to Norwegians, like fish dumplings and lutefisk.[1] Even former vegetarian dishes like vegetable soup are presented with added sausage meat. A diet that used to be rich in fish and cereals has become meat rich: In 1959, Norwegian farmers produced 2.9 million kilos poultry per annum. By 2017, the number had risen to 104.1 million kilos. The numbers for pork show a similar development in the same time period; the production of pork went from 48.2 to 137.3 million kilos. If we take all categories of meat into consideration, the expansion in the same period was from 118.9 to 354.5 million kilos (Helsedirektoratet 2017). Most of this is consumed domestically, and Norway imports considerably more meat than it exports (Animalia 2020). Norway has recently approached the average European level of meat consumption. The sociologists Gunnar Vitterso and Unni Kjærnes explain this astonishing growth by the particular political economy of meat in Norway, in which "concrete political measures combined with extensive marketing" have led to a "politics of meat promotion." Until fairly recently, neither the environmental nor consumer movements have addressed this issue (Vitterso and Kjærnes 2015).

It might seem peculiar to project the changes in culinary culture in a large Asian country and small Scandinavian country to exemplify our claim. However in all its diversity, if there is one thing food practices globally have in common, it is that they on average have become increasingly meat-intense and that this meat comes from industrial animal killing. For example, an estimated 75 percent of pig and poultry production globally comes from industrial systems (Herrero et al. 2015). This in turn has implications for a complex web of factors, including health, animal well-being, and environmental impacts (see Winders and Ransom 2019; Godfray et al. 2018).

INDUSTRIALIZED ANIMAL KILLING

The number of animals killed for human consumption annually is still on the rise almost everywhere and is now the highest it has ever been in history. Food and Agriculture Organization of the United Nations (FAO) (2021) estimates that in 2019, the more than 80 billion animals slaughtered globally included 130,000 mules, 3 million camels, 4.9 million horses, 27.7 million buffalos, 324.5 million cows, 502.8 million goats, 603.2 million sheep, 633 million rabbits, 636 million turkeys, 723.6 million geese and guinea fowl, 1.3 billion pigs, 3.3 billion ducks, and a staggering 72.1 billion chicken. The numbers are hard to fathom. But so is the speed of the increase of the global meat industry. If we compare the numbers to 1979, there has been a quadrupling of animals slaughtered in 40 years. By comparison, the global population less than doubled in the same period, from 4.4 billion to 7.7 billion (World Bank 2021).

Scholarship on the meat industry has expanded in recent times, with scholars mapping and investigating the histories (Josephson 2020; Specht 2019), political economies (Howard 2019; Weis 2013), geographies (Jakobsen and Hansen 2020; Neo and Emel 2017), and political ecologies (Emel and Neo 2015) of industrial meat, as well its impacts on human and nonhuman animals and environments (Blanchette 2020, 2018; Winders and Ransom 2019). Others have investigated the trends and drivers of changing meat consumption patterns (Sans and Combris 2015; Milford et al. 2019), and their connections to changes in the production and provision of meat (Hansen and Jakobsen 2020). Simultaneously, large fields of research have developed around Human-Animal Studies and Critical Animal Studies (see Calarco 2021), where particularly the latter tend to directly challenge dominant meat cultures (Potts 2016; Calarco 2020). In this book, we build on existing scholarship to investigate changing meat cultures from a range of disciplines and in widely different contexts. The contributors investigate both meatification and demeatification, and topics range from global trade flows to local eating practices, and from meat production to alternative proteins. The contributions look into the normalization of meat eating in key emerging economies in Asia, as well as the international impacts of these changes. They look into the histories and potential futures of meat. But they all have in common the focus on changing meat cultures in the context of global capitalist expansion.

FOOD PRACTICES, GLOBAL CAPITALISM, AND THE CONSUMPTION OF ANIMALS

Industrial animal agriculture generally reduces the lives of animals to that of things. Many find this practice hard to justify morally, and the effects of industrial animal husbandry on animal welfare were first made public by Ruth Harrison. In 1964, in her now classic statement *Animal Machines*, she argued that industrial agriculture inflicted severe suffering on farm animals (Harrison 1964). In part due to Harrison's intervention, the field of animal ethics would later form, starting with philosopher Peter Singer's (1975) *Animal Liberation*. While certain steps have been taken toward improving the welfare of animals in industrial meat production in later years, these efforts are local rather than global, and we argue that industrial meat production still represents a moral problem both in the Global North and the Global South.[2]

The increasingly industrial character of meat production has entailed significant changes to the relations we have to the animals we eat. In the chapter that follows, Bjørkdahl and Syse describe some of the practices and rituals that characterized farm slaughter in rural Norway up to the first decades of the twentieth century. In this period, Norwegians drew on various cultural tools like rituals to make the killing of an animal meaningful and acceptable. Then, by exploring the original impetus toward "humane slaughter" in the early to mid-twentieth century, they show how the ritual transformations of animals into meat gave way to laws and regulations to justify animal killing. The idea that one needed a justification to transform animals into meat has been left in what today is a secular society. As long as the laws and regulations are in place, and the actors in the meat industry abide by them, the problem is culturally "outsourced" and judicialized; a process that has enabled the widespread denial of the animal origin of meat. One might ask whether this is a wider, international trend. Has a transition from cultural justification to judicialized legal frameworks for the humane treatment of animals enabled more people to turn a blind eye to the global meat industry? And has this process been significant for consumers to become easy receptacles to the meat industries' massive growth?

As stated in the beginning of this chapter, while the most affluent countries consume much more meat per capita than the rest of the world, it is the Global South that drives the current expansion in global meat production and consumption. In the subsequent chapter, Hansen, Jakobsen, and Wethal use Tony Weis's (2013) concept of the "industrial grain-oilseed-livestock complex" to analyze the increasingly important role of the South in the global meat industry. By analyzing the meat complex in five leading emerging economies, the so-called BRICS (Brazil, Russia, India, China, and South Africa), the authors show how emerging economies are ever more dominant in the ongoing reconfiguration of the global food system. By examining the role of states and businesses within the BRICS, they explore what increasing multipolarity in global meat entails and how it unfolds. They analyze the role of the BRICS countries in feed crops and the production and consumption of pork, beef, and poultry; systematically disaggregate key patterns of meatification; and demonstrate how BRICS play a central role in structuring the global production network of meat through south-south trade relationships. Finally they point toward the increasing dominance of chicken globally, through what they label as *poultryfication*.

Weis's idea of a meat complex points beyond the animals to the agri-industry that feeds industrialized meat production. The importance of high protein animal feed from mainly soy and maize has accelerated immensely during the past five decades (see Weis 2013; Jakobsen and Hansen 2020). In recent decades, the United States almost doubled its soy productions from 49 million tons in 1980 to about 97 million tons in 2019. During the same period, Brazil became the world's leading soy producer, with annual production increasing from 15 million to 114 million tons. Argentina has also taken up the race, and its comparable numbers are from 3.5 million tons in 1980 to 55 million tons in 2019 (FAO 2021). Soy is "big business" and has become an accessible and cheap commodity in both emerging economies and in well-established industrialized countries. Kristi Anne Stølen's chapter in this volume exemplifies how even a traditional beef producing country like Argentina, at one point the world's largest exporter of beef, has become a soy producing country relying highly on international export. The cultural image of cattle grazing freely on the vast pampas has long been part of Argentine cultural imagery. Its pastoral image of animals grazing in open fields remains an image, while in reality farmers have moved their free-range cattle off Argentina's most fertile lands and into confinement. Through the export-oriented soy boom, during the last two-and-a-half decades, soybeans production has expanded to the best agricultural land. Livestock farming has been relegated to feedlots and marginal areas. A number of factors have contributed to this extraordinary growth of soybean production and the transformation of the Argentine countryside, but an international market for the soybean chain and rising prices in the global grain markets over the past decades have made it far more profitable to grow soybeans than to raise cattle. The need for feed to fuel China's massive meat industry is a central factor in all of the above.

Industrially driven meatification has become a global problem of quite immense scale and difficulty. In the course of the twentieth century agriculture has turned into agribusiness in most of the world. Farms have gone from being more or less self-contained units to becoming part of a national and global business venture involving global feed supplies, biotechnology, and the industrialization of sentient animals. What Barbara Noske (1989, 22) called the "Animal-Industrial Complex" is indeed "embedded in a capitalistic fabric." This essentially mirrors the author and critic John Berger's argument that industrialization marked "the beginning of a process, today being completed by 20th century corporate capitalism, by which every tradition which has previously mediated between man and nature was broken" (1980, 3). The break between humans and nonhuman nature has only become clearer since then. If we return to the chicken, Blanchette (2018) discusses in his review of the global meat industry how the enlarged "industrial chicken"—which has undergone a dramatic transformation from an egg-laying farm animal to the most populous species of bird on earth—is being mass-fossilized though billions of chicken skeletons are accumulating across the world (see also Bennett et al. 2018; Patel and Moore 2017). These, Blanchette argues, come to symbolize global capitalism and our relationship to animals:

> It is likely that the earth now contains many billions of poultry skeletons whose shape and density disproportionately reflect the proprietary genetics, feed rations, and capitalist strategies of specific agribusiness corporations such as Tyson Foods or Pilgrim's Pride. The stratigraphic record may be legible as a kind of branded entity, reflecting a moment in time when a handful of corporations competed to monopolize the raising and killing of a species. (Blanchette 2018, 186)

The treatment of chickens as industrial meat machines is also symptomatic of late capitalism, as neoliberalism has deepened the expansion of global capitalism and created new opportunities for "cheap food" that fundamentally depends on the exploitation of workers and the environment (Moore 2015).

Nowhere are these impacts more severe than in China, both in terms of local environmental damage and the global impacts of the meatification of Chinese diets. As Korsnes and Liu explore in their chapter, China has seen an explosion in the amount of animal products of late, and they explore meat's historical role in Chinese food and eating practices as well as its role in contemporary Chinese food culture. The dietary codes within Buddhism, Daoism, and Confucianism have all advocated restraint with regards to meat eating. Vegetarianism was widely practiced, and meat was consumed very sparingly by Chinese people, more often used as a condiment than the main part of a dish. In fact, the manure from domesticated animals was a fertilizer which was considered more important to agriculture than their flesh was to provide meat. However, meat has assumed a new role in contemporary Chinese eating habits during the economic growth and transformations since 1978. Traditional values of frugality and vegetarianism have been put under pressure as agriculture has been rapidly industrialized and intensified. New class distinctions have appeared, and related food practices such as dining out, ordering takeaway, and eating fast food have become part of a new Chinese food culture, and have in part been enabled through a shift from small-scale farmers to large agro-industrial complexes, the end result of which has been a general increase in meat consumption. A nationwide concern for food safety and health is found to distinguish China from Western countries where the meat-eating discourse is dominated by issues relating to animal ethics and environmental sustainability. This is also highly visible in the renewed popularity of vegetarianism and meat reduction among segments of the urban population.

Vegetarianism is also regaining popularity in China's neighboring country, Vietnam. But, as touched on earlier, Vietnam has seen among the fastest increases in meat consumption in the world the past decades. In his chapter, Hansen shows how Vietnam's food systems and urban foodscapes have undergone radical changes, and explains how these changes have contributed to changing meat cultures. Vietnam's capitalist transformation has brought along rapid meatification, an ongoing process toward the industrialization of the meat industry, and a certain tendency toward a standardization of meat cultures. That said, the country's meat cultures are also characterized by continuation. Hansen argues that any claims of an ongoing "Westernization" of diets must disregard deeply embedded and embodied foodways, including the widespread concern for balancing meals according to *am duong* (yin and yang) principles and a rich diversity of dishes and ingredients. Still, the changes in "meatscapes" (Hansen and Jakobsen 2020), particularly supermarkets and new middle-class food spaces, bring along highly different scripts and practices for producing, trading, and eating meat. The chapter shows how meat-related food practices in Vietnam are undergoing complex and often contradictory changes. It seeks to unveil some of this complexity, revisiting how and why meat consumption has increased so rapidly in Vietnam and analyzing how and why meat cultures change. Using the concept of "variegated capitalism" as a starting point (Peck and Theodore 2007), Hansen shows how the capitalist transformation of food and meat systems allows contextually distinct food cultures to evolve within structural-institutional homogenization.

As the chapters on China and Vietnam show, local meat cultures have a mediating effect on the impact of global capitalism and the industrialization of meat production on consumption patterns. Nowhere is this more obvious than in India. As mentioned earlier, India is the odd one out in the story of global meatification. Indeed, the country contradicts any claims of an automatic or "natural" relationship between affluence and increasing meat consumption. There are deep cultural and religious reasons that explain why this is so. In the stereotypical popular perception, India is the land of holy cows, revered by the nation's vegetarian Hindu majority. At the same time, but perhaps lesser known to the world, India is also a world-leading exporter of beef, mainly in the form of buffalo meat, which accounts for as much as 20 percent of global exports. India's apparently paradoxical relationship with beef is the starting point of Jakobsen and Nielsen's chapter. They analyze how India's bovine contradiction is expressive of deeper contradictions within the broader hegemonic project of India's Hindu nationalist government. This hegemonic project is centered on the twin ideological agenda of Hindu nationalism and Hindu majoritarian statecraft, and neoliberal economic policies that seek to create new spaces for capitalist accumulation. Meat and bovine bodies are, they argue, crucial sites where this contradictory hegemonic project plays out. On the one hand, the

Hindu nationalist component of this hegemonic project is furthered through a mix of legal and extralegal cow protection measures, while, on the other, the meatification of Indian agricultural exports and their integration into global value chains furthers the neoliberalization of the Indian agrarian economy.

The way in which Hindutva religion dominates Indian food culture and India's agricultural exports shows that religion and justification for meat eating or vegetarianism go hand in hand both in the past and present. Other contemporary examples of this are Kosher and Halal slaughter practices and rituals. Hibba Mazhary's chapter discusses halal meat as an object of both public scrutiny and contestation, in the intersection of food, faith, and ethics. Halal constitutes an increasing share of worldwide meat production, and represents a highly interesting case within the growing global meat industry. Although dominant meat cultures in high-income countries are often characterized by increasing intensification and the distancing of consumers from the sites of meat production (Serpell 1986; Vialles 1994), countercultures have also emerged to resist such processes (Syse 2017). Mazhary's chapter examines the alternative British halal meat movement as such a countercultural movement, seeking to resist growth and rising consumption and rather reconnect consumers with spaces of food production. The movement is characterized by higher-welfare standards, free-range or organic certification, and small-scale operations, although it still remains a niche movement in which consumers seek to reconnect with the animal death. Mazhary questions the entanglement of religion, production, and the consumers' motivations for wishing to reconnect to animals' death in the first place.

The philosopher Sophia Efstathiou's chapter, on the other hand, asks if it is a disconnection rather than reconnection that has enabled animals to become mere objects in the industrialized system of meat production. She contends that the technological intensification of livestock production and slaughter has withdrawn the animal subject from its body, and effaced them. She argues that this has opened a sphere in which animal products become animal-free. Architecture, uniforms, and various identification protocols for animals, which were initially developed with manifest aims like expediency, hygiene, or safety in mind, have in practice blocked humans and animals from facing each other, as morally significant "Others" (Levinas 1969; Efstathiou 2019). By leaving the animals and the humans working in slaughterhouses to turn them into food out of the public eye, the public are given a chance to escape the realities of slaughter, and dislocate the associating between animals and meat (Bjørkdahl and Syse 2013). Terms like "milk," "sausage," "burger," "mince," which were originally reserved for animal-based foods, have in turn been further disconnected from the animal, allowing an alternative approach to occur, and plant-based meat products take on the labeling of what used to be food made from animal flesh.

Another cultural and material approach to the problem of killing animals for their meat is *not* to kill them and rather let the brave new world of biotechnology take care of meat production. In the final chapter of this volume, Volden and Wethal ask what happens when cultured meat meets meat culture? Although in vitro, or cultured, meat might sound like a sci-fi solution to this problem, to many people, it is framed by its supporters as the ultimate solution to ensure global food security. These supporters claim it can mitigate the severe impacts conventional meat production has on human health, animal welfare, and the environment. Since the first hamburger grown directly from animal cells was created by scientists in 2013, the technology has developed rapidly, and cultured meat might take the leap from laboratory bioreactors to dinner plates soon. According to Volden and Wethal, cultured meat can in principle enable a convenient transition to sustainable food consumption by simply replacing the meaty components in established meat practices. Nevertheless, several social and cultural factors might put spanners in the wheels for a smooth transition. Consumers are skeptical, and many perceive cultured meat to be unnatural and unappetizing.

While modern food systems have become increasingly industrialized and technical and factory farms treat animals like machines, this response might seem paradoxical. Yet at this point, the current entrenched systems and cultures surrounding modern foodways bar consumer acceptance of such "technotopian" alternatives to conventional meat. However alternatives are needed. While certain technological solutions might indeed be utopian, one thing is certain—the toll on people's health, the suffering of animals, and the large-scale environmental destruction caused by contemporary meat systems cry for global change.

NOTES

1. Stockfish reconstituted in lye.

2. Singer's classic utilitarian statement *Animal Liberation* marked the utilitarian stance within animal ethics, followed by Tom Regan's deontological position, in *The Case for Animal Rights* (Berkeley: University of California Press, 1983). For a more popular meditation on the issue, see Jonathan Safran Foer, *Eating Animals* (New York: Little, Brown and Company, 2009).

REFERENCES

Animalia. 2020. *Kjøttets tilstand 2020: Status i norsk kjøtt- og eggproduksjon*. Oslo: Norway. kt20-komplett-origi-web.pdf (animalia.no).

Bennett, Carys, Richard Thomas, Mark Williams, Jan Zalasiewicz, Matt Edgeworth, Holly Miller, Ben Coles, Alison Foster, Emily J. Burton and Upenyu Marume. 2018. "The Broiler Chicken as a Signal of a Human Reconfigured Biosphere." *Royal Society Open Science* 5: 1–11. http://dx.doi.org/10.1098/rsos.180325.

Berger, John. 1980. "Why Look at Animals?" In John Berger (ed.) *About Looking.* London: Writers & Readers, 3–30.

Bjørkdahl, Kristian and Karen Lykke Syse. 2013. "Death and Meatereality." In Rane Willerslev and Dorthe Refslund Christensen (eds.) *Taming Time, Timing Death. Death, Materiality and the Origin of Time.* Farnham: Ashgate, 213–230.

Bjørkdahl, Kristian and Karen Lykke Syse. 2021. "Welfare Washing: Disseminating Disinformation in Meat Marketing." *Society & Animals*: 1–19. Published online.

Blanchette, Alex. 2018. "Industrial Meat Production." *Annual Review of Anthropology* 47: 185–199.

Blanchette, Alex. 2020. *Porkopolis: American Animality, Standardized Life, and the Factory Farm.* Durham and London: Duke University Press.

Bourdieu, Pierre. 1984. *Distinction: A Social Critique of the Judgement of Taste.* London: Routledge.

Braudel, Fernand. 1982. *The Structures of Everyday Life: Civilization and Capitalism, 15th–18th Century.* Harper and Row.

Brillat-Savarin, J. A. 1848. *Physiologie du Goût, Ou Méditations de Gastronomie Transcendate.* Paris: Gabriel de Gonet.

Calarco, Matthew. 2020. *Beyond the Anthropological Difference. Elements in Environmental Humanities.* Cambridge: Cambridge University Press. https://doi .org/10.1017/9781108862769.

Calarco, Matthew R. 2021. *Animal Studies: The Key Concepts.* Oxon: Routledge.

Douglas, M. 1975. "Deciphering a Meal." In Mary Douglas (ed.) *Implicit Meanings; Essays in Anthropology.* New York: Routledge, 249–275.

Efstathiou, S. 2019. "Facing Animal Research: Levinas and Technologies of Effacement." In P. Atterton and T. Wright (eds.) *Face-to-Face with Animals: Levinas and the Animal Question.* New York: SUNY Press, 139–163.

Emel, Jody, and Harvey Neo, eds. 2015. *Political Ecologies of Meat.* Routledge Studies in Political Ecology. London and New York: Routledge and Taylor & Francis Group.

FAO. 2021. *FAOSTAT.* http://www.fao.org/faostat/en/#data

Fiddes, Nick. 1991. *Meat: A Natural Symbol.* Abingdon: Routledge.

Hansen, Arve. 2018. "Meat Consumption and Capitalist Development: The Meatification of Food Provision and Practice in Vietnam." *Geoforum* 93: 57–68.

Hansen, Arve and Jostein Jakobsen. 2020. "Meatification and Everyday Geographies of Consumption in Vietnam and China." *Geografiska Annaler: Series B, Human Geography* 102 (1): 21–39. https://doi.org/10.1080/04353684.2019.1709217

Harrison, Ruth. 1964. *Animal Machines.* London: Vincent Stuart.

Helsedirektoratet. 2017. *Utviklingen i norsk kosthold: Matforsyningsstatistikk og forbruksundersøkelser.* Report. Oslo: Helsedirektoratet, 19.

Herrero, Mario, Stefan Wirsenius, Benjamin Henderson, Cyrille Rigolot, Philip Thornton, Petr Havlík, Imke de Boer, and Pierre J. Gerber. 2015. "Livestock and the Environment: What Have We Learned in the Past Decade?" *Annual Review of Environment and Resources* 40 (1): 177–202. https://doi.org/10.1146/annurev-env iron-031113-093503.

Howard, Philip H. 2019. "Corporate Concentration in Global Meat Processing: The Role of Feed and Finance Subsidies." In Bill Winders and Elizabeth Ransom (eds.) *Global Meat: Social and Environmental Consequences of the Expanding Meat Industry*. Cambridge: The MIT Press, 31–53.

Jakobsen, Jostein and Arve Hansen 2020. "Geographies of Meatification: An Emerging Asian Meat Complex." Globalizations 17 (1): 93–109.

Josephson, Paul R. 2020. *Chicken: A History from Farmyard to Factory*. Cambridge: Polity.

Joy, Melanie. 2010. *Why We Love Dogs, Eat Pigs and Wear Cows: An Introduction to Carnism*. San Francisco: Conari.

Lévi-Strauss, Claude. 1970. *The Raw and the Cooked*. New York: Harper & Row.

Levinas, E. 1969 [1961]. *Totality and Infinity*. Trans. A. Lingis. Pittsburgh, PA: Duquesne University Press.

London, Jonathan D. 2020. "China and Vietnam as Instances of Consolidated Market-Leninism." In Arve Hansen, Bekkevold Jo Inge and Kristen Nordhaug (eds.) *The Socialist Market Economy in Asia*. Singapore: Palgrave Macmillan, 69–114. https ://doi.org/10.1007/978-981-15-6248-8_3.

Milford, Anna Birgitte, Chantal Le Mouël, Benjamin Leon Bodirsky, and Susanne Rolinski. 2019. "Drivers of Meat Consumption." *Appetite* 141 (October): 104313. https://doi.org/10.1016/j.appet.2019.06.005.

Moore, J. 2015. "Cheap Food and Bad Climate: From Surplus Value to Negative Value in the Capitalist World-Ecology." *Critical Historical Studies* 2 (1): 1–43.

Mylan, Josephine. 2018. "Sustainable Consumption in Everyday Life: A Qualitative Study of UK Consumer Experiences of Meat Reduction." *Sustainability* 10 (7 July): 1–13.

Neo, Harvey and Jody Emel. 2017. *Geographies of Meat: Politics, Economy and Culture*. London: Routledge.

Noske, Barbara. 1989. *Humans and Other Animals: Beyond the Boundaries of Anthropology*. London: Pluto Press.

Patchirat, Timothy. 2013. *Every Twelve Seconds: Industrialized Slaughter and the Politics of Sight*. Yale University Press.

Patel, Raj and Jason W. Moore. 2017. *A History of the World in Seven Cheap Things*. Oakland, CA: University of California Press.

Peck, Jamie, and Nik Theodore. 2007. "Variegated Capitalism." *Progress in Human Geography* 31 (6): 731–772. https://doi.org/10.1177/0309132507083505.

Potts, Annie. 2016. "What is Meat Culture?" In Annie Potts (ed.) *Meat Culture*. Leiden and Boston: Brill, 1–30.

Ruby, Matthew B. 2012. "Vegetarianism. A Blossoming Field of Study." *Appetite* 58 (1): 141–150. https://doi.org/10.1016/j.appet.2011.09.019

Sans, Pierre and Pierre Combris. 2015. "World Meat Consumption Patterns: An Overview of the Last Fifty Years (1961–2011)." *Meat Science* 109 (Supplement C): 106–111.

Schneider, Mindi. 2017. "Wasting the Rural: Meat, Manure, and the Politics of Agro-Industrialization in Contemporary China." *Geoforum* 7: 89–97.

Schneider, Mindi. 2019. "China's Global Meat Industry: The World-Shaking Power of Industrializing Pigs and Pork in China's Reform Era." In Bill Winders and Elizabeth Ransom (eds.) *Global Meat: Social and Environmental Consequences of the Expanding Meat Industry*. Cambridge: The MIT Press, 79–100.

Serpell, James. 1986. *In the Company of Animals: A Study of Human-Animal Relationships*. New York: Cambridge University Press.

Singer, Peter. 1975. *Animal Liberation: A New Ethics for Our Treatment of Animals*. New York: New York Review.

Specht, Joshua. 2020. *Red Meat Republic: A Hoof-to-Table History of How Beef Changed America*. Princeton and Oxford: Princeton University Press.

Syse, Karen Lykke. 2017. "Looking the Beast in the Eye: Re-animation of Meat Eating in Food Prose." In Michael Lundblad (ed.) *Animalities: Literary and Cultural Studies Beyond the Human*. Edinburgh: Edinburgh University Press, 168–189.

Syse, Karen Lykke and Kristian Bjørkdahl. 2021. "The Animal that Therefore was Removed from View: The Presentation of Meat in Norway." In Tomaž Grušovnik, Karen Lykke Syse and Reingard Spannring (eds.) *Environmental and Animal Abuse Denial: Averting Our Gaze*. London: Lexington Books.

Vialles, Noelie. 1994. *Animal to Edible*. Cambridge: Cambridge University Press.

Vittersø, Gunnar and Unni Kjærnes. 2015. "Kjøttets politiske økonomi—usynlig-gjøring av et betydelig miljø- og klimaproblem." *Sosiologi i dag* 45 (1): 74.

Weis, Tony. 2013. *The Ecological Hoofprint: The Global Burden of Industrial Livestock*. New York and London: Zed Books.

Winders, B. and Ransom, E. 2019. "Introduction to the Global Meat Industry: Expanding Production, Consumption, and Trade." In B. Winders and E. Ransom (eds.) *Global Meat: Social and Environmental Consequences of the Expanding Meat Industry*. Cambridge, MA: The MIT Press, 1–23.

World Bank. 2021. *World Development Indicators*. https://data.worldbank.org/

Chapter 2

From Ritual Loss of Life to Loss of Living Rituals

On Judicialization of Slaughter and Denial of Animal Death

Kristian Bjørkdahl and Karen Lykke Syse

As per 2019, approximately 80 billion animals are killed for human consumption annually (Ritchie and Roser 2019). That number has been on the rise almost everywhere and is now the highest it has ever been. What the author Upton Sinclair once described as a continuous "stream of animals" and "a very river of death" today runs very deep indeed (1906, 41). As historian Paula Young Lee argues, the modern slaughterhouse has become "a social instrument" that responds "to the demands of a gargantuan belly," consequently producing "serial death along with saleable meat" (2008, 2).

The increasingly industrial character of meat production has entailed significant changes to the relations we have to the animals we eat. Perhaps most strikingly, a far smaller number of those who eat animal flesh today have ever witnessed animal slaughter, and much less performed one. Only a select few have ever been inside a modern slaughterhouse. One would perhaps think that, because we now consume a greater number of animals than ever before, we would be increasingly preoccupied with how we make sense of this unprecedented scale of animal death. The killing of an animal is, after all, an action charged with moral ambiguities, and practically everywhere and at all times people have felt a need to justify the fact that we kill animals to consume them. As we will suggest in this chapter, however, quite the opposite appears to be the case: There are now mechanisms in place that allow us *not* to think of how, or how many, animals are killed for our consumption.

At least in part because animal killing has been morally and emotionally difficult, it has often been ritualized, and thus, placed within a cultural context which meaning went far beyond a need for nutrition. In order to cope with the transition from caretaking to lifetaking, various cultures have erected different rituals, taboos, and traditions that helped remove some of the moral and emotional burden of the killing (see Mazhary this volume; Archetti 1997; Vialles 1994; Willerslev et al. 2015; Willerslev 2007). As Hibba Mazhary points out in this book, slaughter rituals are still an important part of halal and kosher meat cultures, but in secular Western societies, we find that such rituals have all but disappeared. While our killing of animals has taken on an increasingly industrial character, we have shed the rituals that once made animal deaths justified and meaningful, and replaced them with technical laws and regulations that allow consumers to maintain their distance from the act of animal killing.

In this chapter, we look at the loss of slaughter rituals in one particular country, Norway, as a case of a phenomenon that several scholars in animal studies and adjacent areas have suggested is characteristic of meat cultures in contemporary society, namely a tendency to deny of the animal origin of meat. As the anthropologist Noelie Vialles points out in her classic study, *Animal to Edible*, the "origin of [. . .] meat is entirely hidden from view" of the modern consumer (1994, 28), and this, she suggests, happens through a series of "dissociations." To the extent modern society fails to confront the issue of animal killing, this is a matter of some moral importance, since "one-to-one slaughter, in which the roles of animal and man persist right up until the act of killing, is easier to accept than industrial slaughter" (1994, 31). As Vialles notes, we find it so hard to accept the unprecedented scale of animal killing, in fact, that we prefer to look away, avert our gaze. Sociologist Robert Chiles has suggested that the tendency to deny the animal origin of meat is neither a coincidence nor a conspiracy, but that there is a "suppressive synergy" at work, in which "industry, mass media, and consumers' everyday habits jointly contribute to the maintenance of" distance to the idea of where meat comes from (Chiles 2016, 793). Norwegian scholars Gunnar Vittersø and Unni Kjærnes (2015) have argued that a similar dynamic is in place also in Norway, as part of what they call a "politics of meat promotion," which on the one hand encourages Norwegians to eat more meat and on the other encourages them to not think about the moral implications of that consumption. Our contribution to research on this issue is to show how our ways of framing animal killing have changed over time—more specifically, how denial of the animal origin of meat has been implicated in a shift from a ritual to a legal justification for slaughter. This focus adds another layer to the existing scholarship, by highlighting the resources we use to frame and make sense of animal deaths, the implication being that the mechanisms we currently use to deny our industrial scale killing of animals are even more numerous and complex than we have thought.

In what follows, we make three plunges into the history of slaughter in Norway: First, we describe some of the practices and rituals that traditionally characterized the act of killing animals in rural Norway, up to the first decades of the twentieth century. In this period, Norwegians who were involved in the act of farm slaughter drew on a ritual vocabulary of animal killing, which they used to make the killing of the animal meaningful and acceptable. Next, we look at how an impulse emerged, from early in the twentieth century, toward "civilizing slaughter." A push to make slaughter "humane" expelled the old rituals, and replaced them with requirements for preslaughter stunning and the reduction of needless animal suffering. Finally, we elaborate on recent Norwegian legislation on slaughter, to show how laws and regulations, in our time, have taken over the job of justifying and framing animal killing almost completely. During the last 100 years or so, the framing of animal deaths has moved from a cultural sphere, which was widely shared, to a legal sphere, which is dominated by technical expertise. By framing slaughter in this thoroughly technical manner, laws and regulations have contributed to removing the need for consumers to confront the fact that animals are killed for their consumption.

As we will show, this technical judicialization of animal killing has become part of Norwegian culture, to the point where it inspires critiques and creates distinctions to the allegedly barbaric ritual slaughtering practices within Jewish or Muslim meat cultures. But while the historical shift toward "humane" slaughter in some ways represents progress, it contributes, at the same time, to averting our gaze from the ever-growing scales of our industrial killing and consumption of animals. As we shall argue, the judicialization of animal killing adds to a wider set of social mechanisms that allow us to deny our own meat-eating practices, and which consequently stand in the way of our developing a responsible way of treating the animals we eat. While the judicialization process has clearly contributed to raising the bar for animal welfare, it has, at the same time, supported a more general tendency of alienation and denial which characterizes our contemporary relations to meat.

ANIMAL KILLING AND RITUAL

Wherever animals are part of the diet, people need to place the killing of animals into a context where their deaths gain meaning, and where that meaning is widely shared and accepted: the living, breathing creature must be transformed—not just physically, but symbolically—into inert matter fit for consumption. The *animal* must be made *edible*, to cite Vialles's telling book title (1994). We should not be perplexed by this need for symbolic transformation:

After all, the animals we eat are much like us, and up until fairly recently, people's everyday lives were lived in close proximity to these animals, who were often considered members of the household. It only stands to reason that we are reluctant to kill and eat our family members.

According to the historian Keith Thomas, rituals were used to appease providence. In his classic work, *Religion and the Decline of Magic*, Thomas explains how rituals can provide confidence and give agency and control to those involved in a practice. Although such agency or control might be illusory, a magical rite "lessens anxiety, relieves pent-up frustration, and makes the practitioner feel that he is doing something positive towards the solution of his problem" (Thomas 1991, 775). Magic, chants, blessings, and other rituals help bridge the gap between what a person can control and what they cannot control. Slaughter was considered an action in which many things could go wrong, and as slaughter transformed animals to a yearly economical surplus within animal husbandry, people relied heavily on this process going well. Moreover, people were dealing with existential matters of life and death: The people involved had to change from caretakers to lifetakers, and ensure that the meat products this transformative act resulted in did not, for any reason, go bad. Thus any action that could tip the scales of fortune, so that things went well, was important.

According to the anthropologist Arnold van Gennep, another function of rituals is to transfer blame and responsibility from the individual to the collective (van Gennep 1999). We find examples of this from Norway, where the killing of "soul-animals," such as horses, cats, and dogs, was taboo (Lid 1924). As if to offer the community an exit from this problem, a special class of horse slaughterers, called *rakkere*, who lived as untouchables, would ambulate in the countryside, offering to slaughter and skin the animals that no one else would kill. In places where there was no *rakker*, the villagers would agree that everyone had to partake in the process, so that no one in particular could be blamed for the heinous deed (Skar 1909, 142). The anthropologist Victor Turner claimed that rituals could also be used to cement conflicting social norms (1995). Using the example mentioned earlier again: if some voices within society regarded the slaughter of a horse with disgust, the ritualization of its slaughter (by including everyone on the farm in the action) still allowed the deed to take place. Rituals were thus tools of agency in situations where people would rather not act, and slaughter was in many cases such a situation.

"DIE! THAT IS WHY YOU ARE HERE"

In Norway, the tendency to envelop slaughter in various rituals go far back in history, and spring out of the fact that, for most Norwegians, animals were a part of everyday life throughout the day, all year, for the duration of their lives (Bjørkdahl and Syse 2019). In 1900, 47 percent of all working Norwegians were still active in the primary industries (Hansen and Skoglund 2009, 25). For these people, countless hours of work were spent carrying water, feeding, and cleaning sties, stables, and byres. Farmers spread dung, milked the cows, clipped the sheep, and worked side by side with the horse. Lambing in the spring and slaughter in the fall was part and parcel of the agricultural cycle (Taksdal 1943). Newborn lambs were tended to with great care and affection, fed, blessed, given names. In some parts of the country, they were even christened (Visted and Stigum 1952, 162). To quote the critic and author John Berger, animals were "with man at the centre of his world" (Berger 2001, 12), and the human-animal relationship was both multisensory and embodied.

Around 1900, this human-animal relationship had already started to change, and this occasioned the scholarly collection of materials on old slaughtering practices, not least by the Norwegian cultural historian and folklorist, Nils Lid. He was himself the son of a slaughterer, and would become Norway's first professor of ethnology. Traditional slaughter practices and rituals were among his main research interests. In this section, we draw on Nils Lid's published thesis (1924) and various archival sources to describe Norwegian slaughtering practices in the decades leading up to and following the turn of the nineteenth and twentieth century.[1] These archives are unique depositories of past and present thoughts, beliefs, memories, and practices in Norway (Kjus 2013, 143; Esborg and Johannsen 2014)

Although slaughter was part of the annual calendar within any traditional rural society, it was still an *extraordinary* part of this cycle. Like other important peaks of the annual calendar, such as sowing or harvesting grain, various traditions and rituals surrounded slaughter, which were connected to each of the phases of the process: preparation, slaughter, and butchering. For instance, in good time before slaughter, one had to make sure unwanted traits from the animal were not passed on to humans through consumption of the meat. Male animals were gelded. This was particularly important for bucks and rams. The practical reason was that the rut would make the meat taste bad. In the same way that people believed that a man would take on the strength of a bull by drinking bull's blood (Lid 1924, 92), he could become horny like a ram by eating the meat of an uncastrated ram. In some districts, an unruly girl would be called a goat.[2] These traits might have been unwanted because they posed a threat to the social structure and stability of society.

Before slaughtering could take place, the timing had to be right. Moon cycles were observed, as it was considered best to slaughter during the first quarter of the waxing moon. People believed the meat was at its fattest this time of the month (Lid 1924, 31). Slaughter at flow tide was deemed beneficial, because something filling up rather than running out seemed good. Finally, certain days were more beneficial than others, and breaching the Sabbath made Saturday night through Monday morning a bad time for slaughter. The term *griseotta* (pig-early) refers to getting up in the middle of the night—a relic from when pig-slaughter was carried out that early.

Once the time of slaughter was established, other rituals needed to be observed. Slaughtering was a serious and risky undertaking, which one thought could influence providence and fortune. The meat could spoil and one's fortune in animal husbandry could be at stake, so people made small offerings to fairies or fortune. Pregnant women had to stay away, since blood stains from the animal could be transferred as birthmarks on the child. Everyone present at the slaughtering scene had to be absolutely silent; this was a solemn act. No strangers could be present, as they might look at the beast with jealousy or the evil eye and thus magically spoil the animal's meat. Another notable rule was not to feel sorry for the animal that was being led to slaughter. Children would be scolded if they shed tears, because this would lengthen the animal's suffering, and its death would be long and painful. If you felt sorry for the animal, people believed that it would understand what was coming, and hence would refuse to let go of its blood. The blood would coagulate, and spoil the meat. Besides, if you felt pity for the animal, this was admitting that it was not right to kill it.

Taking pity on the beast about to be slaughtered did not seem to be a prevalent issue in some of the earliest quotes in the material we have studied. In Lindås outside Bergen an informant states that "they thought that if you chased the animal before you slaughtered it, the blood would leave the body faster. So the pigs were ridden hard before they were slayed." In Fjærland in Southwest Norway "one would pull at the harness, the other in the tail, and they would pull the pig around and upset it so it would bleed a lot." A bit further west, in Gulen, "they pulled the pig and topped it over until it was totally exhausted." Perhaps the most disturbing quote comes from the south of Norway, from Håland, in Jæren:

> Before the [time of the] enclosures, the village would share a pig and would take turns feeding it. When it was time to slaughter it, the whole village got together. It was time to "knead" it. They would get sticks and branches and would beat and whip it, they would run around the farmhouses and across the fields, beating when they could, and when they finally had kneaded it well enough, they would beat it with sticks until it collapsed.

Then they would say, "This is not for hatred, but for food," to confirm that it was right to kill it (Lid 1924, 78), something which was likened to a source from Sweden, who says that if it took too long before the animal died, the person who held the rope should shout "Die! That is why you are here" (Lid 1924, 79). It was common to say "In the name of Jesus" before stabbing the animal, as a kind of blessing. The slaughterer himself could say "Glorify my stroke." Other blessings were physical in nature, and involved drawing a cross on the animal's back with a piece of coal, or crossing their foreheads with a hand movement.

Until the early 1900s, it was common to strangle smaller animals such as sheep and even pigs by hanging them. Pigs were scolded while they were hanging. In certain areas, newborn calves were deemed unclean, and were slaughtered at a different site on the farm, away from the usual place of slaughter. There are descriptions of hanging and in part skinning calves before slitting their throats, and also accounts of decapitation (Lid 1924, 123). Another practice was to bleed the animal to death, by slitting it open without stunning it. Slitting or bleeding smaller animals like sheep and pigs without stunning was a practice common all over Norway, and was not restricted to certain districts. It was maintained for the longest period with pigs. There are accounts of scalding the pig around the neck before slitting its throat. In fact there are several references to scalding the pig before the life ebbed out, since pig's bristle was supposedly easier to remove on a live animal. Later in the century, larger animals were stunned while smaller animals were still often slaughtered simply through stabbing with a knife. The variation in terminology reflects this, as larger animals are "beaten" while smaller animals were "slaughtered" (Lid 1924, 75). The sources show a lot of references to blood. Blood from some animals was occasionally ritually drunk by the slaughterer, as it spewed out of the wound. Most of the informants who refer to this ritual, believe it is something hunters and semiprofessional slaughterers do to demonstrate bravery, rather than a common practice among farmers.

A certain part of the heart (the *auricula cordis*) of any slaughtered animal was cut off and thrown away. It was not, like other unwanted offal, fed to the pig or to domestic foxes, it was simply cut off and discarded. None of the informants in the source material know why they do this. However, a well-argued explanation with historical depth (Lid 1925) traces it to a pagan offering to either the Norse god Odin or the god Ull: it is called "the raven's bit" (Odin had two ravens that would keep him informed about everything in the world) or Ullsøyro (Ull's ear). The spleen was also disposed of in this manner. Several other rituals were carried out while the butchering took place. A part of cartilage connected to the ribs was cut off and tossed with force against a wall. If it stuck it meant good fortune. A cross was scored in the liver using the butcher knife.

Anthropologists Lykkegård and Willerslev (2016) explain that killing a sacrificial victim is associated with moral ambivalence, and this had to be dealt with by observing a set of rituals to maintain a balance between taking and giving from nature. In the material we have studied, we find a constant underlying anxiety about provoking destiny and chance which is often solved by sacrifice, such as the ritual disposal of the *auricula cordis* described earlier. One of the informants warns that it is dangerous to make use of "the animal or animal parts that *should be wasted*," (emphasis ours) as this may lead to death and destruction.[3] The words "should be wasted" are key, because they signify that there is a strong incitement to perform this little sacrifice. Again, this is a little bit of surviving magic—it was important to play along with the forces of fate, and to give the offering that is required (see also Visted and Stigum 1952, 281).

Many of these practices, customs, and rituals spring from the circumstance that those who were tasked with killing animals had also often been the caretakers of those animals, and had lived in close, everyday proximity to them. To take off some of the discomfort of killing a creature that had been almost like a family member, some sort of symbolic transformation thus had to take place. For instance, the beating and chasing ritual described earlier may be a way of transforming the animal from a subject with *personhood*, which has been fed and probably cherished by the whole village, to an edible object devoid of human traits. The collective beating might be a way of beating this personhood or soul out of the animal. It is a social ritual, thus slaughtering the pig is something everyone takes part in. No individual was responsible for eating an animal friend; a ritual of maltreatment transformed the friend to foe, and this ritual was acted out collectively.

CIVILIZING SLAUGHTER

Most of the practices and rituals we have just described would over time disappear, and in fact, the scholarly effort to collect material on the old slaughtering practices in the early 1900s was itself an attempt to capture a way of life that was now going extinct. When Norwegians gradually shed their old slaughtering rituals, this change was arguably due to a number of complex causes related to various aspects—practical and economic, as well as political and moral—of modernization. As several scholars have pointed out, however, a particularly important impetus was the growing focus on "civilizing slaughter" (Otter 2008)—an attempt to regulate, more strictly and in formal terms, *how* animals could be killed, *where*, and *by whom*.

The push to establish public slaughterhouses, wherein the process of killing could be monitored and controlled, was one important part of this program, for as long as slaughter was done by private individuals or by small slaughtering outfits, one could not trust the killing to be performed according to the emerging standards of hygiene, cleanliness, and concern for animal suffering. As historian Dorothee Brantz notes, slaughterhouse reforms "were a European-wide phenomenon in the nineteenth century," starting with the first public slaughterhouse in Paris in 1818, and spreading to most major cities of Europe as the century progressed (Brantz 2008, 71). The process was set in motion by urban development, that is, by the fact that growing numbers of people were now living in ever more densely populated—and often quite unsanitary—areas, which increasingly were populated also with animals meant for slaughter (Brantz 2008; see also Cronon 1991). The many practical problems that ensued from this situation merged with moral motives, however, and together they formed a vision of a civilized modernity.

In the early 1900s, legislation was established in Norway which established that animals were to be slaughtered in municipal slaughterhouses. A newspaper article in connection with the opening of the grand municipal slaughterhouse in the capital, Kristiania, is illustrative:

> It is well known that several of the private slaughterhouses in this city have been in a condition that have made it a sanitary necessity to move beyond the present state, as they, by their location, were a great annoyance to their surroundings. Conditions have been wretched and primitive, unworthy of a big city. It is apparent that meat made by slaughter in tight, miserable, and overfilled (and for that reason insufficiently cleaned) venues, will be a less valuable and healthy food than meat produced under good conditions. In addition, animals for sale and slaughter are also kept tight and miserable styes and byres. The new central slaughtering facility with the adjacent cow market, which was opened yesterday, is a definitive step out of this accumulation of sanitary wretchedness, over into timely and modern care. (Muri 2005, 121)

An important aspect of modern animal killing was the idea that slaughter should be "humane," which one could recognize first and foremost by its use of preslaughter stunning—and, over time, with other forms of anesthetics—which removed needless infliction of pain on the animal (Otter 2008). In Norway, the authorities were central actors in the push toward making slaughter more civilized and humane. In a booklet published by the Ministry of Agriculture in 1923, for instance, Norway's "public veterinarian" E. Laukvik regretted the fact that, for the lack of public slaughterhouses, "people have to slaughter at home, both for their own consumption and to sell" (Laukvik 1923, 3). In the book's preface, the director of Agriculture wrote that, still, "slaughter is often done in such a way that needless suffering is inflicted upon the animals. This is a form of animal abuse which cannot be excused, as it can easily be avoided with some care and caution," and he explained that this was precisely the purpose of the book: "The present text aims to better these conditions, as far as both the humanitarian and the economic aspects are concerned" (Norway's director of Agriculture, in Laukvik 1923, 2). The book was, in effect, a manual in how to perform humane slaughter, and it was not the only one (see, for example, Blomqvist 1917).

The book's author went on to give a series of concrete requirements and suggestions, shifting constantly between economic and moral justifications. For instance, he would explain that the animals needed to rest for a specific period of time before being killed, as the meat would be tough and not very durable if one failed to do so. He would also list the practical requirements for performing slaughter in a clean and orderly fashion, by making lists of the necessary equipment: "Tools to keep at hand include: gun, axe, sharp knife, saw, butcher's bench, pulley; tray, bucket and whisk for the blood; a cart or a trough for the entrails; washbasin, soap, towels, and plenty of water" (ibid., 5).

At the same time, Laukvik would emphasize the need for humane treatment of the animal to be slaughtered: "The law mandates that when slaughtering livestock or reindeer, the animal is to be stunned before the bloodletting. The effect of the stunning should be so immediate that the animal loses consciousness before any sensation of pain sets in" (ibid., 3). The moral injunction was somewhat more complex than simply to avoid inflicting pain upon the animal, however, as the author adds,

> During the killing, other livestock and children under the age of 14 must not be present. A slaughtered animal should not be flayed, scalded or ribbed until one can ascertain death. The slaughter should be performed by an adult, and as far as possible a competent, person. (ibid., 3)

With the new Animal Protection Act of 1935, which shifted the weight from injunctions against abuse of animals toward a positive obligation for their welfare, the principle of humane treatment of animals was firmly established in Norway. The central paragraph in that Act held that "animals are to be treated with care, so that they are not exposed to unnecessary suffering" (Njaa 1940, 13).

Surely, sentiments such as those expressed by Laukvik, and codified in the Act of 1935, created a push toward more humane treatment of animals. Such legal notions were motivated by ideals of civilization—by ideas that said that to treat animals as one had in the past, amounted to a form of barbarism, a vulgarity (see, for example, Blomqvist 1917). It was certainly not the kind of thing one would want children to witness. The act of killing animals increasingly became something to be "cleaned up," and the main way to do this was to make it into a professional practice, which was performed by especially trained people (slaughterers) at designated sites (public slaughterhouses). This process did not remove animal killing, but it did remove animal killing from sight. As Chris Otter points out, this process is thus part of what the sociologist Norbert Elias called the civilizing process, where "civilization

[. . .] advances by distancing itself not from killing itself but from the perception and reminder of it" (Otter 2008, 90).

JUDICIALIZATING DEATH

The push to civilize slaughter would rely heavily on *legislation*, and with the coming of formal laws to regulate our treatment of animals, slaughter would be moved, more decisively, out of the widely shared cultural sphere of ritual and into the more technical sphere of legal expertise. In Norway, there was a watershed in 1935, when the abovementioned Animal Protection Act went into effect. Since then, this law has been replaced twice, first in 1974, and then in 2009, as the Animal Welfare Act. Today, this law—which the minister of Agriculture incidentally declared would make Norway a world leader in animal welfare—is the main frame with which Norwegians justify and make sense of the killing of the animals they consume.

The law and its attendant regulations are expressions, we argue, of a *judicialized transformation of animals into meat*—where the emotional and moral distress that used to be solved by a ritual of some sort is now, largely, taken care of by law. If one gives any credence to this reading, it may be argued that slaughter is one of many practices that participate in a more general shift in our society toward the judicialization of politics, which is defined by Law Professor Ran Hirschl as "the reliance on courts and judicial means for addressing core moral predicaments, public policy questions, and political controversies," and which he argues is "one of the most significant phenomena of late twentieth- and early twenty-first-century government" (Hirschl 2008, 119).

When juxtaposed with the description we gave earlier, of Norwegians' traditional slaughtering customs and rituals, the laws and regulations point to radical changes in how we relate to animal deaths over the last 100 years or so. In the law itself, the killing of animals is mentioned at various points, including in a separate paragraph on the taking of animal lives, that is, slaughter. The main ordinance is that "the killing of animals and the handling of animals in connection with the killing must *responsibly secure the animal's welfare*" (emphasis ours). The law further orders that any animal to be put down "must be stunned before slaughter," and that "the method of stunning must procure a loss of consciousness,"[4] which must endure throughout the act of killing. Alternatively, the animal can be killed with a method that causes immediate loss of consciousness.

Clearly, this paragraph primarily responds to a moral call for humane treatment of animals, not just because it opens with the general requirement about securing the animal's welfare, but also because it establishes that "animals are not to be slaughtered as an independent part of any entertainment or a competition" (ibid.). The law disallows the killing of animals for fun or for sport, and hence acknowledges that animals are more than commodities. In fact, the law states in a central earlier paragraph that "animals have an intrinsic value which is independent of the utility they offer humans." In this way, the Norwegian law rests on the idea of humane slaughter as outlined by Burt, which is (supposedly) a form of slaughter that answers "only to the abstractly conceived higher cause of humanity" (2006, 129–130). The whole purpose of the law is to make sure that slaughter does not inflict pain, or at least no needless pain, on the animal. This ordinance, then, has a function that is in many ways similar to old rituals. Both remove some of the moral and emotional stress associated with taking the life of an animal, since they allow Norwegians to tell themselves that, while they do in fact kill, they are the type of people who kill humanely—they bring death, but not pain, on the animals. Because it strictly and successfully removes animals from "sources of pain and distress," this judicialized humanitarianism allows us to "slaughter without quite the horror the word 'slaughter' should connote" (Burt 2006, 131).

This, however, is only the first, the humanitarian, aspect of the judicialized transformation of animals into meat, the other being the hygienic and economic. We can get an idea of how slaughter is circumscribed in our time by looking not only at the law but also at the more concrete, lower-level regulations relating to this activity. In Norway, the entity responsible for these regulations is the Norwegian Food Safety Authority (NFSA). While the Animal Welfare Act comes across as a fairly readable document for regular citizens, the information offered by the NFSA illustrates just how far into a specialized, technical sphere slaughter has moved today.

NFSA's webpages on "production of meat and meat products" begin by announcing that "there are comprehensive regulations in the area of foodstuffs, and there are special rules for foods of animal origin" (NFSA 2019), which communicate well enough, but then quickly turn to listing a selection of the various regulations concerning slaughter. One such says, for example,

> The requirement is for one stamp mark on each part of the slaughtered carcass. When pigs are divided in two, each half requires only one single stamp. Sheep are not divided, and in that case, one stamp suffices.

> See the regulation on special rules for implementation of public control of productions of animal origin destined for consumption (the animal control regulation), cf. 854/2004 (H3) addendum I paragraph I chapter III (2) (b). (Ibid.)

Another says,

On slaughtered cattle, SRM is to be removed.

> See the regulation on prevention, control, and eradication of transferable spongiform encephalopathies (TSE), cf. 999/2001 addendum IV (4.1) (b) and (11.3). (Ibid.)

These excerpts are not terribly informative to the general consumer and citizen, but that is precisely our point. The context in which we find these regulations is NFSA's version of a FAQ, which is addressed to specialists in the agricultural sector, or even, to slaughtering professionals. What is significant for our purposes is not so much what these regulations—actually say—that is, how they regulate slaughter—but the fact that ordinances concerning slaughter are couched in highly technical language that tells the ordinary citizen and consumer of meat very little indeed. For most people, an attempt to interpret this text would be like trying to get a handle on the *Corpus Hermeticum*. As discourse, these ordinances are highly esoteric; they communicate exclusively to a small group of specialized professionals.

The highly technical nature of these regulations is particularly interesting when one considers that these regulations are about the only thing we have to take the place of the rituals of old. While the emergence of laws to regulate animal welfare are in themselves a sign of judicialization of animal killing, the Norwegian act, as we saw, does appeal to public morality with its universalist statements concerning animals' intrinsic value, and so on. Meanwhile, the regulations that actually determine how slaughter should take place illustrate how the symbolic transformation of animals into meat has moved away from being a public issue to being a specialized, technical one.

The symbolic transformation of meat today takes place not with blessings or sayings or excuses, with offerings or particular uses of the animal, or with particular ways of comporting oneself during slaughter. In other words, slaughter does not involve widely shared and practiced rituals that justify to all (or many) of us that we may rightfully take the life of an animal. Rather, it takes the form, on the one hand, of a judicialized morality—what Burt calls "human slaughter"—and, on the other, of regulative hygiene—that is, of specialized rules and instructions concerning how slaughter should take place in order to ensure food safety. Gone with the old rituals, then, is much of the messiness of slaughter. The act of taking an animal's life has been cleansed, one could say, on both a moral and a practical level.

LAWS AND REGULATIONS AS SMOKE SCREENS

What emerges from the three plunges we have made in this chapter is that we have gone, over time, from *ritual loss of life to a loss of living rituals*. While the laws and regulations of today still regulate, specify, and justify, like the old rituals did, we argue that the shift toward a legal paradigm goes hand in hand with, and might even enhance, the modern alienation from animal killing. Laws and regulations, while they undoubtedly incentivize animal welfare and help us avoid the worst cases of animal abuse—and hence, represent real progress—also have another, and more insidious, function: they act as an efficient smoke screen for the industrial scale of current meat production and consumption, and allow us to deny the moral questions raised by this industrial scale of killing. As the French anthropologist, Noelie Vialles, argues,

> This killing is something we would rather know nothing about. In former times, sacrifices were solemn occasions celebrated in public. Later, slaughterhouses operated in the middle of towns, when animals were not actually killed in the street. Nowadays, slaughtering has become an invisible, exiled, almost clandestine activity. We know it goes on, of course, but it is an abstract kind of knowledge. [. . .] We demand an ellipsis between animal and meat. (Vialles 1994, 5)

The replacement of ritual by law enhances this "invisibilization" of animal killing, since when this killing is regulated merely by law, there is nothing—or at least nothing much—that forces us to confront the fact that we kill an animal to eat it. Laws about animal welfare ordain that animals are to be treated, and killed, in particular ways, but they do not offer us any incentive to confront our own practices. To the contrary, those laws tend to restrict access to the sites where animals are killed, and their overall effect, we submit, is a certain moral outsourcing: As long as the taking of an animal life is regulated by law, we—consumers and citizens—do not have to ponder that act any further. In this sense, the judicialization of the ritual, which we can see as a loss of a *living* ritual, functions as a smoke screen for the act itself. The existence of a law that regulates the killing actually contributes, in its way, to making the killing less visible and, one might say, less visceral.

In this regard, the cultural shift we have described, from ritual to juridical, has run in parallel with a spatial and social shift, from private home slaughter to professional slaughter taking place in industrial slaughterhouses. As Vialles (1994) and Pachirat (2011), among others, have pointed out, this spatial and social shift has also meant that the killing of animals is removed from sight, in a process Lee refers to as the "the extraction of animal slaughter from quotidian experience" (2008, 6). Modern slaughterhouses, she argues, were invented "to eliminate the mundane horror of encountering hand-slaughter in the streets by displacing it to the urban outskirts, where the geometry of the killing system could expand without restrictions" (ibid.). As we have tried to show, this shift has been consolidated in the cultural sphere, as the act of killing has increasingly moved out of folk or popular culture and into the technical, specialized domain of legal expertise. The result of this process is that the ordinary consumer and citizen no longer "owns" the meaning and the justification of his killing of animals—a killing which is now of course only indirect. This means in turn that the ordinary consumer and citizen is in no position to prevent that the "very river of death" described by Upton Sinclair continues to run wild.

MERCIFUL NORWAY VERSUS MUSLIMS AND JEWS

While there has been a shift from a widely shared ritual frame around slaughter to a more exclusive technical-legal frame, which allows the average consumer to retain a distance to animal killing, this technical-legal frame has, interestingly, itself become a part of culture—even, one might say, of Norwegian identity. When Norway's discrimination ombudsman proposed, a few years ago, that Norway should take a more lax—or rather, more generous—approach to so-called ritual slaughter, that is, slaughter which for religious reasons is performed without prior stunning, Norwegians had evidently forgotten about their own not-so-distant past. This proposal infuriated a few Norwegian commentators, many of whom used the occasion to "nationalize" the legally mandated, pre-stun, slaughter as a civilized alternative in contrast to the more primitive, ritual, even barbaric, form of slaughter favored by some Muslims and Jews.

One example of this was the philosopher, author, and cow farmer, Tore Stubberud, who began one of his op-eds on the issue by noting that while there was a long philosophical tradition of considering the moral status of animals, "in traditional halal and kosher animals have no moral standing. On the butcher's block they are nothing but objects for the archaic, religious needs of Muslims and Jews." Stubberud compared conventional Norwegian slaughter with halal and kosher slaughter thus, "Two animals are to be slaughtered and are met with rules and guidelines concerning animal welfare up to their killing. But now, one animal is led into panic and the religious sphere, while the other is gently anesthetized," he wrote, adding, with some pathos, "But does not the animal too have a face?" Apart from the note about animals being "gently anesthetized," he neglected to engage in depth with the realities of conventional slaughter: he spent several graphic paragraphs laying out the cruel consequences of halal and kosher, describing how "the artery is throttled and loss of consciousness delayed" and how the result is "blood, slime, and vomit." By marginalizing any real description of conventional slaughter, he arguably validated a sort of nonconcern for the context around this "normal" practice. The contrast he drew up allowed those who identify with conventional, Norwegian slaughter to remain unconcerned, since the attention is uniformly focused on the cruel practices of a set of villainized "others." While we do not know how this op-ed was read, an effect of it could be a disburdening of responsibility for animal killing onto other people, who demonstrably were killing more brutally than what we are. This too is a sort of denial mechanism, we would argue, which encourages us to dispel any thought of the bad things that *we do*, by focusing on what even worse things that certain *others* are doing.

CONCLUSION

In many countries, including Norway, the laws and regulations that were introduced in the early 1900s, and which since then have only grown in scope and complexity, have indeed lead to less suffering in connection with animal killing. The designation "humane slaughter" is not entirely wrong. With the coming of laws to protect animals, many of the ritual practices that we described in the first part of this chapter were cataloged as animal abuse, and rightly so. We believe, in other words, that the drive to civilize slaughter is a form of progress. At the same time, this progress has been double-edged, since alongside the emergence of more humane ways of slaughter, we have moved toward an increasingly industrial, large-scale—and therefore indirect and impersonal—relation to the animals we eat. By focusing on the objectionable nature of ritual slaughter in Kosher or Halal meat cultures, one might overlook, as Burt argues, that "the phrase 'humane slaughter,' when considered in the light of the scale of killing for meat and the deanimalizing (and dehumanizing) technologies that meat production entails, is a contradictory one" (2006, 126). Although the old ways of animal abuse have long since disappeared, some would argue that "the distinction between what is civilized and what is barbaric—mainly on the grounds of whether a creature is stunned before slaughter or not—takes place within a system that is deeply inhumane by virtue of its scale" (Burt 2006, 126).

When we, over the last 100 years, have put in place a set of strict laws and regulations that aim to "civilize" slaughter, we have removed many sources of animal suffering. But these laws and regulations might be what, at the same time, allow us to turn a blind eye to the industrial scale of slaughter today. The judicialization of animal killing thus appears to have contained one source of animal suffering only to better accommodate another.

NOTES

1. Between 1917 and 1920, Nils Lid initiated a series of questionnaires which were distributed all over Norway, with additional series of questionnaires distributed in

1930/1931 and 1943, deposited in the archive Norsk folkeminnesamling (Norwegian Collection of Folk Memory). Then, in 1950, a second cultural archive, Norsk etnologisk granskning (Norwegian Ethnological Research) was established. The first questionnaire resulted in Lid's published doctoral thesis, "Norske Slakteskikkar" (Norwegian Slaughter Customs) (Lid 1924). The other series were *Innsamling av tradisjon um slakt* (Collecting traditions about slaughter), in 1930/1931; *Ord og Sed, Avliving av slaktedyr 89* (Killing animals for slaughter), in 1943; and *NEG Norsk Etnologisk Granskning 19 Slaktedyr* (Norwegian Ethnological Research 19, Animals for slaughter).

2. Source from NEG questionnaire no. 25.

3. Norwegian "Død og fordervelse." Source from NSF cabinet 5 drawer 2.

4. Lov om dyrevelferd (Animal Welfare Act). Online: https://lovdata.no/dokument /NL/lov/2009-06-19-97.

REFERENCES

Amundsen, Arne Bugge. 2006. "Kulturhistoriske ritualstudier." In Arne Bugge Amundsen, Bjarne Hodne, and Ane Ohrvik (eds.) *Ritualer: Kulturhistoriske studier*. Oslo: Universitetsforlaget, 7–28.

Archetti Eduardo. 1997 [1992]. *Guinea-Pigs: Food, Symbol, and Conflict of Knowledge in Ecuador*. Oxford: Berg.

Berger, John. 2001. *Why Look at Animals?* London: Penguin.

Bjørkdahl, Kristian and Karen Lykke Syse. 2019. "Kjøtt, fremmedgjøring og fornek-telse." *Nytt Norsk Tidsskrift* 36 (3): 255–267.

Blomqvist, Axel. 1917. *Dyrenes bok: Hjembygdenes dyr, deres vern og røgt*. Kristiania: Grøndahl & Søns forlag.

Burt, Jonathan. 2006. "Conflicts around Slaughter in Modernity." In The Animal Studies Group (ed.), *Killing Animals*. Champaign: University of Illinois Press, 120–144.

Chiles, Robert Magneson. 2017. "Hidden in Plain Sight: How Industry, Mass Media, and Consumers' Everyday Habits Suppress Food Controversies." *Sociologia Ruralis* 57: 791–815.

Cronon, William. 19991. *Nature's Metropolis: Chicago and the Great West*. New York: W.W. Norton & Co.

Ehn, Billy, Löfgren Orvar and Richard Wilk. 2016. *Exploring Everyday Life: Strategies for Ethnography and Cultural Analysis*. London: Rowman & Littlefield.

Esborg, Line and Dirk Johannsen, eds. 2014. *"En vild endevending av al virkelighet" – Norsk Folkeminnesamling i hundre år*. Oslo: Novus.

Hansen, Stein and Tor Skoglund. 2009. *Sysselsetting og lønn i historisk nasjonalregn-skap. Beregninger for 1900–1930. Notater 2009/38*. Oslo: Statistisk Sentralbyrå.

Hirschl, Ran. 2008. "The Judicialization of Politics." In Gregory A. Caldeira, R. Daniel Kelemen, and Keith E. Whittington (eds.) *The Oxford Handbook of Law and Politics*. Oxford: Oxford University Press, 119–141.

Kjus, Audun. 2013. "Nils Lid (1890–1958)." In Bjarne Rogan and Anne Eriksen (eds.) *Etnologi og folkloristikk: En fagkritisk biografi om norsk kulturhistorie*. Oslo: Novus, 137–152.

Laukvik. E. 1938. *Heimeslakting*. 2nd ed. Oslo: Ministry of Agriculture.

Lee, Paula Young, ed. 2008. *Meat, Modernity, and the Rise of the Slaughterhouse*. Durham: University of New Hampshire Press.

Lid, Nils. 1924. *Norske slakteskikkar med jamføringar frå nærskylde umråde*. Kristiania: Dybwad.

Lid, Nils. 1925. "Ullins Øyra." In *Heidersskrift til Marius Hægstad*. Oslo: Norli, 128–144.

Lykkegård, Jeanette and Rane Willerslev. 2016. "Regenerating Life in the Face of Predation: A Study of Mortuary Ritual as Sacrifice among the Siberian Chukchi." *Sibirica* 15 (2): 1–39.

Muri, Beate. 2005. *Kristiania for 100 år siden*. Oslo: Schibsted.

NFSA. 2019. "Produksjon av kjøtt og kjøttprodukt." https://www.mattilsynet.no/mat _og_vann/produksjon_av_mat/kjott_og_kjottprodukter/produksjon_av_kjott_og_k jottprodukt.4625. Accessed 21 June 2019.

Pachirat, Timothy. 2011. *Every Twelve Seconds: Industrialized Slaughter and the Politics of Sight*. New Haven: Yale University Press.

Ritchie, Hannah and Max Roser. 2019. "Meat and Seafood Production & Consumption." *OurWorldInData.org*. https://ourworldindata.org/meat-and-seaf ood-production-consumption.

Sinclair, Upton. 1906. *The Jungle*. Minneapolis: First Avenue Editions.

Skar, Johannes. 1909. *Gamalt or Sætesdal*. Vol. 4. Oslo: Norli.

Thomas, Keith. 1991 [1971]. *Religion and the Decline of Magic*. London: Penguin.

Turner, Victor. 2017 [1969]. *The Ritual Process. Structure and Anti-Structure*. Routledge: New York.

Van Gennep, Arnold. 1999 [1908]. *Rites de passages. Overgangsriter*. Oslo: Pax.

Vialles, Noelie. 1988. "La viande ou la bête". *Terrain* 10: 86–96.

Vialles, Noelie. 1994. *Animal to Edible*. Cambridge: Cambridge University Press.

Visted, Kristofer and Hilmar Stigum. 1952. *Vår Gamle Bondekultur*. Vol. 2. Oslo: Cappelen.

Vittersø, Gunnar and Unni Kjærnes. 2015. "Kjøttets politiske økonomi – usynlig-gjøring av et betydelig miljø- og klimaproblem." *Sosiologi i dag* 45 (1): 74–97.

Willerslev, Rane. 2007. *Soul Hunters: Hunting, Animism, and Personhood among the Siberian Yukaghirs*. Berkeley: University of California Press.

Willerslev, Rane, Piers Vitebsky and Anatoly Alekseyev. 2015. "Sacrifice as the Ideal Hunt." *Journal of Royal Anthropological Institute* 21: 1–23.

Chapter 3

New Geographies of Global Meatification

The BRICS in the Industrial Meat Complex

Arve Hansen, Jostein Jakobsen, and Ulrikke Wethal

INTRODUCTION

Daily consumption of meat used to be confined to rich countries, but has over the past 50 years become a global phenomenon.[1] As the geographer Tony Weis (2013) puts it, meat has moved from the periphery to the center of human diets, a process he conceptualizes as "meatification." Meat consumption remains highly uneven, and inhabitants of high-income countries continue to consume significantly more meat than the rest of the world (Hansen 2018). But most of the increase in global meat consumption takes place in the "Global South," a trend that is expected to persist over the coming decades (OECD/FAO 2020; Henchion et al. 2014). More precisely, major increases have taken place in middle-income countries in Eastern Asia and Latin America, while there has been little increase in per capita meat consumption in Sub-Saharan Africa and South Asia (Godfray et al. 2018; Sans and Combris 2015; MacLachlan 2015).

Although there is significant regional variety in the types of meat consumed, global production, trade, and consumption patterns focus upon three categories of meat: pork, poultry, and beef. Centered on these three categories, the vast meat industry behind such patterns has taken an increasingly integrated and properly *global* position (Weis 2013; Blanchette 2018; Winders and Ransom 2019). "The production and consumption of meat," a recent assessment holds, "has reached such a global scale that a hamburger can link together people and businesses across the globe" (Winders and Ransom 2019, 1). This is not merely in terms of the meat commodities themselves, but in a more encompassing sense as global meatification unfolds in and through what

Weis (2013) calls the "industrial grain-oilseed-livestock complex" involving numerous commodities and thus of crucial importance to the entire global agrifood system. At the same time, both the global economy and the global food system have been changing, with significant "global shifts" toward the east and south (Belesky and Lawrence 2019; McMichael 2020). A range of so-called emerging economies plays central roles in what has been labeled the "rise of the South" (UNDP 2013; Hansen and Wethal 2015). While global meatification necessarily reflects the mentioned geographical unevenness in consumption patterns, it is more and more shaped by new dynamics within an increasingly multipolar global political economy. Asia unsurprisingly plays a central role, and Jakobsen and Hansen (2020) have shown how an Asian meat complex is emerging, involving, and depending upon the development of cash crops for feed in Latin America (see also Oliveira 2016; Stølen this volume). Yet there is a lack of studies systematically exploring the increasing multipolarity of the global meat industry and how the rise of the South is reflected in processes of global meatification.

In this chapter, we focus on production, trade, and consumption in five leading emerging economies, the BRICS (Brazil, Russia, India, China, and South Africa). The BRICS has received significant attention as a political-economic cooperation bloc on the global arena (Cousins et al. 2018), and the mere size of this constellation underlines its importance at a global scale—together comprising around 40 percent of the world's population and accounting for over 25 percent of global GDP and land area (Belesky and Lawrence 2019). Still, the changing role of the BRICS in global meat systems has received surprisingly little attention. The BRICS is increasingly interconnected through the "industrial grain-oilseed-livestock complex," and scholars have argued that China, Brazil, Russia, and India are ever more dominant in the ongoing reconfiguration of the global food system, as "emerging nodes of power" and "'hubs' of capital" (Belesky and Lawrence 2019, 1120; see also Escher 2021). Moreover, both private and state actors in each country are central in structuring production and trade of meat in their respective regions. South African actors are less dominant in global networks, but are nonetheless central within the African region and crucial for understanding how meat production and consumption on the African continent co-shape with global reconfigurations. By examining the role of states and businesses within the BRICS, we explore what increasing multipolarity in global meat entails and how it unfolds. The differences between the BRICS countries also allow us to highlight how aspects of interconnectedness, variation, and centralization are all integrated parts of meatification in the Global South.

The empirical analysis in the chapter draws on secondary literature, media reports, and statistics compiled by the authors. We start by giving a broad outline of global meatification, the role of countries in the "South," and the

BRICS' characteristics and distinct positions in the world economy. Having done so, we proceed to our main analysis of the role of BRICS in global meat systems. We organize the analysis by focusing first on feed crops, before we look at the production and consumption of pork, beef, and poultry in turn. This allows us to disaggregate key patterns systematically, while demonstrating the role of BRICS countries in the global feed and meat industry. Moreover, we illustrate how BRICS plays a central role in structuring the global production network of meat through South-South trade relationships. We conclude by discussing the centrality of the BRICS in processes of meatification, with particular consideration of global *poultryfication*.

UNPACKING GLOBAL MEATIFICATION

In a joint report in 1999, the United Nations Food and Agriculture Organization (FAO), the International Food Policy Research Institute, and the International Livestock Research Institute (ILRI) located a "livestock revolution" in developing countries at the center of the massive transformations in global agriculture. They interpreted this as a demand-driven process that would bring major benefits for consumers and producers alike (Delgado et al. 1999; ILRI 1999). However, critical scholars have pointed to how the above narrative fails to grasp the spatially uneven patterns of global meatification (MacLachlan 2015), and the ways in which these are entwined with capitalist expansion. A leading proponent of such critical approaches is Tony Weis (2007, 2013, 2015). He rejects the nutrition/health argument brought forth in the "livestock revolution" narrative, where such demand is understood as mainly concerning palate pleasure and culture. Weis argues for understanding meatification through an industrial complex where demand for more meat is fortified by powerful economic motivations on the production side (2015, 297).

South-South Relations and Global Meat

Several scholars have pointed to the centrality of meatification to accumulation in the broader global agro-food system (McMichael 2013; Neo and Emel 2017; Jakobsen and Hansen 2020). Others have explored how meatification develops through capitalist geographies at national scales. Notably, Schneider's (2014, 2017a, b, 2019) work on China shows how the rapid meatification process has involved reorganization of its agricultural sector toward large-scale and unsustainable capitalist agriculture (see also Korsnes and Liu, this volume). Moreover, through a series of in-depth reports, the Institute for Agriculture and Trade Policy has examined the role of China in what they refer to as "the global meat complex" (Sharma 2014; Sharma and Rou 2014; Schneider and Sharma 2014; Rou and Horowitz 2014). Neo and Emel (2017) examine how foreign direct investment flows have led to the restructuring of Poland's pork industry, while Hansen (this volume) finds that meatification in Vietnam has depended upon capitalist transformations across domestic food systems.

The term "BRICS," starting as an acronym created by Goldman Sachs investor Jim O'Neill in 2001 to signal where investors should look for the next fast-growing economies, materialized into a political constellation in 2006. Since then, this relatively odd grouping of Brazil, Russia, India, China, and South Africa has held biannual meetings, sought to work toward similar goals in international meetings, and created joint financial institutions set to rival Bretton Woods institutions. Economically, however, the group is much less coherent and increasingly competing rather than cooperating.[2] Yet they have each engaged in extensive economic activities both intra- and interregionally, seeking to expand control over natural resources central to meat production and consumption. In two special issues from 2016 and 2018, a set of scholars from the BRICS Initiatives in Critical Agrarian Studies sought to unpack the role of BRICS in global agrarian transformations, excluding India (McKay et al. 2016; Cousin et al. 2018). These studies focused on national agrarian dynamics within Brazil and Russia (Andrade 2016; Nikulin and Trotsuk 2016); the dominating role of South Africa, Brazil, and China in their respective regions (Martiniello 2016; Zhou 2016; Hall and Cousins 2018; Mills 2018; Sauer et al. 2018); and new South-South connections (Campbell 2016; McKay et al. 2016; Milhorance 2016; Wilkinson et al. 2016). Across cases, they find a "general pattern of extractivism, large-farm development often through contested land deals or 'land grabbing,' the expansion of corporate agribusiness and agro-processing, consolidated and vertically integrated value chains, right through to the supermarketisation of food retail" (McKay et al. 2016, 587). Cousins and colleagues (2018) focus on similar processes within and between BRICS countries, while connecting the role of the BRICS countries to the rise of other key middle-income countries (Craviotti 2018; McKay 2018).

In this chapter, we build on the conceptualizations and findings outlined earlier for analyzing interconnections between geographies, economic developments, and changing meat cultures—focusing on the role of the BRICS. While much of the literature has centered around production (Hansen and Jakobsen 2020), we need to acknowledge that meatification occurs through patterns of food provision that shape, while being shaped by, uneven consumption patterns across the world (Hansen 2018; Hoelle 2017; Weis 2013).

BRICS and the Global Meat Complex

The BRICS occupies a rapidly increasing share of global meat trade. In 2019, exports from BRICS countries represented 15 percent of global meat flows, mainly due to Brazil, while imports to BRICS countries accounted for 17 percent of all trade in meat—with 15 percent of global flows directed to China alone (Chatham House 2021). All five countries are home to large meat industries, with the partial exception of South Africa, as we will show, and combined they represented 38 percent of global meat production in 2019 (FAO 2021).[3] That said, China's massive meat industry clearly dwarfs the others, as illustrated in figure 3.1.

In terms of consumption, BRICS has seen highly uneven patterns, as revealed by the consumption numbers in table 3.1. Four out of five BRICS countries consume well above the world average per capita meat consumption in 2019 of 34 kilograms (OECD 2021). Brazil is even high above the OECD average annual meat consumption per capita of 70.1 kilograms[4] (OECD 2021). Meanwhile, India consumes very little meat in per capita terms.

The most striking difference is indeed between the two largest countries—India and China—with remarkably different patterns of meatification. According to FAOSTAT food supply numbers, China's per capita meat consumption increased sixfold from 1978, the year market reforms were initiated, to 2013 (FAO 2021). This increase drove and was driven by an immense increase in domestic meat production (Schneider 2017b) and meat imports (Cheng et al. 2015). The latter trend has intensified alongside the outbreak

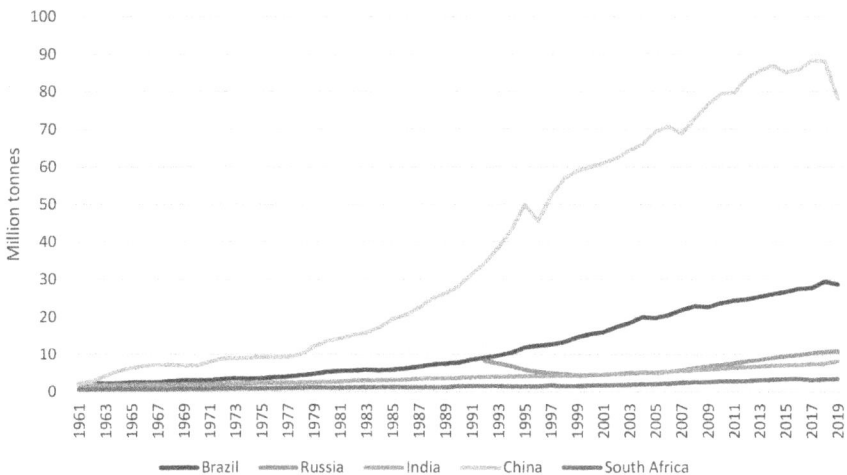

Figure 3.1   Total Annual Meat Production, BRICS, 1961–2019.

Table 3.1   **Meat Consumption Per Capita (kilograms), 2019**

	Beef	Pork	Poultry	Sheep meat	Annual total
Brazil	25.2	12.8	40.3	0.5	78.8
Russia	10.1	20.6	30.6	1.3	62.6
India	0.5	0.2	2.4	0.5	3.6
China	4.1	24.4	14.0	3.2	45.7
South Africa	11.1	3.7	34.2	2.6	51.6

of African Swine Fever (ASF), and China imported 37 percent more meat in 2019 than in 2018 (FAO 2020). China has gone from being a major soy producer to outsourcing this production to countries in Latin America, including Brazil (Hairong et al. 2016; Stølen, this volume), and become one of the largest meat producers globally.

In India things look very different. Although the popular depiction of India as a vegetarian country is misleading, and meat consumption is increasing among parts of the population (Jakobsen and Nielsen, this volume), the country hardly saw any increase in per capita meat consumption between 1978 and 2013, from 3.6 kilograms to 3.69 kilograms (FAO 2021). According to OECD numbers, per capita meat consumption has increased slightly for poultry since 1990s, but has in fact decreased for all other meat types (OECD 2021). Indeed, India has among the lowest rates of per capita meat consumption in the world and acts as a reminder of the shortcomings of strictly income-based explanations of meat consumption (see Hansen 2018). Yet India is a significant meat producer, and the industrial grain-oilseed-livestock complex in the country has expanded in recent years (Jakobsen and Hansen 2020; Jakobsen 2020).

Brazil is a massive soy producer, with Brazilian capital also dominating production in other Latin American countries, such as Bolivia (McKay 2017). Moreover, Brazil is the world's second largest producer of beef and poultry, third of maize, and forth of pork (Sharma and Schlesinger 2017), signifying Brazil's central positioning in several parts of the production chain. The Brazilian company JBS-Friboi (JBS) is the largest meat company in the world, operating in production and trade of beef, pork, and poultry, as well as feed. Marfrig and Brasil Foods is one of the top five meat companies in the world. State support has been instrumental in supporting Brazilian actors' move toward the core of global meat production, pushed forward by the Brazilian National Development Bank's policy (2007–2013) of turning Brazilian companies into leading transnational companies (Sauer et al. 2018).

South Africa is the odd one out on the production side. It has a comparatively very small meat sector, although many have argued for a significant potential for expansion. Instead, South Africa imports meat to feed booming levels of meat consumption. According to FAOSTAT data, per capita meat consumption remained fairly stable from the 1960s until the 1990s, then started booming in the 2000s. The average South African consumed 32 kilograms of meat in 1961 and 37 kilograms in 1999. By 2013, however, the figure had reached 65 kilograms (FAO 2021). The massive increases in meat consumption have first and foremost occurred through poultry, with consumption tripling already in the years between 1970 and 2002 (Delport et al. 2017). Ronquest-Ross et al. (2015) further found that between 1994 and 2009, consumption of poultry and pork increased by 109 percent and 119 percent respectively, whereas the consumption of red meat remained stable. South Africa has also played a key role in the restructuring of regional agrarian change and consumption patterns, leading major land acquisitions (Martiniello 2016), concentrating corporate power within the agrifood system (Greenberg 2017), and being central to the expansion of supermarkets and fast-food chains within Sub-Saharan Africa (Campbell 2016; Hall and Cousins 2018).

Since around 2000, Russia's consumption of meat and meat products has risen markedly, from 50 kilograms per capita in 2000 to 85 kilograms in 2014 (Wegren et al. 2018, 104). Russia has become a major meat importer, and between 2006 and 2010, it was indeed the largest meat importer in the world (Prikhodko and Davleyev 2014). In the recent decade, however, Russia's meat imports have been decreasing at a rapid pace, from a value of 7.1 billion USD in 2012 to 1.8 billion USD in 2019 (Chatham House 2021). Over the same period, exports have been surging, albeit still at a relatively low value, from 106 million USD in 2012 to 539 million USD in 2019 (Chatham House 2021). This is related to Russia's import trade embargo for a number of agricultural items including meat from the EU, United States, and other Western countries first introduced in 2014. It also clearly signals that Russia's meat industry is undergoing change. Poultry and pork are the main components of meat production systems in Russia, with a few companies—OJSC Cherkizovo Group being the lead—increasingly consolidating their hold over the Russian meat industry (Flanders 2020). The meat industry thus partakes in the broader change in Russian agriculture toward mega-farms (known as "agroholdings") running integrated and concentrated operations (Wegren et al. 2018). Interestingly, the Russian Ministry of Health has established a "rational meat consumption norm" of 72 kilograms of meat per person per year, which marks the goal for domestic meat consumption (Prikhodko and Davleyev 2014).

THE BRICS IN GLOBAL MEATIFICATION

As demonstrated earlier, the BRICS countries play increasingly important roles across the global "industrial grain-oilseed-livestock complex." We proceed by mapping and analyzing these roles, starting with the feed crops, especially soybean and maize, that make industrial meat possible.

Feed crops

Brazil's emergence as a soybean powerhouse has attracted much scholarly attention (see, for example, Oliveira and Hecht 2016; Oliveira 2016). While the rapid increase of soybean production to cater to global demands—especially China's—for animal feed in their growing meat industries has been a regional phenomenon involving what has been called an integrated "Soybean Republic" in Latin America (Turzi 2011), Brazil's developments outsize nearby countries. Soy represents around 52.9 percent of the total grain area in Brazil (Escher et al. 2018), and in 2016 it was estimated that Brazil supplies 40 percent of the global market in soybean, coupled with being the world's second largest exporter of maize (Oliveira 2016). Soybean has been crucial to Brazil's role within broader geopolitical changes such as the rise of the BRICS, serving as a key arena where Brazilian state and agribusiness interests seek to challenge Western agro-food dominance in a context of increasing multipolarity (ibid). Clearly, the Brazil-China trade relationship is central to this pattern of agro-industrial transformation, yet this relationship has been far from unproblematic, with recent studies emphasizing frictions and seeming "Sinophobic" sentiments in Brazil due to the (perceived or real) influence of Chinese agribusiness *within* Brazil, including in the form of contested land grabs (Oliveira 2018). Brazil's trade in maize is rather different, with the largest flow by far going to Iran, followed by Vietnam and Spain (Chatham House 2021).

The rising meat production in Russia is coupled with increase in imports of soybeans, primarily from Brazil and Paraguay (followed by Belarus) at an annual value of almost one billion USD. Since 2014, however, imports have declined due to a new import substitution program aimed at increasing domestic production of feed crops (Rau and Frolova 2019). This is paralleled by steeply rising exports of soybeans, at an annual value of 762 million USD, to a number of countries but with the main flows being to China and Algeria. Increased soybean production for feed has been the stated aim of state policies in Russia for the last few years, leading to soybeans rapidly overtaking acreage from other oilseeds in the country (ibid). Moreover, as Chinese imports of U.S. soybeans have sunk markedly as a consequence of U.S.-China "trade wars," Russia seems to have stepped in—or the other way around. Indeed, one of the key soybeans producing regions of Russia is Amur Oblast, bordering to China. In 2019, it was reported that "buyers from neighboring Chinese towns have flocked to the Russian region, clearing out all their soybean stocks" (Milenkovic 2019, no page). This is not an entirely new phenomenon, as bordering regions have for some time seen Chinese investments and leased cultivation of farmland, including run by Chinese agribusiness. These regions have offered opportunities for Chinese agrarian capitalism that were otherwise curtailed by state policy in China (Zhou 2016). In 2018, it was reported that Chinese investors were looking at investing further in the Amur Oblast region for the purpose of soybean cultivation. This includes large Chinese agribusinesses such as the Dongjin Group, leasing 66,667-hectares land in Russia's Far East for soybean exports since 2017 (*Global Times* 2018).

The ways in which Chinese actors are entering into Russian and Brazilian feed production (in addition to feed production in Africa, Southeast Asia, and Eastern Europe) illustrate the massive demand from China's meat industry. China is the world's largest importer of soy, buying 60 percent of all traded soybeans on the global market in 2012 (Escher et al. 2018). China's soy imports increased more than eightfold between 2000 and 2019, from 11 million tons to 91 million tons, the main exporters being Brazil, the United States, and Argentina (Chatham House 2021, see also Stølen, this volume). With help of China's "going out" policies, formalized in 2001, Chinese companies are increasingly establishing themselves overseas to take advantage of the demand for soybeans and take control over the soybean import system to China (Giraudo 2020). According to Escher et al. (2018), Chinese private companies, so-called dragon-head enterprises,[5] and specialized supply-and-marketing cooperatives control 60 percent of the soy traded to China (see also Schneider 2017b). Moreover, 70 percent of China's domestic maize production is used for feed, yet is nowhere near covering the demand for maize. To meet the increasing demand and due to competition from cheap soy imports from Latin America, many Chinese farmers have switched from soy to maize production which is rapidly transforming the grain production landscape (Sharma 2014).

In India, maize has been booming in the last few decades, increasing to becoming one of the foremost "food crops" grown in the country—a government terminology that hides the fact that 60 percent of it is estimated to go into animal feed, primarily for poultry. Hence, maize is becoming a key aspect of the expansion of the industrial grain-oilseed-livestock complex in the country (see Jakobsen 2020; Jakobsen and Westengen 2021). This has also implications for India's relation to other countries, including by way of trade with countries in Asia, but noticeably not with China (see Jakobsen and Hansen 2020). Instead, while soybeans are exported to the United States and other parts of Asia, the Indian maize industry—in terms of private companies, governmental agencies, and their affiliated international advisory bodies—has expressed strategic interest in Southeast Asian markets as export destinations, publicly expressing the aim of becoming an "export hub" for the region (CGIAR 2015).

South Africa has a surplus of maize production, while experiencing a deficit in soy- and feed-related products, such as oil cake. Consequently, the latter products have largely been imported from South America (Ncube 2018), mainly Argentina (Chatham House 2021). Imports of soybeans, mainly from South America, increased from less than 2 million USD in 2013 to over 100 million USD in 2016 (ibid). However, South Africa is currently "spearheading the intensification of soybean production in Africa," which is considered a direct outcome of growing demand for meat and dairy products of growing middle classes, in combination with increasing biofuel production (Foyer et al. 2018). Soy is considered a very attractive crop across Africa, given the growing regional and international demand (mainly from China), which has made the government strongly incentivize a soybean-maize rotation where possible (ibid). These processes are largely driven by an increasing regional demand for poultry, where a small number of large South African corporations are seeking to establish and control supply chains for animal feed in the Southern African region (Ncube 2018).

Pork

China is central at all stages of the global pork industry: half of the world's pigs are bred, produced, and eaten in China (Schneider 2019); it is the most popular type of meat among Chinese consumers; and production is well ahead of the other BRICS countries (see figure 3.2).

The pig has traveled from being an important and integrated part of many Chinese households to becoming commodified and industrialized particularly after Deng Xiaoping's "Reform and Opening" in 1978 (see Lander et al. 2020; Korsnes and Liu, this volume). The pork industry has received massive governmental support, particularly through finance subsidies and investments, which in turn has been instrumental in reducing smallholder producers from 74 percent to 37 percent of production between 2000 and 2010 (Howard 2019). Three companies dominate the market and account for 68 percent of total sales and 86 percent of profits for the top 10 Chinese producers (Schneider 2019). With the purchase of U.S.-based Smithfield in 2013, Chinese WH Group also became the largest pork enterprise in the world. Moreover, this purchase made it possible for China to take advantage of subsidized feed and vertically integrate its supply chain for feed in the United States (ibid). Chinese per capita pork consumption peaked at 32.7 kilograms in 2014. It has declined somewhat since then, before falling to 24.8 kilograms in 2019 following the ASF outbreak that caused major disruptions to the domestic industry (OECD 2021). Estimations suggest that the ASF led to the culling of more than 100 million

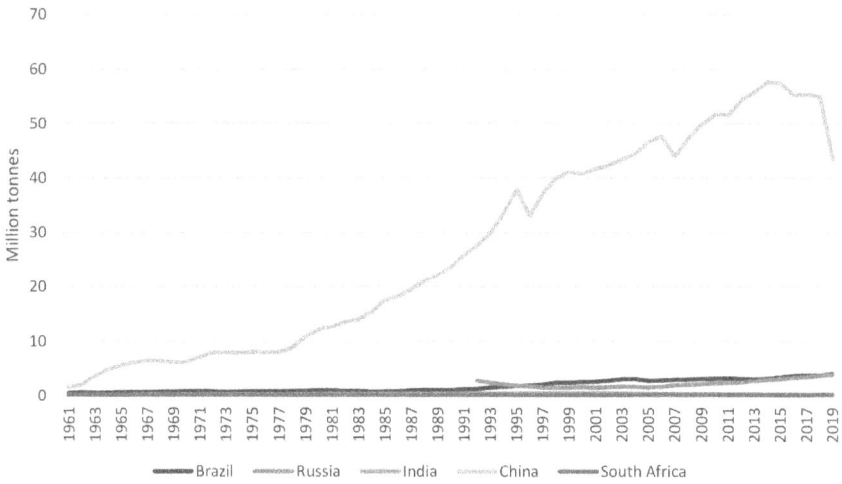

Figure 3.2   Annual Pork Production, BRICS, 1961–2019.

pigs (He 2019), causing a major decrease in pork output. While imports have soured seeking to meet Chinese pork demand, USDA/GAIN (2020a) estimates a supply gap of 18 million tons pork. That said, both production and consumption are picking up again and are expected to grow significantly in 2021.

In South Africa, pork makes up only 7 percent of meat consumption. The traditionally low consumption of pork is connected to cultural and religious beliefs, but pork consumption is increasing, partly explained by favorable prices in comparison to beef and lamb (USDA/GAIN 2017). Delport et al. (2017) divide pork consumption roughly into two income groups, fresh pork being consumed by low-income consumers and processed products such as bacon being consumed by higher-income groups. The domestic pork industry has remained small, only 0.2 percent of global pork production, mostly absorbed by domestic consumption (BFAP 2014; Bhorat et al. 2019). Less standardized production and high entry barriers have concentrated the sector, with only two firms accounting for 80 percent of production (Bhorat et al. 2019). Still, pork production has had a 4.5 percent annual increase since mid-2000s. While markets in China, India, and Vietnam are singled out as lucrative for South African pork exports, this is dependent on South African economies of scale. A more accessible export route is through the Southern African region, but the high degree of informality involved in meat trade in the region, and the length of time for transport, currently represents a barrier for such an expansion (ibid).

Although Brazil is one of the world's top pork producers, pork accounts for only 13 percent of domestic meat consumption (Sharma and Schlesinger

2017). Many Brazilian consumers seem to consider pork a less healthy option. Combined with the low cost and high availability of beef and poultry, pork has remained a less popular meat choice (Nogueira 2015). Consequently, three quarters of domestic produce is exported. Indeed, the main global pork trade flows are located from Brazil to Hong Kong, Brazil to China, China to Hong Kong, Brazil to Singapore, and Brazil to Argentina, illustrating the centrality of Brazil in the global pork industry (Chatham House 2021).

Brazil has also tapped into the Russian meat market. After EU exporters diverted their exports away from Russia and toward China after the 2014 Russian embargo, Brazil has moved up as one of the main exporters of pork to Russia. In fact, pork exports to Russia constituted half of Brazil's export of pork in 2015 (Szűcs and Vida 2017). However, imports are currently decreasing as Russian pork production is on the rise. Government support and trade measures have been important components in seeking to reverse the massive decreases in meat production from the 1990s and far into the 2000s. Already from 2005, there were signs of a turning tide fueled through "intensified pork production, shorter growing cycles and faster animal turnover in swine production facilities" (Prikhodko and Davleyev 2014, 21). Between 2005 and 2010 pork production expanded by 49 percent, accompanied by a 38 percent increase in consumption (ibid, 20).

Beef

Beef has varied histories in the BRICS countries. Brazil has a long history of producing and consuming beef in a region known for very high levels of beef consumption (see Stølen, this volume), whereas cows are politically contested in India (see Jakobsen and Nielsen, this volume) and beef used to be known as the millionaire's meat in China. This clearly shows in consumption statistics, where the average Brazilian ate 25.2 kilograms of beef in 2019 (10 kilograms more than the OECD average), the average South African ate 11.1 kilograms, the average Russian ate 10.1 kilograms, the average Chinese ate 4.1 kilograms, and the average Indian ate 0.5 kilograms (OECD 2021). Together, BRICS exports represent 19 percent of global beef trade, with main flows going from Brazil to China, Hong Kong, and Egypt, and from India to Vietnam. India is among the world's leading beef exporters, a striking fact in view of the politically sensitive nature of beef in the country (see Jakobsen and Nielsen, this volume). Moreover, BRICS imports represent about one-tenth of all beef trade, with China being the main importer, followed by Russia. Beef imports to China are indeed growing at an astounding pace, with almost a third of imports stemming from Brazil (Chatham House 2021), reflecting a rapid increase in domestic beef consumption. Due to the ASF outbreak depressing domestic pork production and affecting prices on pork,

Chinese consumers are also expected to replace some pork consumption with beef. Although this rise will initially be covered by imports, this could also boost domestic cattle production in China over the long run (USDA/GAIN 2020a) (figure 3.3).

South Africa has traditionally been a net importer of beef (DAFF 2018), but has recently been ramping up red meat production. This is visible, for example, through the recent establishment of what is reputedly the world's largest single feedlot site, south of Johannesburg, housing as much as 160,000 cattle for beef production. According to a 2018 news report, this single feedlot accounted for as much as 70 percent of South Africa's beef exports and 30 percent of the local market (Bloomberg 2018). Although South Africa has primarily exported to neighboring African countries (DAFF 2018), expansion of production capacity seeks to tap into Asian markets, primarily Chinese (Bradfield 2017). In fact, already in 2015 and 2016, South Africa exported more beef to Asia than to the African continent (DAFF 2018).

Brazil is the second largest producer of beef in the world (behind the United States), and the major beef exporter globally (Vale et al. 2019). This has triggered critical attention to the role of the country's beef industry in deforestation, with some assessments holding that as much as 80 percent of new deforestation in the Amazon is directly linked to land for cattle operations (Kuepper et al. 2018). Brazilians eat most of the produce (81 percent) on the domestic market, the rest exported; the "rest" here amounting to no less than 20 percent of the entire global beef production (Sharma and Schlesinger 2017). In both domestic and export markets, there is heavy corporate

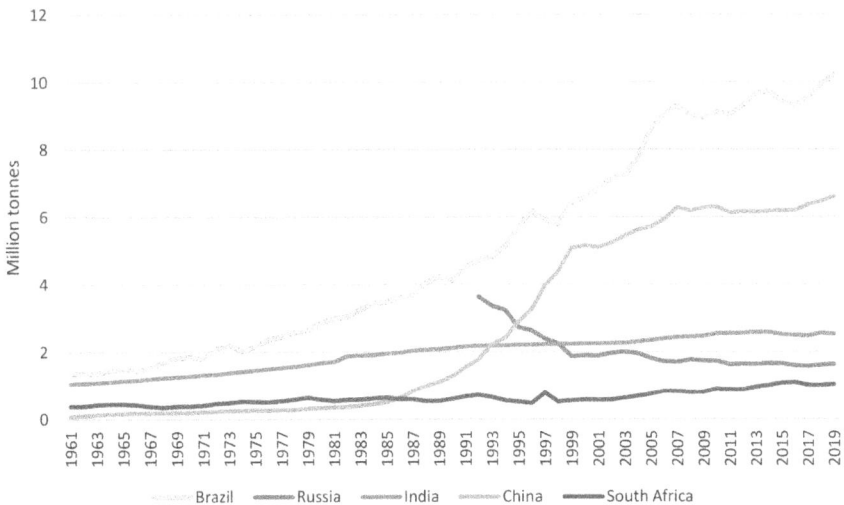

Figure 3.3   Annual Beef and Buffalo Meat Production, BRICS, 1961–2019.

concentration with JBS and Marfrig controlling 30 percent of the beef slaughterhouses (Benítez 2018). Through massive government support deployed to develop export firms into major transnational corporations, JBS has risen to the position of the largest meat processing company in the world, and has expanded from a specialization in beef into poultry and pork (Almanza et al. 2018; Vale et al. 2019).

Poultry

The global increase in poultry production and consumption during the past 70 years has been extreme. In 1961, a total of 6.5 billion chickens were slaughtered in the world. In 2019, the number was a staggering 72 billion (FAO 2021). BRICS countries play a central role in global poultry production and consumption. China alone slaughtered 11 billion chickens in 2019, Brazil 5.8 billion, India 2.7 billion, Russia 2.5 billion, and South Africa almost 1 billion. In other words, BRICS slaughtered about a third of all chickens globally in 2019 (FAO 2021).

In total, BRICS exports represented 26 percent of global poultry exports in 2019, but almost all of this (in value terms) comes from Brazil (6.5 billion dollars of a total of 7.2 billion USD) followed by China and Russia. Brazil exports frozen chicken all over the world. China, after Saudi Arabia, represents the second largest importer of Brazilian chicken (Chatham House 2021). Although Brazil is a leading global exporter of poultry, 70 percent of production is consumed domestically, illustrating the massive size of Brazil's industry (Sharma and Schlesinger 2017).

China is also a substantial producer of chicken, but most is consumed in the domestic market. By 2014, China produced 18 percent of all poultry in the world (Pi et al. 2014). China's poultry sector has transformed at rapid pace, and especially consumption and production of chicken have been expanding very rapidly. As part of these transformations, the sector has gone through dramatic industrialization, upscaling, and consolidation. Pi et al. (2014) have showed how the number of broiler farms decreased by 75 percent between 1996 and 2011, as 70 million small-scale farmers left the sector between 1985 and 2005. Poultry production indeed transformed from a sideline activity for rural households to a colossal industry. By 2009, intensive broiler farms represented almost 70 percent of total supply, mainly met by large, private operations, including many foreign corporations, replacing state-owned poultry companies (ibid). Due to rising pork prices after the ASF outbreak, the government is also actively encouraging consumers to eat more poultry (USDA/GAIN 2020a).

Over the past decades, the Russian meat market has transformed through a shift from the consumption of beef to that of poultry, as well as a major increase in production capacity. Russia's poultry production increased by 180 percent from the early 1990s to 2010 (Prikhodko and Davleyev 2014), and reaching the capacity to fully meet domestic demand in 2017 (USDA/GAIN 2020b). Still, Russia has continued as a major export destination for Brazilian frozen chicken meat (ibid), while the increased production capacity has been directed to rapidly rising poultry exports. Especially since the Chinese market opened for Russian trade in 2019, Russian poultry companies have eyed this as an opportunity for expansion. Indeed, 62 percent of Russian poultry exports went to China during first half of 2020, up from 29 percent in 2019 (USDA/GAIN 2020b).

Also in South Africa, there has been a major boom in the consumption of poultry over the past decades. In 1970, annual per capital consumption of poultry meat was 7.7 kilograms, increasing to almost 40 kilograms in 2015 (Delport et al. 2017). Between 2000 and 2014 this meant an increase of almost 80 percent (USDA/GAIN 2017), and in 2015, poultry totaled to 59 percent of the meat consumed in South Africa (Davids and Meyer 2017). The popularity of poultry, mainly chicken, is commonly explained by the importance of price and income for South African consumers (Erasmus and Hoffman 2017). Although only 1.8 percent of global production, the broiler industry still represents the largest agricultural subsector in South Africa and 16.5 percent of the gross value of agricultural production (Davids and Meyer 2017). Moreover, while South Africa is importing large amounts of poultry from Brazil (amounting to 168 million USD in 2019, Chatham House 2021), the government has in recent years sought to meet rising consumer demand and boost domestic production by introducing higher tariffs on imports (Ncube et al. 2018; Naidoo 2020).

The last BRICS country, India, also makes part of the broader trend of poultryfication, with surging production, especially since around 2000. Total poultry production increased by more than 400 percent from 2000 to 2019, reaching 4.2 million tons annually (FAO 2021). While still low in comparative terms, India's poultry sector is booming. According to Khara et al. (2020), India is turning into one of the fastest growing markets for consumption of poultry, with its popularity being connected to how poultry is less associated with religious and cultural taboos (Bruckert 2021). The poultry sector also differs from other meat sectors in India by being more industrialized (see Jakobsen 2020).

CONCLUDING DISCUSSION: BRICS, MEATIFICATION, AND GLOBAL POULTRYFICATION

Processes of meatification persist globally. While inhabitants in rich countries on average consume much more meat than inhabitants in less affluent countries, most of the growth in meat consumption globally takes place in middle-income countries, and countries in the "South" are increasingly important meat producers. This chapter has shown how Brazil, Russia, India, China, and South Africa in variegated ways have taken the center stage in the global "industrial grain-oilseed-livestock complex." Brazil and China stand out as massive producers, and Brazil also as a central meat exporter. Russia and South Africa have also seen a rapid expansion in meat production and consumption, particularly in poultry. India is the odd one out, but is home to a large beef industry that tends to go under the radar. Moreover, the BRICS countries and regions in the South are continuously weaved together through production and export of crops that feed into booming meat sectors. The role of Brazil and Brazilian capital is significant here, being a global soybean powerhouse, expanding industrially throughout Latin America, and playing a central role in meat production processes in China, Russia, and South Africa. Strong demand from China has been particularly central in dethroning the United States as *the* main exporter of soy and maize.

Despite variegation, global meatification still involves a certain global homogenization of meat cultures toward industrially produced beef, pork, and chicken (Winders and Ransom 2019). While all represent significant industries, chicken is increasingly dominating and a global process of poultryfication is obvious. Chicken, and the prevalence of chicken bones in the geological record, has indeed become the "ultimate symbol of the Anthropocene" (Bennett et al. 2018a). Broiler chickens, unable to survive without human intervention, now have a combined mass larger than that of all other birds on Earth and "vividly symbolize the transformation of the biosphere to fit evolving human consumption patterns" (Bennett et al. 2018b, 9; see also Patel and Moore 2017). While chicken tends to be portrayed as a healthier and even more environmentally friendly form of meat, the poultry industry is intertwined with a range of capitalist processes and their despoliations of nature, as chicken consumption expands across a wide range of different meat cultures (Josephson 2020). Global poultryfication warrants much more academic attention, particularly in terms of its impacts on animal welfare and local and global environments. Furthermore, as Patel and Moore (2017) write, the continuation of global poultryfication will demand enormous amounts of labor, with the present global poultry industry documented to be significantly based upon underpaid, frequently migrant, and racialized labor forces (see also Silbergeld 2016). Global poultryfication is certainly deeply problematic.

Additionally, there is a clear tendency of consolidated corporate power within each meat type, as well as important alliances forged between global meat companies and feed traders. Consequently, a few very large economic actors are given great power in shaping the dynamics of "industrial grain-oilseed-livestock complex," keeping meat relatively cheap and accessible

(Howard 2019). The largest meat processors globally have concentrated markets

> (1) horizontally, through acquiring direct competitors in their initial processing sectors [such as the Chinese WH group]; they have also grown (2) concentrically, by branching into the processing of additional livestock species [such as Brazilian JBS]; and (3) vertically, by taking over upstream suppliers [such as Chinese and South African corporations]. (ibid, 31)

In the BRICS countries, this centralization of power seems to be heavily state-backed, with national policies being tailored to make the meat industry globally competitive, in line with how emerging and developing states have tended to play a more dominant role in national economic and industrial development processes more broadly. In China, "dragon-head enterprises" control around 70 percent of pork and poultry production (Escher et al. 2018), and Brazilian JBS, Marfrig, and Minerva control 50 percent of the country's beef market (Vale et al. 2019).

The future of meatification, however, is uncertain in important ways. The meat industry has experienced a series of disruptions in recent years in the form of the Covid-19 pandemic and repeated outbreaks of avian influenza and ASF. The consequences of these are complex and largely unknown. After a decline in global meat production and consumption in 2019 and 2020, 2021 was forecasted to break new records in global meat consumption at the time of writing (Euromeatnews 2021). These disruptions could also have far-reaching consequences through stricter quality controls that eventually could favor industrialized meat production (see Hansen and Jakobsen 2020b). However, meat reduction and vegetarianism are global trends that potentially could have an impact on meatification. For example, meat reduction is a prevalent new practice among the rapidly expanding Chinese middle classes. This practice received some perhaps unexpected governmental support, when the Chinese government's dietary guidelines targeted a cut in meat consumption by 50 percent (Milman and Leavenworth 2016; Korsnes and Liu, this volume). Moreover, the role of alternative meats, such as plant-based (see Efstathiou, this volume) or cultured meats (see Volden and Wethal, this volume), could become more important parts of global diets in the future.

That said, evidence from affluent countries where meat reduction has been on the agenda for many years shows that such trends do not necessarily lead to a reduction of meat consumption in practice. Furthermore, the meat industry is a highly profitable business that keeps targeting new markets and opportunities. And while there is much discussion of the need for creating more sustainable food systems globally, most of the world is arguably moving in the opposite direction toward less healthy and less sustainable diets

(Swinburn et al. 2019). Taking into account how much higher average meat consumption is in affluent countries than in large parts of the world, there is obviously potential for a further intensification of meatification. Knowing the range of impacts industrial meat has on human and nonhuman animals and on the global environment, and knowing that we are already in the middle of what a recent Lancet report referred to as a "global syndemic of obesity, undernutrition and climate change" (Swinburn et al. 2019), such an intensification gives much reason for concern.

NOTES

1. We would like to thank Desmond McNeill and Karen Lykke Syse for constructive feedback on earlier versions of this chapter.
2. Arguably also in political terms, but at least there are attempts to unify political interests through the political constellation of BRICS.
3. Combined, the BRICS countries produced 128 million tonnes meat in 2019, while the global total was 337 million tones (FAO 2021)
4. Including 14.5 kg of beef and veal, 23 kg of pork, 31.3 kg of poultry and 1.3 kg of sheep meat (OECD 2020).
5. The concept "dragon-head enterprises" refers to agribusinesses appointed by the state to take lead in processes toward agricultural modernity. For more detail, see Scheider (2017b).

REFERENCES

Almanza, Jonathan, Douglas H. Constance and Francisco Martínez (2018). "Poultry Grabs and Agri-Food Financialization: The Case of JBS of Brazil." In Hilde Bjorkhaug, André Magnan and Geoffrey Lawrence (eds.) *The Financialization of Agri-Food Systems: Contested Transformations*. Routledge: Oxon, 176–197.

Andrade, Daniela (2016). "'Export or Die': The Rise of Brazil as an Agribusiness Powerhouse." *Third World Thematics: A TWQ Journal* 1 (5): 653–672.

Belesky, Paul and Geoffrey Lawrence (2019). "Chinese State Capitalism and Neomercantilism in the Contemporary Food Regime: Contradictions, Continuity and Change." *The Journal of Peasant Studies* 46 (6): 1119–1141.

Benítez, Galia J. (2018). "Business Lobbying: Mapping Policy Networks in Brazil in Mercosur." *Social Sciences* 7 (10): 1–30.

Bennet, Carys, Jan Zalasiewicz, Mark Williams and Richard Thomas (2018a). "How Chickens Became the Ultimate Symbol of the Anthropocene." *The Conversation*. https://theconversation.com/how-chickens-became-the-ultimate-symbol-of-the -anthropocene-108559.

Bennett, Carys, Richard Thomas, Mark Williams, Jan Zalasiewicz, Matt Edgeworth, Holly Miller, Ben Coles, Alison Foster, Emily J. Burton and Marume Upenyu

(2018b). "The Broiler Chicken as a Signal of a Human Reconfigured Biosphere." *Royal Society Open Science* 5: 1–11. http://dx.doi.org/10.1098/rsos.180325

BFAP (2014). *Evaluating the Competitiveness of South African Pork Production within the Global Context.* First annual progress report, The agri benchmark project. The Bureau for Food and Agricultural Policy (BFAP) in collaboration with the Thünen Institute in Braunchweig, Germany.

Bhorat, Haroon, Arabo Ewinyu, Kezia Lilenstein, Christopher Rooney, François Steenkamp and Amy Thornton (2019). *Economic Complexity and Employment Expansion: The Case of South Africa.* Report for "Building economic complexity in Africa: Laying the foundation for expanding economic opportunities for women and youth in Africa." IDRC/CRDI, Development Policy Research Institute.

Blanchette, Alex (2018). "Industrial Meat Production." *Annual Review of Anthropology* 47: 185–199.

Bloomberg (2018). "World's Largest Feedlot Leads South African Beef Export Push." *Engineering News.* https://www.engineeringnews.co.za/article/worlds-largest-feedlot-leads-south-african-beef-export-push-2018-11-28/rep_id:4136

Bradfield, Michael (2017). "2020 & Beyond: A Vision for the SA Beef Industry." *Farmers Weekly.* https://ruvasa.co.za/wp-content/uploads/2019/08/Beef-Vision-for-the-future.pdf

Bruckert, Michaël (2021). "Chicken Politics: Agrifood Capitalism, Anxious Bodies, and the New Meanings of Chicken Meat in India." *Gastronomica* 21 (2): 33–46.

Campbell, Melodie (2016). "South African Supermarket Expansion in Sub-Saharan Africa." *Third World Thematics: A TWQ Journal* 1 (5): 709–725.

CGIAR Research Program on Maize (2015). "India Has Potential to Become Export Hub for Maize in South East Asia." http://maize.org/india-has-potential-to-become-export-hub-for-maize-in-south-east-asia/

Chatham House (2021). *Resource Trade Database.* https://resourcetrade.earth/

Cousins, Ben, Saturnino M. Borras Jr, Sergio Sauer and Jingzhong Ye (2018). "BRICS, Middle-Income Countries (MICs), and Global Agrarian Transformations: Internal Dynamics, Regional Trends, and International Implications." *Globalizations* 15 (1): 1–11.

Craviotti, Clara (2018). "Agrarian Trajectories in Argentina and Brazil: Multilatin Seed Firms and the South American Soybean Chain." *Globalizations* 15 (1): 56–73.

DAFF (2018). *A Profile of the South African beef Market Value Chain. Directory of Agriculture, Forestry and Fisheries.* Republic of South Africa.

Davids, Tracy and Ferdi H. Meyer (2017). "Price Formation and Competitiveness of the South African Broiler Industry in the Global Context." *Agrekon* 56 (2): 123–138.

Delgado, Christopher, Mark Rosegrant, Henning Steinfeld, Simon Ehui, and Claude Courbois (1999). "Livestock to 2020: The Next Food Revolution." *IFPRI Food, Agriculture, and the Environment Discussion Paper.* Washington, DC: IFPRI.

Delport, Marion, Marlene Louw, Tracy Davids, Hester Vermeulen and Ferdi Meyer (2017). "Evaluating the Demand for Meat in South Africa: An Econometric Estimation of Short Term Demand Elasticities." *Agrekon* 56 (1): 13–27.

Erasmus, Sara W. and Louwrens C. Hoffman (2017). "What is Meat in South Africa?" *Animal Frontiers* 7 (4): 71–75.

Escher, Fabiano (2021). "BRICS Varieties of Capitalism and Food Regime Reordering: A Comparative Institutional Analysis." *Journal of Agrarian Change* 21: 46–70.

Escher, Fabiano, Sergio Schneider and Jingzhong Ye (2018). "The Agrifood Question and Rural Development Dynamics in Brazil and China: Towards a Protective 'Countermovement'." *Globalizations* 15 (1): 92–113.

Euromeatnews. 2021. *Meat Consumption Set for a New Record Year.* https://www.euromeatnews.com/Article-Meat-consumption-set-for-a-new-record-year/4706?utm_source=Euromeatnews+-+Newsletter+Subscription&utm_campaign=b7a3a1c25e-EuromeatNewsletter_05_02_COPY_01&utm_medium=email&utm_term=0_fe20153ae3-b7a3a1c25e-36945927

FAO (2020). *Meat Market Review: Overview of Global Meat Market Developments in 2019.* http://www.fao.org/3/ca8819en/ca8819en.pdf

FAO (2021). *FAOSTAT Database.* Accessed from: http://www.fao.org/faostat/en/#data

Flanders (2020). "Meat Sector in Russia and North-West Region." *Flanders Investment & Trade Market Survey.* https://www.flandersinvestmentandtrade.com/export/sites/trade/files/market_studies/2020_Russian%20and%20North-West%20region%20meat%20sector_0.pdf

Foyer, Christine H., Kadambot H. Siddique, Amos PK Tai, Sven Anders, Nándor Fodor, Fuk-Ling Wong, Ndiko Ludidi, Mark A. Chapman, Brett J. Ferguson, Michael J. Considine, Florian Zabel, P. V. Vara Prasad, Rajeev K. Varshney, Henry T. Nguyen and Hon-Ming M. Lam (2019). "Modelling Predicts that Soybean is Poised to Dominate Crop Production across Africa." *Plant, Cell & Environment* 42 (1): 373–385.

Giraudo, Maria E. (2020). "Dependent Development in South America: China and the Soybean Nexus." *Journal of Agrarian Change* 20 (1): 60–78.

Global Times (2018). *Chinese Farmers Could Cultivate Soybeans in Russia's Far East to Replace US Soybean Imports.* https://www.globaltimes.cn/content/1116091.shtml

Godfray, H. Charles J., Paul Aveyard, Tara Garnett, Jim W. Hall, Timothy J. Key, Jamie Lorimer, Ray T. Pierrehumbert, Peter Scarborough, Marco Springmann, and Susan A. Jebb (2018). "Meat Consumption, Health, and the Environment." *Science* 361 (6399): 1–10.

Greenberg, Stephen (2017). "Corporate Power in the Agro-Food System and the Consumer Food Environment in South Africa." *The Journal of Peasant Studies* 44 (2): 467–496.

Hairong, Yan, Chen Yiyuan and Ku Hok Bun (2016). "China's Soybean Crisis: The Logic of Modernization and its discontents." *The Journal of Peasant Studies* 43 (2): 373–395.

Hall, Ruth, and Ben Cousins (2018). "Exporting contradicTions: The Expansion of South African Agrarian Capital Within Africa." *Globalizations* 15 (1): 12–31.

Hansen, Arve (2018). "Meat Consumption and Capitalist Development: The Meatification of Food Provision and Practice in Vietnam." *Geoforum* 93: 57–68.

Hansen, Arve, and Jostein Jakobsen. (2020a). "Meatification and Everyday Geographies of Consumption in Vietnam and China." *Geografiska Annaler: Series B, Human Geography* 102 (1): 21–39.

Hansen, Arve and Jostein Jakobsen (2020b). "Covid-19 and the Asian Meat Complex." *East Asia Forum*, 29.09.2020. https://www.eastasiaforum.org/2020/09/29/covid-19-and-the-asian-meat-complex/

Hansen, Arve, and Ulrikke Wethal (2015). "Emerging Economies and Challenges to Sustainability." In Arve Hansen and Ulrikke Wethal (eds.) *Emerging Economies and Challenges to Sustainability: Theories, Strategies, Local Realities.*Oxon: Routledge, 3–18.

He, Laura (2019). "China Could Release Emergency Pork Reserves after Losing 100 Million Pigs to Swine Fever." *CNN Business*. https://edition.cnn.com/2019/09/04/business/china-pork-swine-fever-pigs/index.html

Henchion, Maeve, Mary McCarthy, Virginia C. Resconi and Declan Troy (2014). "Meat Consumption: Trends and Quality Matters." *Meat Science* 98 (3): 561–568.

Howard, Philip H. (2019). "Corporate Concentration in Global Meat Processing: The Role of Feed and Finance Subsidies." In Bill Winders and Ransom Elizabeth (eds.) *Global Meat: Social and Environmental Consequences of the Expanding Meat Industry*. Cambridge: The MIT Press, 31–53.

ILRI (1999). *Making the Livestock Revolution Work for the Poor*. https://cgspace.cgiar.org/bitstream/handle/10568/2868/ILRIAR1999.pdf?sequence=1&isAllowed=y

Jakobsen, Jostein (2020). "The Maize Frontier in Rural South India: Exploring the Everyday Dynamics of the Contemporary Food Regime." *Journal of Agrarian Change* 20 (1): 137–162.

Jakobsen, Jostein and Arve Hansen (2020). "Geographies of Meatification: An Emerging Asian Meat Complex." *Globalizations* 17 (1): 93–109.

Jakobsen, Jostein and Ola T. Westengen (2021). "The Imperial Maize Assemblage: Maize Dialectics in Malawi and India." *The Journal of Peasant Studies*: 1–25, DOI: 10.1080/03066150.2021.1890042.

Josephson, Paul R. (2020). *Chicken: A History from Farmyard to Factory*. Cambridge: Polity.

Khara, Tani, Christopher Riedy and Matthew B. Ruby (2020). "'We have to Keep it a Secret'–The Dynamics of Front and Backstage Behaviours Surrounding Meat Consumption in India." *Appetite* 149: 1–11.

Kuepper, Barbara, Matt Piotrowski and Tim Steinweg (2018). *Cattle-driven Deforestation: A Major Risk to Brazilian Retailers*. Washington, DC: Chain Reaction Research.

Lander, Brian, Mindi Schneider and Katherine Brunson (2020). "A History of Pigs in China: From Curious Omnivores to Industrial Pork." *The Journal of Asian Studies* 79 (4): 865–889.

MacLachlan, Ian (2015). "Evolution of a Revolution: Meat Consumption and Livestock Production in the Developing World." In Jody Emel and Harvey Neo (eds.) *Political Ecologies of Meat*. Routledge, London.

Martiniello, Giuliano (2016). "'Don't Stop the Mill': South African Capital and Agrarian Change in Tanzania." *Third World Thematics: A TWQ Journal* 1 (5): 633–652.

McKay, Ben M. (2018). "Control Grabbing and Value-Chain Agriculture: BRICS, MICs and Bolivia's Soy Complex." *Globalizations* 15 (1): 74–91.

McKay, Ben M., Alberto Alonso-Fradejas, Zoe W. Brent, Sérgio Sauer, and Yunan Xu. (2016a) "China and Latin America: Towards a New Consensus of Resource Control?" *Third World Thematics: A TWQ Journal* 1 (5) (September 2, 2016): 592–611. https://doi.org/10.1080/23802014.2016.1344564.

McKay, Ben M., Ruth Hall and Juan Liu (2016b). "The Rise of BRICS: Implications for Global Agrarian Transformation." *Third World Thematics: A TWQ Journal* 1 (5): 581–591.

McMichael, Philip (2020). "Does China's 'Going Out' Strategy Prefigure a New Food Regime?" *The Journal of Peasant Studies* 47 (1): 116–154. DOI: 10.1080/03066150.2019.1693368

Milenkovic, Aljosa (2019). "B&R Forum: Russia Expects More Agricultural Exports to China." *CGTN.* https://news.cgtn.com/news/3d3d774e306b544e334 57a6333566d54/index.html

Milhorance, Carolina (2016). "Growing South-South Agribusiness Connections: Brazil's Policy Coalitions Reach Southern Africa." *Third World Thematics: A TWQ Journal* 1 (5): 691–708.

Mills, Elyse N. (2018). "Framing China's Role in Global Land Deal Trends: Why Southeast Asia is Key." *Globalizations* 15 (1): 168–177.

Milman, Oliver and Stuart Leavenworth (2016). "China's Plan to Cut Meat Consumption by 50% Cheered by Climate Campaigners." *The Guardian.* https://www.theguardian.com/world/2016/jun/20/chinas-meat-consumption-climate-change

Naidoo, Prinesha (2020). "South African Poultry Industry Invests $60 Million in Expansion." *Bloomberg.* https://www.bloomberg.com/news/articles/2020-09-22/south-african-poultry-industry-invests-60-million-in-expansion

Ncube, Phumzile (2018). "The Southern African Poultry Value Chain: Corporate Strategies, Investments and Agro-Industrial Policies." *Development Southern Africa* 35 (3): 369–387.

Neo, Harvey and Emel, Jody (2017). *Geographies of Meat: Politics, Economy and Culture.* London: Routledge.

Nikulin, Alexander Mikhailovich Nikulin and Irina Vladimirovna Trotsuk (2016). "Utopian Visions of Contemporary Rural-Urban Russia." *Third World Thematics: A TWQ Journal* 1 (5): 673–690.

Nogueira, Antonio Carlos Lima (2015). "Agricultura: O Agronegócio da Suinocultura Brasileira." *Analíse de conjuntura.* Informacões FIPE. https://www.fipe.org.br/Content/downloads/publicacoes/bif/2015/3-5-agr.pdf

OECD (2021). *Meat Consumption (Indicator).* doi: 10.1787/fa290fd0-en (Accessed on 25 May 2021).

OECD/FAO (2020). *OECD-FAO Agricultural Outlook 2020–2029,* FAO, Rome/OECD Publishing, Paris. https://doi.org/10.1787/1112c23b-en.

Oliveira, Gustavo de L. T. (2016). "The Geopolitics of Brazilian Soybeans." *The Journal of Peasant Studies* 43 (2): 348–372.

Oliveira, Gustavo de L. T. (2018). "Chinese Land Grabs in Brazil? Sinophobia and Foreign Investments in Brazilian Soybean Agribusiness." *Globalizations* 15 (1): 114–133.

Oliveira, Gustavo de L. T. and Susanna Hecht (2016). "Sacred Groves, Sacrifice Zones and Soy Production: Globalization, Intensification and Neo-nature in South America." *The Journal of Peasant Studies* 43 (2): 251–285.

Patel, Raj and Jason W. Moore (2017). *A History of the World in Seven Cheap Things: A Guide to Capitalism, Nature, and the Future of the Planet.* Oakland: Univ of California Press.

Pi, Chendog, Zhang Rou and Sarah Horowitz (2014). "Fair or Fowl? Industrialization of Poultry Production in China." In Shefali Sharma and Lilliston Ben (eds.) *Global Meat Complex: The China Series.* Washington, DC: Institute for Agriculture and Trade Policy, 1–40.

Prikhodko, Dmitry and Albert Davleyev (2014). *Russian Federation: Meat Sector Review.* Rome, Italy: FAO.

Rau, V. V. and E. Y. Frolova (2019). "Agrarian Sector: New Points of Growth." *Studies on Russian Economic Development* 30: 154–161.

Ronquest-Ross, Lisa-Claire, Nick Vink and Sigge Gunnar O. (2015). "Food Consumption Changes in South Africa since 1994." *South African Journal of Science* 111 (9–10): 1–12.

Sans, Pierre and Pierre Combris (2015). "World Meat Consumption Patterns: An Overview of the Last Fifty Years (1961–2011)." *Meat Science* 109 (Supplement C): 106–111.

Sauer, Sérgio, Moisés V. Balestro and Sergio Schneider (2018). "The Ambiguous Stance of Brazil as a Regional Power: Piloting a Course Between Commodity-Based Surpluses and National Development." *Globalizations* 15 (1): 32–55.

Schneider, Mindi (2014). "Developing the Meat Grab." *Journal of Peasant Studies* 41 (4): 613–633.

Schneider, Mindi (2017a). "Wasting the Rural: Meat, Manure, and the Politics of Agro-industrialization in Contemporary China." *Geoforum* 7: 89–97.

Schneider, Mindi (2017b). "Dragon Head Enterprises and the State of Agribusiness in China." *Journal of Agrarian Change* 17 (1): 3–21.

Schneider, Mindi (2019). "China's Global Meat Industry: The World-Shaking Power of Industrializing Pigs and Pork in China's Reform Era." In Bill Winders and Elizabeth Ransom (eds.) *Global Meat: Social and Environmental Consequences of the Expanding Meat Industry.* Cambridge: The MIT Press, 79–100.

Schneider, Mindi and Shefali Sharma (2014). *China's Pork Miracle? Agribusiness and Development in China's Pork Industry.* Institute for Agriculture and Trade Policy. *EUR-ISS-PER.*

Sharma, Shefali (2014). *The Need for Feed: China's Demand for Industrialized Meat and Its Impacts.* IATP. Institute for Agriculture and Trade Policy. *EUR-ISS-PER.*

Sharma, Shefali and Sergio Schlesinger (2017). *The Rise of Big Meat: Brazil's Extractive Industry.* IATP. Institute for Agriculture and Trade Policy. *EUR-ISS-PER.*

Silbergeld, Ellen K. (2016). *Chickenizing Farms and Food: How Industrial Meat Production Endangers Workers, Animals, and Consumers.* Baltimore: Johns Hopkins University Press.

Szűcs, István, and Viktoria Vida (2017). "Global Tendencies in Pork-production, Trade and Consumption." *Applied Studies in Agribusiness and Commerce* 11 (3–4): 105–111.

Swinburn, Boyd A., Vivica I. Kraak, Steven Allender, Vincent J. Atkins, Phillip I. Baker, Jessica R. Bogard, Hannah Brinsden, et al. (2019). "The Global Syndemic of Obesity, Undernutrition, and Climate Change: The Lancet Commission Report." *The Lancet* 393 (10173) (February 23, 2019): 791–846. https://doi.org/10.1016/S0140-6736(18)32822-8.

UNDP (2013). *The Rise of the South: Human Progress in a Diverse World. The Rise of the South: Human Progress in a Diverse World* (March 15, 2013). UNDP-HDRO Human Development Reports.

USDA/GAIN (2017). *The South African Pork Market.* Global Agricultural Information Network. Pretoria. https://apps.fas.usda.gov/newgainapi/api/report/downloadreportb yfilename?filename=The%20South%20African%20pork%20market%20_Pretoria _South%20Africa%20-%20Republic%20of_9-5-2017.pdf

USDA/GAIN (2020a). *Livestock and Products Semi-Annual.* People's Republic of China. https://apps.fas.usda.gov/newgainapi/api/Report/DownloadReportByFile-Name?fileName=Livestock%20and%20Products%20Semi-annual_Beijing_China %20-%20Peoples%20Republic%20of_02-15-2019

USDA/GAIN (2020b). *Poultry and Products Annual. Russian Federation.* Report Number: RS2020-0042. https://apps.fas.usda.gov/newgainapi/api/Report/Dow nloadReportByFileName?fileName=Poultry%20and%20Products%20Annual _Moscow_Russian%20Federation_08-15-2020

Vale, Ricardo, Petterson Vale, Holly Gibbs, Daniel Pedrón, Jens Engelmann, Paulo Barreto and Ritaumaria Pereira (2019). "Expansion and Market Concentration of Brazil's Beef Industry." http://www.gibbs-lab.com/wp-content/uploads/2019/01/Vale _etal_2019_Expansion_and_market_concentration_of_Brazils_beef_industry.pdf

Wegren, Stephen K., Alexander Nikulin and Irina Trotstuk (2018). *Food Policy and Food Security: Putting Food on the Russian Table.* Rowman and Littlefield.

Weis, Tony (2007). *The Global Food Economy: The Battle for the Future of Farming.* London, New York, Halifax and Winnipeg: Zed Books & Fernwood Publishing.

Weis, Tony (2013). *The Ecological Hoofprint: The Global Burden of Industrial Livestock.* New York & London: Zed Books.

Weis, Tony (2015). "Meatification and the Madness of the Doubling Narrative." *Canadian Food Studies/La Revue canadienne des études sur l'alimentation* 2 (2): 296–303.

Wilkinson, John, Wesz Junior, Valdemar João and Anna Rosa Maria Lopane. (2016). "Brazil and China: The Agribusiness Connection in the Southern Cone Context." *Third World Thematics: A TWQ Journal* 1 (5): 726–745.

Winders, Bill and ELizabeth Ransom (2019). "Introduction to the Global Meat Industry: Expanding Production, Consumption and Trade." In Bill Winders and Elizabeth Ransom (eds.) *Global Meat. Social and Environmental Consequences of the Expanding meat Industry.* Cambridge: The MIT Press.

Zhou, Jiayi (2016). "Chinese Agrarian Capitalism in the Russian Far East." *Third World Thematics: A TWQ Journal* 1 (5): 612–632.

Chapter 4

From Pastures to Feedlots, from Beef to Soybeans

Changing Meat Culture in Argentina

Kristi Anne Stølen

INTRODUCTION

For a long time Argentina was the world's largest exporter of beef, and cattle grazing freely on the vast pampas have long been part of Argentine cultural imagery. Because of a confluence of factors including climate and a diversity of grass species, Argentina was known as the producer of the world's best beef. Extensive livestock farming and its pastoral image of animals grazing in open fields is becoming less and less common, as farmers move their free-range cattle off Argentina's most fertile lands and into confinement. Through the export-oriented soy boom, during the last two-and-a-half decades, soybeans production has expanded to the best agricultural land at the expense of livestock farming, which is relegated to feedlots and marginal areas. A number of factors have contributed to this extraordinary growth of soybean production and the transformation of the Argentine countryside: changes in the global food system influencing the dynamics of the international market for the soybean chain, the technological and organizational innovations associated with the introduction of GM soybeans, and public policies favoring the expansion of this crop. The transition has been driven by rising prices in the global grain markets over the past decades, making it far more profitable to grow soybeans than to raise cattle.[1]

In this chapter, I will discuss the transformation of the Argentine agrarian sector in view of changes in the global food and fodder industry, especially the role of China, currently Argentina's most important trade partner. Then I will focus on changes in Argentine meat culture, how Argentines historically became passionate meat lovers, and presently remain among the world's most voracious meat consumers. Whereas the global meat consumption has increased a lot over the past decades, consumption of meat in Argentina has been relatively stable. The impact of the passage from grass-fed to grain-fed cattle on the quality of beef does not seem to bother most Argentines. In contrast they are continuously complaining about beef prices. Due to economic instability and rising beef prices relative to poultry and pork over the past decades, cheaper meat has been replacing their beloved beef.

INCREASING APPETITE FOR MEAT

With rising incomes in a number of countries worldwide, the appetite for meat and milk and eggs has generated an enormous growth in animal products. Between 1961 and 2011 there has been a fourfold increase in global meat consumption. In 1961 beef and pork dominated, poultry was number three, but far behind. From 1950 to 1980, beef and pork increased more and less at the same pace, but due to land scarcity in many countries, more cattle was moved from grassland to feedlots. Because cattle, in contrast to poultry, are not efficient in converting grain into meat, world beef production has not increased much after 1990. Poultry production has accelerated overtaking beef in 1997 (see also Hansen, Jakobsen, and Wethal, this volume).

China and the United States are the top meat consuming countries, the United States leading until 1992, when it was overtaken by China. In 2017, more than twice as much meat was consumed in China as in the United States. However, in terms of average per person intake China lags behind, but there has been remarkable increase over time. In 1961, a Chinese consumed barely above 3 kilograms, which implies a 15-fold rise compared to the 61 kilograms in 2017, while in Argentina, which historically has been a "meat country," the corresponding increase during the same period was 7 kilograms (Ritchie and Roser 2019).

As people move up the food chain, consuming more animal products, indirect grain consumption rises. Both pork and poultry depend heavily on grains, beef and milk production more on a combination of grass and grains. Worldwide approximately 35 percent of the annual grain harvest goes to animal feed. In contrast, 85 percent of the soybean harvest ends up as feed (Voora et al. 2020). Consumption trends vary significantly across the world. In China, beef consumption is low; pork meat accounts for around two-thirds of per capita meat consumption, poultry for 11 percent. In Argentina, beef meat still dominates, accounting for about half of meat consumption (Ritchie and Roser 2019).

The increase in Chinese meat consumption alone has created a huge international demand for grains, and especially for soybeans. China does not have enough land to produce grains to cover the internal demands and prioritizes the production of rice and other grains at the expense of oilseeds (O'Connor 2013). There has also been a big rise of demand for soybeans in other Asian countries, especially Vietnam and India, going into domestic feed production (Jacobsen and Hansen 2020). These countries are both major importers of Argentine soybeans and contribute to the Argentine soy boom (Resourcetrade .earth 2019). However, their influence on Argentine economy is much weaker than that of China.

Global meat production has increased rapidly over the past 60 years and has more than quadrupled since 1961. Production has increased in terms of kilos in all continents, but the increase in Asia is by far the most remarkable, 15-fold compared to 1961, now accounting for around 40 percent to 45 percent of total meat production (Jacobsen and Hansen 2020). The average increase in Latin America has been sevenfold, though with great differences between countries. Argentina, traditionally a meat and wheat country has only doubled its production, while the rise is Brazil has been exceptional with 13-fold, approaching Asian numbers (Ritchie and Roser 2019). The distribution of meat types also varies significantly across the world. Land-rich countries like Argentina with vast grasslands depend heavily on cattle, while countries that are more densely populated and lack extensive grazing lands have historically relied more on pork.

This enormous rise in demand for animal feed due to the increase in meat consumption and the industrialization of the meat sector in many countries changed the export potentials for Argentina and contributed to the soy boom and the changes in cattle raising.

THE EXPANSION OF SOY IN ARGENTINA

By the turn of the twenty-first century Argentina was in the midst of a profound socioeconomic crisis, the result of more than 10 years of neoliberal policies comprising wholesale privatization, deregulation of all kinds, and an indiscriminate opening to the world economy. The Argentine government, eager to pull the country out of a deep economic recession that culminated in full-scale depression in 2001 to 2002, restructured its economy around GM soy grown for export. The GM soy was considered an ideal crop, practically all for export, high prices, high demands, it did not interfere directly with food prices/workers' wages which had always been a problem in Argentina where food crops and export crops used to be the same (Brambilla et al. 2018; Richardson 2008).

Monsanto's GM soy variety Roundup Ready engineered to be tolerant to Roundup (Monsanto's formulation of the glyphosate herbicide) was introduced in Argentina during the Menem government in 1996, the same year as it was released for international commercialization. The new biotechnology was conceived as a welcome development that offered the prospect of extracting greater profits from using land more efficiently, but with fewer inputs, therefore reducing production costs. Unlike other developing countries whose view of the new biotechnology has been informed by concerns of food security, Argentina has embraced this technology on grounds of its export potentials (Newell 2009).

Due to high prices and high demands at the international market, soybeans production offered much higher profits than the traditional crops and cattle farming. Another advantage associated with this crop was the no-tilling practice and the chemical cleaning of the fields. Due to its resistance to glyphosate, soybeans could be sown directly on stubble fields and survive the herbicide spraying that would kill the weeds. Before the introduction of the RR soy, the fields had to be cleaned mechanically, which implied endless hours on the tractor, plowing and harrowing, as well as higher fuel costs.

Another advantage was that the soybean cycle is complementary to the wheat cycle; both can be grown in the same year, with wheat in the winter and soy in the summer. This enhanced profitability by having two harvests a year with the wheat-soybeans combination. Therefore, in contrast to other crops and meat production, the rise of soy did not compete with wheat, that is one of the staple foods in Argentina. Moreover, as a measure of promotion from the agribusiness companies, farmers received advancement of input packages to be paid upon delivery of crops after the harvest, important in a country where access to credit is limited (OECD 2018).

In contrast to other soy producing countries, Argentina did not recognize intellectual property protection of the RR seeds, since the national seed law allowed farmers to use farm-saved seeds. Thus, the RR technology was not patented and seeds were relatively cheap, something that implied a comparative advantage regarding production costs for Argentine farmers and a long-lasting judicial conflict with Monsanto (Qaim and Traxler 2005).

The Kirchner/Fernandez governments (2003–2015) more attuned to the social responsibilities of the state than the previous ones, increased the export tax on agricultural products to raise more funds for public spending, such as subsidies and social programs aimed at redistribution of incomes and alleviation of poverty. The export tax on soy reached 35 percent during Christina Fernandez's government (2007–2015). In 2008, the international price of oilseeds reached record levels. The government attempted to introduce a new sliding-scale taxation system for soybean and sunflower exports that would raise tax to 44 percent on soybeans. The farmers responded with a nationwide four-month lockout. For the first time in history, the farmers' organizations representing different segments of the agrarian sector united in a successful struggle to stop it (Barsky and Dávila 2020; Leguizamón 2014).[2]

The technological transformation of agriculture, especially in the pampas, has been outstanding, with a very rapid rate of adoption of the new technologies. Until recently, there has been a steady increase in soy production. The top was reached in the 2015/2016 agricultural season when soybeans were planted on 20.5 million hectares, more than 60 percent of Argentina's cultivated land. Soybeans and its derivatives represent almost 50 percent of agro-food exports, make up more than half of Argentina's crop production and a fourth of its total exports. Soy has become the country's most important export commodity and Argentina is now the world's third largest soy producer and number one exporter of processed soy (oil, meal, and biodiesel) (INDEC 2020).

Agricultural producers and their associated industrial and commercial sectors celebrate the incorporation of new productive areas to the country's agricultural map and the income they generate. An almost unreserved optimism has been associated with the expansion of soybeans. The public debate, strongly influenced by agribusiness companies, focuses on the merits of biotechnology as an economic and developmental strategy. The governments implement measures to deal with undesirable impacts to maintain national food security but these measures have not been efficient in limiting the expansion of soy at the expense of other crops and cattle farming. The government depends on soy exports to collect taxes and keep the economy alive. Newell argues that the desirability of the GM-based growth strategy has been secured in material, institutional, and discursive arenas of power, producing a particular expression of what he calls bio-hegemony (Newell 2009).

In contrast to other grain crops such as maize and wheat that are both for export and domestic consumption, soy is almost exclusively for export. Historically, the main export products, beef, wheat, and maize, were also the primary consumption goods of the country's well-organized and combative urban workers. Because soybeans are not consumed by the working class, the government could both promote and tax export, generating fiscal revenues for the state while not harming the effective purchasing power of the urban workers and thereby creating social upheavals or provoking a balance of payment crisis (Richardson 2008).

During the past decades bovine meat as well as maize and wheat have been subject to export curbs to ensure affordable domestic food supplies, by keeping certain amounts of these products in the country, immune to rising international prices. There are no such curbs on soy export, which contributes to steer farmers even further toward planting heavily taxed soybeans. Bovine meat production has been one of the areas most damaged by this policy, with the country losing its position in the international meat market. Both the livestock sector and some crops other than soybeans have struggled to be competitive due to low investment and low productivity growth. Bovine meat production experienced a significant decrease between 1990 and 2016. This decrease was due to a reduction in the number of animals, resulting from policies such as an export ban, taxes, and macroeconomic policy uncertainty. These policies discouraged domestic livestock production and favored crop production, which has shorter cycles and requires less upfront investment (Lema et al. 2018; OECD 2019).

ARGENTINA-CHINA—"A MARRIAGE OF CONVENIENCE"

China, with its enormous demand for animal feed, has played a decisive role in Argentina's soy boom. Like in other Latin American countries, China's economic presence has become very significant over the past two decades. China's trade with Latin American countries has been increasing quickly, especially the imports of raw materials, concentrated on grains and oilseeds, and to a lesser degree some agricultural industrialized food such as meat, dairy, selected fruits and vegetables, fish, and shellfish. Agricultural trade is an increasing component of the trade with China, even though the importance of it varies between countries (Oliveira and Schneider 2016).

The traditional agricultural and food destinations for Argentine exports, mainly Britain and other European countries, as well as trade within the continent have now been surpassed by the increasing demand from Asia, especially China. China has become the main export destination for Argentina's soy products. This increase of demand for soybeans on the international market is a consequence of China's decision to "sacrifice" soybeans to keep land and water for rice, wheat, and maize (O'Connor 2013). Increasingly, Argentina is also becoming a strategic location for investment by Chinese firms. Since 2016 China has also turned into Argentina's main importer of bovine meat (Donaubauer et al. 2015).

The relationship between Argentina and China has been characterized as a "marriage of convenience" (di Paola 2020). In 2020, China ascended as Argentina's top trade partner, replacing Brazil to a second position. China is a fundamental ally for Argentina's national economic growth. Recently a number of agreements have been signed deepening Argentina's role in international trade as a supplier of raw agricultural materials and minerals, most of them with a low level of added value. Environmental considerations were not included in the agreements signed by Argentina and China. In order to attract investments, the agreements allow for the direct acquisition of contracts and preferential conditions for companies of Chinese origin. This means that approval procedures such as environmental impact evaluations and citizen consultations, for example, can be simplified. There is currently a tendency to reverse civic protection standards in Latin America and Argentina is no exception (di Paola 2020).

CHANGES IN LAND USE

Only 25 years ago, virtually all of Argentina's cattle still grazed freely. But as global agriculture markets boomed, it became harder for cattle farmers to resist the quick profit from soy and wheat. Hastened by the financial crisis in 2001, many cattle ranchers sold their cattle and turned over their land to soybeans. Whereas grass-fed cows take three to five years to be ready to sell, a farmer can turn around a soy or maize crop in a matter of months. Cropland area has increased twofold and crop production has increased fivefold in the past decades, trends driven by the increased value of crops, especially soybeans relative to livestock (Lence 2010). More crops are now produced and higher yields obtained, while livestock farming has been replaced or shifted to marginal areas less suitable for agricultural production.

The most significant change in land use has taken place in the pampas where big cattle estates, historically dedicated to fattening of cattle, went through a rapid process of modernization during the 1990s, converting pastures into soybeans cultivation and incorporating the new technological package. According to Slutzky (2012), in most cases, the traditional land-owners manage these enterprises themselves. However, some new actors of more urban, sometimes foreign extraction have entered the agricultural scene, investors who participate in agricultural business through new forms of production management, the so-called the "sowing pools" (Sosa Varrotti 2019).

Initially the sowing pools consisted of agricultural producers who joined resources and efforts to increase scale. Gradually this changed. Today the "pools" are characterized by the key role played by finance capital and the organization of a transitional enterprise system that takes control of agricultural production, by leasing large tracts of land. They buy sowing, spraying, harvesting, and transport services in order to generate economies of scale and high yields. At the end of the harvest, profits are distributed to the investors of the pool. Since profits are much higher in soybean than in wheat production they often opt for mono-cropping of soy creating land deterioration problems. Technological innovation and entrepreneurial skills, rather than land ownership, have become the most important assets in today's agriculture (Slutzky 2012). "What you need to establish a big enterprise today is no more than two persons, one agronomist and one with financial skills and contacts each with a laptop and smartphone" a farmer told me. The sowing pools played a key role in agricultural expansion and have contributed to the demise of family farmers.[3]

A number of studies from the pampa region have examined the dynamics of farm exits and adjustments (Gras 2009; Gras and Hernández 2009). They show that the strong growth of export production, an increasing demand for capital investment, and technological incorporation have resulted in substantial changes in the social and economic structure of agricultural production, such as reduction in farm numbers, an increase in the average size of farms, a concentration of production, and new tenure patterns. This is also the case in areas outside the pampas, such as the northern part of Santa Fe Province, where I have carried out longitudinal anthropological research on agrarian change (Archetti and Stølen 1975: Stølen 1996). Until the soy boom this region was dominated by vigorous family farms producing cotton and sunflower for the national market. Soy expansion has been a success in terms of increased production and productivity, all the land is used and produces more efficiently, but most farmers have left the countryside, renting out or selling their land to the few who have been able to make the transition to agribusiness (Stølen 2015).

Success in soy production requires access to larger tracts of land and new expensive technology, which implies investments beyond the possibilities of most small- and medium-sized family farms with very limited access to credits. Moreover, as tractors and other equipment get bigger and technologically more advanced, specialized skills are necessary to operate them. The same happens with the planning of production and commercialization of products. These skills cannot be acquired in the family and the community; they must be acquired through formal education. Due to high demand and competitive pressure for land, only those who have been able to pool resources, accumulate land (own or rented) and capital, and adopt a capitalist management strategy continue farming, but they are no longer working as farmers, rather as managers, and do not live in the countryside. Those who survive often diversify their production combining soybean/wheat production with cattle in feedlots and/or industrial poultry breading (Stølen 2015). To keep beef prices low on less land, the Argentine government provided subsidies for the grain-fed feedlot cattle from 2007 to 2009. Both INTA and the Argentine Beef Promotion Institute touted use of the feedlot for quick, effective production. Now, an increasing share of the country's beef has been through a feedlot.

In the northern parts of the country, rapid rates of deforestation have resulted in habitat loss, biodiversity loss, and also loss of livelihoods. Deforestation is mainly caused by the expansion of cattle ranching. This process has been incited by the soybean expansion in other regions. Cattle ranchers that have been "replaced" from traditional livestock land by soybeans have moved to the northern parts, where land prices still are significantly lower, land is fertile, labor and input costs are low (Ortega 2012).

HOW ARGENTINA BECAME A MEAT POWER

Cattle raising for beef is closely related to the economic, social, and cultural development of Argentina. In the sixteenth-century Spanish conquistadores brought domesticated animals, including cattle, sheep, and horses that were released on the pampas, at that time sparsely inhabited by indigenous hunters and gatherers. The grassland was an ideal environment for these new species, and big herds grew which wandered freely across the region. This feral cattle *cimarrón* became the basis for cattle raising in Argentina. Due to a small population facing an area overflowing with cattle, ever since the early colonial times, a consumption pattern based on beef was established; beef offered ecological, economic, and nutritional advantages and became the staple ingredient in all meals. The archaeologist Mario Silveira estimated that in the seventeenth and eighteenth centuries, annual per capita beef consumption in Buenos Aires was as high as an average 220 kilograms (Pavan et al. 2017).

Until the first *saladeros* (salting houses) were established in Argentina in the early nineteenth century, opening for the conservation of meat, hides rather than meat were the added value of the cattle. Meat was abundant and available for everyone. The consumption of meat by the rising, but still small population was limited, while leather was an export product. It is reported that approximately one-fourth of the animals slaughtered was enough to cover the consumption needs of the population. During the seventeenth and eighteenth centuries, *vaquerías*' true hunting expeditions of *cimarrón* cattle were carried out by gauchos—men on horseback, hunting the animals with lasso, knife, and *boleadoras*, a device made of leather cords and three iron balls that was thrown at the legs of an animal to entwine and immobilize it. The cattle was slaughtered, the skin and tallow removed, and the carcasses left on the field to be devoured by vultures and wild animals, except for the share they were able to eat themselves. The gauchos subsisted largely on meat and were the creators of the asado, the Argentine way of roasting meat that has become a symbol of "Argentineness" (Archetti 2000). The *vaquerías* were initially organized to populate the new colonial estates "estancias" that were beginning to emerge in these immense territories, but it was also part of an active and very profitable legal and illegal trade of hides. The arrival of the *saladeros* put an end to this practice. Meat could now be conserved and exported, mainly to feed slaves in Brazil and the Caribbean (Montoya 1956).

The introduction of cooling technology made it possible to reach new markets for Argentine meat in Europe, especially in Great Britain. However, certain changes of cattle breed had to be made in order to succeed in the European market. The traditional criollo cattle of Spanish origin did not satisfy the palate of the European consumer. Therefore, pedigrees were imported from England/Scotland. The first pedigree was a Shorthorn bull imported by a landowner of British origin in 1826. In the 1860s and 1870s, Hereford and Aberdeen Angus pedigrees arrived. This gave the origin to the bovine mixture that improved the quality of Argentine meat and gave it the reputation of the best meat in the world (Krebs 2011).

Argentina was able to compete well in the international meat market, because of the fact that its production costs were significantly lower than costs in Europe, due to lower wages and the breeding in open fields as opposed to that of barns. The first exports to Britain in 1880 contained live animals transported by stable ships. This kind of shipping was soon replaced after the establishment of the first refrigerator plant in the province of Buenos Aires in 1882, financed by American capital. From this plant, the first export of chilled meat was sent to London in 1883 (Gebhardt 2000). This initiated a rapid increase in cattle raising and from the early twentieth century Argentina dominated the world's beef market, and its meatpacking plants became one of the country's major industries employing immigrant workers.

Changes in the world economy had created new opportunities for Argentine exports. During the nineteenth century, the capitalist world economy was increasingly shaped by industrialization. The revolution of overland transport was particularly important for the exporting countries like Argentina. It enabled the prairies of Argentina like the ones of Australia, Canada, and the United States to become the world's major exporters of grain and meat to Europe, which was rapidly urbanizing and increasingly dependent on imports of staple food (Bernstein 2010, 66–70). The building of the railway in Argentina from the 1860s not only reduced the cost of transport, that previously had been based on horses or mules, but also stimulated the cultivation of land located at longer distances from the harbors. Between 1860 and 1930, exploitation of the rich land of the pampa strongly pushed economic growth. During the first three decades of the twentieth century, Argentina outgrew Canada and Australia in population, total income, and per capita income. By 1913, Argentina was the world's 10th wealthiest nation per capita (Taylor 1948).

The economic prosperity of Argentina in the decades before and after the turn of the twentieth century was based on a massive arrival of European immigrants who were to "populate the desert," the vast territories to the north and the south of the pampa region as well as the growing cities, especially Buenos Aires. Scarcity of labor was acute and since independence from Spain in 1816 there was a constant agitation for attracting immigrants. Argentine politicians were inspired by the North American model, and also carefully followed the development of Australia and Canada (Taylor 1948; Ferrer 1972). Before independence only the central part of the pampa, the shores of La Plata River and the hinterland of Buenos Aires, was controlled by the Spaniards and their descendants. The vast areas to the northeast often referred to as the Litoral, comprising the provinces along the Paraná river, were controlled by indigenous tribes, as were the vast areas to the south including Patagonia. After independence military campaigns were initiated to take control over these territories.[4] *Gobernar es poblar* (to govern is to populate) was a dominant political doctrine of the period. As the army expanded into these territories indigenous people who were not willing to "become integrated and civilized" were killed or fled to more marginal areas.

The so-called liberated territories were gradually populated by European immigrant settlers, who were offered land on favorable terms: low prices and down-payment arrangements without interests, on the condition that they produced wheat, maize, and flax that in addition to meat were the main export crops of the period. In the settler areas cattle was only raised for subsistence and the local market. In this way agricultural land was expanded by 30 million hectares, however not of the same quality as the land of the pampas (Aguirre 2007). Even though the main objective of the immigration was to "populate the desert" the majority of the newcomers was absorbed by the growing cities, especially Buenos Aires, where labor was badly needed.

High levels of urban salaries and low food prices compared to those of their home countries permitted a diet previously unattainable for the immigrants, most of whom originated from rather poor conditions. It is reported that the foreigners were especially astonished by the quantities of meat served (Silveira 2003, 22). The combination of low meat prices and good salaries became the basis for the dominant consumption pattern and the construction of the cultural representation of what was to become the signature plate of Argentines, *el asado* (Aguirre 2007).

The immigrants, the majority of whom were Italian and Spanish, replaced their grain-based Mediterranean diet, considered a diet of scarcity, for a meat-based diet. As a result of beef's historical high consumption in the twentieth century, it became identified as a meal in itself; beef was considered the core of all dishes. Vegetables and starchy foods were seen as garnishes, which meant that a dish without beef was not food. Vegetables, potatoes, and pasta lacked the status of food in the culinary imagination (Pavan et al. 2017).

In the imagery of the first half of the twentieth century, characterized by the influence of recent immigration of poor Europeans, a major concern was that there should be no shortage of food, food should be varied, and it should be abundant. According to Aguirre (2007), frugality was never a norm, to eat was synonymous with eating a lot, and to be fat was a symptom of physical and economic health. This was a perception shared by the working class as well as the upper classes, even though the latter were more refined in their gastronomy, inspired by French cuisine. Slim bodies were associated with scarcity, hunger, and poverty, while fat bodies were a symbol of health and beauty.

THE ROLE OF MEAT IN THE NATIONAL KITCHEN

One of the consequences of the Great Depression (1929) was the decrease in international trade. Demand for the traditional Argentine export products decreased dramatically. The cutback in exports combined with continued demand for imported products led to serious deficits on the balance of payment. Anticipating a long-lasting international crisis, the Argentine government initiated an economic reorganization, with a strong emphasis on import substitution through the development of national industries, concentrating on the production of consumption goods and production of machinery and equipment that required relatively simple technology, and small- to medium-scale production (Ferrer 1972, 177–179). The development of local industry required supply of raw materials that had not previously been produced in Argentina. According to the national development plans of the period, industrial growth was to be based on a division of labor within the agricultural sector. Industrial inputs such as cotton and oil seeds should be produced by the settler farmers outside the pampa region, while the pampa should continue the production of meat and grains for export. This process stimulated internal migration of labor surplus from rural areas to the industrializing towns, where the migrants were offered formal wage work. The establishment of a welfare state model during the Peronist governments (1946–1955) contributed to the continuity of the upward mobility of the working class from the previous decades (Torrado 2003, 52).

During this period the role of the agrarian sector was to supply cheap food for the growing working classes and to generate positive trade balances. However, in spite of the decline in exports of agrarian products, meat continued to be perceived as an economic factor of first importance. Basically meat, but also wool and hides, constituted approximately half of Argentine exports during almost two-thirds of the twenty-first-century, which undoubtedly contributes to explain the strong influence of the large cattle owners in politics, the economy, and society (Azcuy Ameghino 2005).

Beef maintained its position as the most important ingredient in the Argentine diet across class differences, but the cuisine had become clearly hybridized, reflecting the influence of immigration. In his analysis of the construction of a national Argentine cuisine Archetti (2000) paraphrasing Levis-Strauss (1965) identifies what he calls "our meat triangle." In this triangle not only has the pampa, with its ecological meat abundance, embraced Italy through the *milanesa*, a thin slice of breaded beef, or Spain through the puchero (cooked meat and vegetables), but the roasted has been combined with the fried and the cooked. The asado is seen as the most "natural" transformation, while the frying and cooking are seen as more cultural, arriving with conquest and immigration. The attributes of the asado, la *milanesa* and the puchero, contribute to the construction of the aggregate and hybrid character of the Argentine cuisine. Moreover, the fried and the cooked belong to the inside, the kitchen, the women, and the family, while the asado belongs to the outdoors and male domain, and constitute a "very Argentine virile ceremony"(Archetti 2000) .

In the first household expenditure polls published in 1965, the consumption of basic products was registered in three income groups (CONADE 1965). This poll shows that there are still few differences in consumption patterns in the three income categories. Rich and poor consume the same products, but the richer consume moderately more of all products and they consume food of better quality (Aguirre 2007, 10). The average annual consumption of meat per capita this year was 120 kilograms with only 3 kilograms difference between highest- and lowest-income groups (Pavan et al. 2017, 45).

DECREASE IN BOVINE MEAT PRODUCTION AND CONSUMPTION

Over the last 60 years Argentina has seen military and civil government with different political agendas, but one thing in common, the opening up to the global economy and increased influence of transnational companies and financial capital leading to a process of downward mobility of the middle and working classes. This is also a period of political instability increasing social and economic differences in access to food and great changes in consumption patterns.

The unified consumption pattern of the previous period has been replaced by a much more differentiated one. Industrialized food is no longer an exceptional resource, it has become a norm, partly because of rise in women's work outside home and less time for cooking. Takeaway and street food have also become much more common as working people normally have at least one daily meal outside home, and increased income differences are reflected in the food consumption.

The notion of the healthy body is turned upside down. For ages it has been associated with being well-fed and fat, now it is associated with being slim and slender. In spite of that overweight and obesity are widespread, especially among the poor, and men more than women. The diet of the poor is one of scarcity in terms of nutritional value being dominated by cheap carb and fat, while more well-off people can afford a more balanced diet including fruit and vegetables that is more expensive than bread and the cheaper meat. There has also been an increase in "lifestyle illnesses" associated with overweight and obesity (Aguirre 2007). In spite of these changes meat consumption has not decreased much over the past decades. Argentines have remained among the most carnivorous people in the world. However, they cannot afford to eat as much beef as they used to and now regularly swap it with less expensive foods. This is problematic for Argentines who are profound beef-lovers and for whom eating beef is part of their cultural identity. It also creates problems for butchers as well as ranchers and meat packers, who have been highly dependent on domestic consumers for most of their sales.

In a nationwide study from 2014, Bifaretti et al. found that price was by far the most important factor regarding consumption of beef. But not only price is influencing its popularity. Other factors such as tradition, taste, that everyone in the family likes it, it is easy to prepare, and it yields more was among the answers in Bifaretti's study. Eight out of ten defined themselves as meat consumers, some 5 percent as vegans and vegetarians, most of them between sixteen and twenty-five years and from higher-income families. Another 15 percent defined themselves as "flexitarians" comprising people who said they would like to reduce their meat consumption. Health and environmental issues did not appear as important concerns in this study.

The Argentine health authorities as well as nutritionists recommend that a daily portion of meat should be included in the diet, but the size of this portion should not be bigger than "the palm of the hand." However, their definition of meat is different from the popular one, since it includes white meat and fish. For most Argentines meat still means beef (Pavan et al. 2017).

However, economic instability and hardships has led consumers to look for other options for their daily meals. Beef is preferred, but due to high prices compared to chicken, the latter has gained ground in the Argentine cuisine. Chicken is the preferred substitute for beef. The first official data informing the annual per capita consumption of poultry (1990) and pork (1992) showed an average of 10.9 kilograms and 5.6 kilograms, respectively. Since then, poultry and pork consumption have increased by a total of four- and twofold, respectively, resulting not only in an overall increase in meat consumption (106.3 kilograms in 2000 to 114.5 kilograms in 2016), but also in a change in the consumption patterns. In 2000, beef represented 62.4 percent (66.4 kilograms) of total meat per capita consumption and, in 2016, less than 50 percent of it (56.7 kilograms) (Pavan et al. 2017). The domestic market for poultry has practically reached its top, at the same time as production is increasing and opening for expansion of new export markets. Pork is conceived as a less attractive alternative to bovine meat, except as in processed products such as ham and sausages. Pork prices are relatively high and many people do not appreciate the taste and think that pork is hard to digest (Bifaretti et al. 2014).

Argentina has a long coastline and one could expect to find high proportion of fish in the diet. This is not the case and fish is, in most cases, not conceived as a substitute for bovine meat. Fish is recognized as healthy and low in calories, but only consumed by high-income groups. Most people are not accustomed to cook and eat fish. High prices, lack of availability, and insecurity regarding freshness as well as smell and taste are working against increased fish consumption (Bifaretti et al. 2014).

CHANGING MEAT CULTURE

The place of meat has always been essential in the diet of the Argentine population. The average quantity of meat per capita consumption has been relatively stable throughout the twentieth century and beef is embedded in the popular culture to such an extent that Argentines would proudly mention "our beef" with a sense of ownership. Argentine beef is also believed to be of superior quality, and this belief extends beyond Argentina.

Until the 1990s, nearly 100 percent of beef cattle were grass-fed, with occasional grain supplementation. Toward the end of the 1990s, feedlots became more frequent. Since then the number of feedlots has gradually grown to between 65 percent and 70 percent of the cattle brought to slaughterhouses, driven by the increase in soybean planting, which substantially reduced the use of grazing land for beef as well as dairy cattle (Gutman 2018).

The importance of the meat chain in the current Argentine economy is certainly not the same as it was in 1920s. Today, meat exports barely reach 3 percent or 4 percent of total exports, when in that decade the percentage was 35. However, even today, when meat production is mainly directed at the domestic market, the largest cattle farmers continue to be export-oriented preferably producing for the Hilton quota for exports to the EU, high-quality beef from grass-fed animals that have not been fed with GM grains.[5] Since 2016 China has been the main destination for Argentine meat in terms of volume, while Europe is dominating regarding the import of high-quality meat. So far the preferred cuts in the Chinese market are of inferior quality, while the European importers demand high-value cuts from grass-fed steers to supply a circuit in which Argentine beef is, and has been for a long time, an undisputed quality mark (Quaizel 2017).

Other destinations for Argentine meat are Chile, Israel, Russia, and Brazil. Importers from these countries demand different cuts, of dissimilar vaccine categories and for different uses. According to the Institute for the Promotion of Argentine Beef this is an advantage because it implies that they can sell cuts rather than whole animals. The asado cuts, which are the ones Argentines appreciate the most, are practically not exported. This implies that Argentina could recover exports not only without affecting the domestic market, but also by increasing the domestic supply of the most consumed cuts.

Argentina is one of the very few places in the world where it still is possible to raise high volume of top quality grass-fed cattle year round, due to the temperate climate, access to water sources, and the rich grasslands. Some producers may export special cuts to high-end markets and restaurants, but since there is no labeling of meat in Argentina, most animals enter the domestic market where there is no certification infrastructure in place for meat. Grass-fed meat is sold alongside meat from feedlots and almost all farmers sell in the same market.

Some Argentine chefs prefer and intentionally serve grass-fed beef. And customers in good relations with their butchers may be able to get it, too. But the vast majority of restaurants as well as butchers and consumers pay little or no attention to the overall tenderness or distribution or color of fat, for instance, which are ways to distinguish feedlot versus grass-fed. This was clearly the case in my area of study. Neither do they have concerns about the fact that the grain-fed is gene modified. Moreover, grass-fed beef has never needed a title or a label since the "grass" used to be implied, and many consumers are not aware of the difference. In contrast to Argentina, Uruguay has not abandoned grass-fed beef. There, the beef industry focused on getting international certification for it, so it could sell to high-end markets in Europe. In Argentina a small, but growing movement of consumers, providers, and environmentalists is also beginning to demand the beef of days past.

NOTES

1. I have carried out research on this recent transition from a provincial perspective, based on fieldwork in the northern area of Santa Fe Province as part of my longitudinal fieldwork of agrarian change in Argentina (Stølen 2015, 1996; Archetti and Stølen 1975). This chapter adopts a national/global focus, building on previous knowledge, secondary data, and studies by other researchers. I would like to thank the editors for valuable comments on earlier drafts of the chapter.

2. Export taxes have been a recurrent mechanism in Argentine economic policy. It was abolished by Menem in the 1990s, and reintroduced in 2002. Tax on soybean started at 20 percent and reached 35 percent by the end of Christina Fernandez's government. During Macri's government (2015–2019), export tax on soy was reduced, by the end of his period it was 24.5 percent. Shortly after the change of government in December 2019, the new Peronist president Alberto Fernandez increased it to 30 percent and later to 33 percent, which is the current rate. The level of export tax

depends, to a large extent, on the Presidency in office and on its attitude toward free trade, exports, and the distributive conflict (Brambilla et al. 2018).

3. The two biggest sowing pools, Los Grobo and MSU, control 250,000 hectares and 210,000 hectares of soy respectively, most of it operate under lease (Gras and Sosa Varrotti 2013, 224).

4. The northwestern provinces of Argentina closer to the Andes had been incorporated into the Viceroyalty of Peru during the sixteenth century. The rest of the country had limited natural resources of interest in the early colonial period. The Viceroyalty of Rio de la Plata, with Buenos Aires as its capital, was not established until 1776 (Nouzeilles and Montaldo 2009).

5. Argentina has two special quotas for the entry of high-value meat in the EU with differentiated tariffs. The "Hilton quota," for grass-fed meat, 29,500 thousand tons per year, with a 20 percent tariff, and the "481" quota comprising 48,200 tons in total of meat finished in feedlots to be shared with Uruguay, Brazil, Paraguay, the United States, Canada, Australia, and New Zealand. There is no tariff on this meat. (Ministerio de Agricultura, Ganadería y Pesca. https://serviciosucesci.magyp.gob .ar/principal.php?nvx_ver=2284.)://serviciosucesci.magyp.gob.ar/principal.php?nvx _ver=2284https://serviciosucesci.magyp.gob.ar/principal.php?nvx_ver=2284https:// serviciosucesci.magyp.gob.ar/principal.php?nvx_ver=2284

BIBLIOGRAPHY

Aguirre, Patricia. 2007. "Comida, cocina y consecuencias: la alimentación de Buenos Aires." S. Torrado In *Población y bienestar. Una historia Social del siglo XX. Tomo 2.* edited by Susana Torrado. Buenos Aires: Editorial Edhasa, 469–503.

Archetti, Eduardo P. 2000. "Hibridación, pertenencia y localidad en la cocina nacional." *Trabajo y Sociedad* II, no. 2: 1–18.

Archetti, Eduardo P. and Stølen, Kristi Anne. 1975. *Explotación familiar y acumulación de capital en el campo argentino.* Buenos Aires: Siglo XXI.

Arelovich, Hugo M., Rodrigo B. Bravo, and Marcela Martínez. 2011. "Development, Characteristics, and Trends for Beef Cattle Production in Argentina." *Animal Frontiers* 1, no. 2: 37–45.

Azcuy Ameghino, Eduardo. 2005. "Crisis y estancamiento del comercio exterior argentino de carnes vacunas." *Ciclos* XV, no. 29: 137–161.

Barsky, Osvaldo, and Mabel Dávila. 2020. "Conflicto agrario del 2008." In *Diccionario del Agro Iberoamericano*, edited by José Muzlera, and Alejandra Salomón. Buenos Aires: Teseopress. https://www.teseopress.com/diccionarioagro/ chapter/conflicto-agrario-de-2008/

Bernstein, Henry. 2010. *Class Dynamics and Agrarian Change.* Sterling, VA: Kumarian Press.

Bifaretti, Adrián E., Eugenia A. Brusca, and Miguel Jairala. 2014. *Cambios socioeconómicos y demanda de carnes: ¿Cómo se construye el mapa del consumo de proteínas cárnicas en el mercado argentino?* http://www.ipcva.com.ar/files/ AAEA2014web.pdf

Brambilla, Irene, Sebastián Galiani, and Guido Porto. 2018. "Argentine Trade Policies in the XX Century: 60 Years of Solitude." *Latin American Economic Review* 27: 4. DOI 10.1007/s40503-017-0050-9

CONADE. 1965. *Encuesta sobre presupuestos de consumo de las familias urbanas por niveles de ingreso para 1963.* Buenos Aires: CONADE.

di Paola, Maria Marta. 2020. "Opinion: China and Argentina's Marriage of Convenience." *Dilogo Chino*, February 11, 2020. https://dialogochino.net/en/trade-investment/33453-opinion-china-and-argentinas-marriage-of-convenience/

Donaubauer, Julian, Andres Lopez, and Daniela Ramos. 2015. "FDI and Trade: Is China Relevant for the Future of Our Environment? The Case of Argentina." *Global Economic Governance Initiative*, Discussion Paper 2015-https://www.researchgate.net/publication/315178787_FDI_and_Trade_Is_China_Relevant_for_the_Future_of_Our_Environment_The_Case_of_Argentina/link/5b785082458 5151fd11f777b/download

FAO. 2016. *The State of World Fisheries and Aquaculture. 2016. Contributing to Food Security and Nutrition for All.* Rome: FAO. http://www.fao.org/3/i5555e/i5555e.pdf

Ferrer, Aldo. 1972. *La economía argentina.* Mexico City and Buenos Aires: Fondo de Cultura Económica.

Gebhardt, Roberto C. 2000. *The River Plate Meat Industry since C. 1900: Technology, Ownership, International Trade Regimes and Domestic Policy.* PhD Thesis, London School of Economics. http://etheses.lse.ac.uk/1512/1/U118849.pdf

Gras, Carla, and Valeria Hernández. 2009 "Reconfiguraciones sociales frente a las transformaciones de los 90: desplazados, chacareros y empresarios en el nuevo paisaje rural argentino." In *La Argentina Rural: de la agricultura familiar a agro-negocios,* edited by Carla Gras and Valeria Hernández, 89–113. Buenos Aires: Editorial Biblos.

Gras, Carla, and Andrea Sosa Varrotti. 2013. "El modelo de negocios de las principales megaempresas." In *El Agro como negocio. Producción, sociedad y territorios en la globalización,* edited by Carla Gras and Valeria Hernández, 215–236. Buenos Aires: Editorial Biblos.

Gutman, Daniel. 2018. "As It Recovers, Argentina's Beef Production Faces Environmental Impact Questions" *IPS*, May 20, 2021. http://www.ipsnews.net/2018/08/argentinas-beef-production-recovers-faces-questions-environmental-impacts/

INDEC. 2020. "Complejos exportadores año 2019." *Comercio Exterior* 4, no 4: 5–8. https://www.indec.gob.ar/uploads/informesdeprensa/complejos_03_201711C CEF8E.pdf

Jacobsen, Jostein, and Arve Hansen. 2020. "Geographies of Meatification: An Emerging Asian Meat Complex." *Globalizations* 17, no 1. https://www.tandfonline.com/doi/full/10.1080/14747731.2019.1614723

Krebs, Miguel. 2011. *Historia de la ganadería y los frigoríficos en Argentina.* https://www.historiacocina.com/paises/articulos/argentina/vacuno.htm

Leguizamón, Amalia. 2014. "Modifying Argentina: GM Soy and Socio-Environmental Change." *Geoforum* 53, May 2014, 149–160. http://dx.doi.org/10.1016/j.geoforum.2013.04.001

Lema, Daniel, Marcos Gallacher, Juan José Egas, and Carmine Paolo de Salvo. 2018. "Analysis of Agricultural Policies in Argentina 2007–2016." *IDB Agricultural Policy Reports 2018*. https://publications.iadb.org/publications/english/document/Analysis_of_Agricultural_Policies_in_Argentina_2007%E2%80%932016_en_en.pdf

Lence, Sergio H. 2010. "The Agricultural Sector in Argentina: Major Trends and Recent Developments" In *The Shifting Patterns of Agricultural Production and Productivity Worldwide*, edited by Julian M. Alston, Bruce A. Babcock and Philip G. Pardey, 409–448. Aimes: Iowa State University.

Lévi-Strauss, Claude. 1965. "Le triangle culinaire." *L'Arc* 26: 19–29.

Montoya, Alfredo. 1956. *Historia de los saladeros argentinos*. Buenos Aires: Editorial Raigal.

Newell, Peter. 2009. "Bio-Hegemony: The Political Economy of Agricultural Biotechnology in Argentina." *Journal of Latin American Studies* 41, no. 01: 27–57.

Nouzeilles, Gabriela and Graciela Montaldo, eds. 2002. *The Argentina Reader: History, Culture, Politics*. Durham, NC: Duke University Press.

O'Connor, Ernesto A. 2013. "China, Brazil and Argentina: Agricultural Trade and Development." *American Journal of Chinese Studies* 20, no. 2: 101–111.

OECD. 2018. *Agricultural Policies in Argentina*. https://www.oecd.org/officialdocuments/publicdisplaydocumentpdf/?cote=TAD/CA(2018)9/FINAL&docLanguage=En

Oliveira, Gustavo de, and Mindi Schneider. 2016. "The Politics of Flexing Soybeans: China, Brazil and Global Agroindustrial Restructuring." *The Journal of Peasant Studies* 43, no. 1: 167–194. doi:10.1080/03066150.2014.993625

Ortega, Lucía. 2012. "El Norte en transformación: propiedad y alquiler en las zonas de reciente expansión agropecuaria." In *Estudios agrarios y agroindustriales,* edited by Azcuy Ameghino, Eduardo, Pedro Castillo, Daniel A. Fernández, Lucía Ortega, José Pierri, Fernando Romero Wimer, and Juan Manuel Villulla, 137–168. Buenos Aires: Imago Mundi.

Pavan, Enrique, Gabriela Grigioni, Patricia Aguirre, and Marcela Leal. 2017. 'What is Meat in Argentina?' *Animal Frontiers* 7, no. 4: 44–47. https://doi.org/10.2527/af.2017.0434

Qaim, Matin, and Greg Traxler. 2005. "Roundup Ready Soybeans in Argentina: Farm Level and Aggregate Welfare Effects." *Agricultural Economics* 32, no. 1: 73–86. https://doi.org/10.1111/j.0169-5150.2005.00006.x

Quaizel, Daniel. 2017. "Qué cortes de carne vende Argentina a qué países." *Noticias Agropecuarias,* August 10, 2017. https://www.noticiasagropecuarias.com/2017/08/10/que-cortes-de-carne-vende-argentina-que-paises/

Resourcetrade.earth. 2019. https://resourcetrade.earth/?year=2019&exporter=32&category=87&units=value&autozoom=1

Richardson, Neal, P. 2009. "Export-Oriented Populism: Commodities and Coalitions in Argentina." *Studies in Comparative International Development* 44: 228–255. DOI 10.1007/s12116-008-9037-5

Ritchie, Hannah, and Max Roser. 2019. "Meat and Dairy Production." *OurWorldInData.org*. https://ourworldindata.org/meat-production.

Silvera, Mario Jorge. 2003. "La cadena alimenticia del vacuno: época colonial y Siglo XIX y su relación con el uso del espacio en la Ciudad de Buenos Aires." *Historia para Arqueólogos*. http://www.iaa.fadu.uba.ar/publicaciones/critica/0134.pdf

Silvera, Mario Jorge. 2005. *Cocinas y comidas en El Río de la Plata*. Neuquen: Editorial Educo.

Slutzky, Daniel. 2012. "Los cambios recientes en la tenencia de la tierra en el país con especial referencia a la región pampeana: nuevos y viejos actores sociales." *Doc. CIEA* 6: 141–173. http://bibliotecadigital.econ.uba.ar/download/docuciea/docuciea_n6_06.pdf

Sly, Maria José Haro. 2017. "The Argentine Portion of the Soybean Commodity Chain." *Palgrave Communications*. https://doi.org/10.1057/palcomms.2017.95

Sosa Varrotti, Andrea P. 2019. "Las megaempresas del agronegocio: Un estudio del modelo agrario a partir de las prácticas empresariales". *Estudios Socioterritoriales* No. 26. DOI:10.37838/unicen/est.26-026

Stølen, Kristi Anne. 1996. *The Decency of Inequality. Gender Power and Social Change on the Argentine Prairie*. Oslo: Scandinavian University Press.

Stølen, Kristi Anne. 2015. "Agricultural Change in Argentina: Impacts of the Gene Modified Soybean Revolution." In *Emerging Economies and Challenges to Sustainability: Theories, Strategies, Local Realities*, edited by Arve Hansen and Ulrikke Bryn Wethal, 149–161. London: Routledge.

Taylor, Carl C. 1948. *Rural Life in Argentina*. Baton Rouge: Louisiana State University Press.

Torrado, Susana. 2003. *Historia de la Familia en la Argentina Moderna (1870–2000)*. Buenos Aires: Ediciones de la Flor.

Voora, Vivek, Christina Larrea, and Steffany Bermudez. 2020. "Global Market Report: Soybeans." *Sustainable Commodities Marketplace Series*. IISD: Winnipeg.

Chapter 5

Meating Demand in China

Changes in Chinese Meat Cultures through Time

Marius Korsnes and Chen Liu

INTRODUCTION

Agriculture is vital to produce foods for humans, but agriculture also impacts Earth's biosphere. About 20 percent of the world's greenhouse gas (GHG) emissions come from agriculture (fao.org 2021). Of these, almost three quarters come from livestock (meat and dairy) alone (Dunne 2020). An overdependence on large-scale intensified meat production is undesirable for several interconnected reasons: sustainability (Willett et al. 2019), food safety (Yasuda 2018), risks of diseases (Wallace 2016), physical health (Myers et al. 2017), and animal welfare (Neo and Emel 2017). The dominance of capitalism, economic growth, and efficiency-thinking makes ideas of limits hard to imagine (e.g. Wilhite 2016), but it is highly doubtful that economic growth can be sustained long-term within planetary biophysical boundaries (Jackson 2017; Raworth 2017). This chapter explores meat production and consumption in China historically and today, with an aim to provide some thoughts about how meat-related food practices have coevolved and co-constituted demand for animals. The chapter looks briefly at the ways in which meat and animals were used in traditional China, when Confucianism, Daoism, and Buddhism gained a foothold in Chinese thought, before we look at the ways in which demand for meat is reproduced in contemporary China, during the period after 1978.

How—if at all—can it be made possible to cover human needs without breaching Earth's ecological boundaries? To us, posing such a question means scrutinizing "human needs" and attempting to understand how demand for meat and animal products has been constituted over time. This is particularly interesting in China, given the rapid increase in meat consumption during the past 40 years, in addition to the centrality of moderation and frugality in Chinese tradition—particularly when it came to food (Sterckx 2019). Today's demand for meat has been thoroughly bolstered through increased industrialization and intensification of production with government's support. Pro-pork policy in China has since 1978 among others aimed to stabilize the price of pork by establishing a pork reserve and providing grants, tax incentives, cheap loans for farms, and free animal immunization (Schneider 2011). Concurrently with the increased industrialization of food in China, public concern for food safety has grown, as, for instance, was the case after the infant formula milk scandal in 2008 (Yasuda 2018). During the past three years, China has experienced a severe disruption in pork production due to the impact of the African Swine Fever (ASF) (fao.org 2020). This has in turn induced extremely unusual fluctuations in pork prices (Zhang et al. 2020) and an increase in meat imports to China from abroad, which has reshaped global meat markets (ft.com 2020). The Covid-19 global pandemic that is currently shaking the world has generated sharp declines in global food production and food trade, the volatility of food prices, and thereby caused food insecurity and further health crisis in low- and middle-income countries (Laborde et al. 2020). This global pandemic is also an effect of human beings increasing industrialization of meat production, which increasingly expands into areas with wild animals (see Wallace 2016). In other words, the meat consumption practices of the Chinese population are of global interest, not only because of climate and environment issues, but also because of a global concern for food security and animal welfare. Food is a particularly interesting topic for analyzing sociocultural images and human-ecosystem interactions since all humans eat, and we eat differently compared to different times and to different places. To mention some examples, dog meat used to be a luxury food in China but is not anymore (Huang 2000), and wild animals (such as snakes, bamboo rats, and pangolins) was a high-status eating behavior but now is avoided because of the rapid rise in animal-related diseases (Klein 2017). Also, using chopsticks and sharing dishes are common in many Eastern countries while knife/fork and individual dishes are common in many Western countries. This chapter shows the ongoing negotiations that are happening in China between a variety of practices from production to consumption that underpin meat eating. In order to do this, we start the chapter by looking at food, eating, and the role of meat in Chinese history and tradition until 1978 when Chinese economic—and nutrition—growth started accelerating. We then outline the role that meat has assumed in contemporary Chinese eating habits during the period of rapid growth, with a particular focus on urban eating, since the turn of the millennium. Lastly, we conclude with some thoughts on how the transformation of foodways might impact meat eating in China and what it would take to downshift demand for meat without compromising the welfare of people.

MEAT IN CHINESE TRADITION

Food and eating has been at the center of human life since the very beginning of our existence. Lin Yutang (1895–1976), a Chinese philosopher and linguist, is known to have said that "it is a pretty crazy life when one eats in order to work and does not work in order to eat" (quoted in Sterckx 2011, 11). Increased urbanization and division between food production and consumption have made the daily toil of food provision for our ancestors a phenomenon long forgotten for many of us. Food is central to Chinese thought and tradition. Chang (1973, 14), for instance, said that "food and eating are among things central to the Chinese way of life and part of the Chinese ethos." Although perhaps unsubstantiated, Sterckx (2019, chap. 9) remarks that "few cultures put more emphasis on the central role of food preparation and consumption than the Chinese in both a secular and religious context." At any rate, the fascination with food that can be observed in China speaks to the Chinese way of life—a life in which animals and meat are deeply entangled.

Looking at the broad canvas of food and eating in Chinese history, there are some particularities that can be outlined, which are of importance to the understanding of meat eating. Basic to any understanding of Chinese food is the distinction between *fan* (饭) and *cai* (菜) dishes. Narrowly speaking the two concepts refer to rice and vegetables respectively, but in a wider sense *fan* dishes include all cereals and starch and are seen as the staple food, while *cai* dishes typically are the ones that make a meal tasty, and can be made of vegetables, meat, or fish (Simoons 1991, 15). A balanced meal includes both *fan* and *cai* dishes (Chang 1977). *Cai* dishes are typically mixed with multiple ingredients and combinations of tastes, and ingredients are cut into smaller pieces ready to be eaten directly with chopsticks. The two should ideally be balanced to get a healthy meal, something which is also closely connected to the balance between *yin* and *yang*; if these forces are not in equilibrium there would be problems such as ill-health or disease (see also Hansen, this volume). Based on the traditional philosophy of medicine food homology, eating certain types of food would be closely associated with one's health (Chang 1977). Meat was sometimes embedded in regimens because of certain therapeutic effects (Li et al. 2020). In short, food in Chinese tradition is "medicine, pleasure, skill, sustenance, ethics, politics and economics rolled into one" (Sterckx 2019, chap. 9). Moreover, taste, rather than nutrition, is considered to be the most important feature of food in China where people treat eating and cooking as an art (Nam et al. 2010).

There is great local and regional variety in Chinese cuisine. A major division is often made between the wheat-eating areas of the north and the rice-eating areas in the south. For instance, Emperor Kangxi in a lecture to his sons allegedly said that "the people of the North are strong; they must not copy the fancy diets of the Southerners, who are physically frail, live in a different environment, and have different stomachs and bowels" (Smith 2015, 415). A classification is also made between the eight different cuisine "schools" of China, namely Shandong (*Lu*—鲁), Jiangsu (*Su*—苏), Guangdong (*Yue*—粤), Hunan (*Xiang*—湘), Zhejiang (*Zhe*—浙), Anhui (*Hui*—徽), Fujian (*Min*—闽), and Sichuan (*Chuan*—川) foods (Nam et al. 2010). Generally, although the majority of meat products in China are prepared from pork, these regional cuisines have their own particular characteristics, tastes, cooking materials, and techniques (Nam et al. 2010). For example, double steaming delicate foods such as bird nests and shark's fins is widely used in Guangdong and Fujian cuisines; panfrying and then red cooking pork belly with soy sauce, sugar, and wine is popular in Zhejiang cuisine; and water-boiled or deep-fried pork slices with chili pepper are famous foods of Human and Sichuan cuisines. Suffice to say here that Chinese food customs are regionally variegated and that we in this chapter do not attempt to provide a comprehensive overview or analysis of all of them. Rather, we here aim to provide a brief snapshot of the way in which meat has figured in Chinese food practices in history.

Food is closely connected to social division in Chinese tradition. The availability of food was associated with economic class, and as pointed out by Spence (1977, 271), who focused on the Qing dynasty (1644–1912), "in the assortments of food there was a wider disparity in China between rich and poor than in any other country of the world." As an example, a common complaint observed in Chinese history, as noted by Chang (1977, 14), shows that food and prosperity are closely intertwined: "While the wine and the meat have spoiled behind the red doors [of rich households], on the road [outside] there are skeletons of those who died of exposure." Going back to the time of the principal Chinese thinkers such as Confucius, Laozi, and Mencius from about 500 BCE, several scholars note a desirability of frugality and moderation concerning food in Chinese tradition. For peasants and the poor, frugality was a necessity, but for the elite frugality was a virtue. According to Wertz (2007), "Frugality with food and eating was one of the things central to the Chinese way of life and a part of the Chinese ethos." In other words, food was to be consumed in moderation, and should not be wasted. Overindulgence was seen as unbalanced and unhealthy. In fact, "excessive consumption of food and liquor was considered a sin so serious that it could even bring down a dynasty" (Simoons 1991, 18). This is also one of the reasons why Chinese food includes all parts of an animal, and traditional recipes also contain leftovers. A common maxim, which Chinese parents apparently have said to their children for millennia, is that the proper amount of consumption is "70 percent" full and not more (Chang 1977, 10). Or, as it was formulated in the *Neiye* (內業), one of the oldest texts in China, "In eating it is best not to fill up; in thinking it is best not to overdo" (quoted in Sterckx 2019, chap. 9).

Overall, the balance between meat- and plant-based foods remained relatively stable for several millennia in China, until large-scale nutritional changes started taking place during the end of 1970s. Smil (2004, 113) notes that

> during the fourth century BCE in the state of Wei, a typical peasant was expected to provide each of his five family members with nearly half a kilogram of grain a day—a total identical to the mean per capita supply of grain in North China during the early 1950s.

On average, Chinese predominately ate vegetarian—although this was out of necessity due to shortage of land and dense populations (Simoons 1991, 293, 295). An example from the Southern Song Dynasty (1127–1279) shows what came to be known as the "seven necessities":

> The things that people cannot do without every day are firewood, rice, oil, salt, soybean sauce, vinegar, and tea. Those who are just slightly better off cannot do without *hsia-fan* ["food to help get the rice down"] and soup [both presumably of vegetables]. (Freeman 1977, 151)

Estimates indicate that in the 1960s and 1970s, 95 percent of food energy in an average Chinese diet came from plant foods, with rice, wheat, and corn as the major staple foods (Smil 2004, 99). There is large agreement that meat was consumed in very small quantities on average in Chinese history (Mote 1977, 200). If there was any meat at all it was "consumed more often as flavoring for vegetables and as the basis of a sauce than as the principal component of a dish" (ibid., 201), or at special occasions such as the Lunar New Year (Simoons 1991). Nevertheless, there was a stark contrast between the elite and the peasants. The wealthy and middle classes could afford, and ate, more meat than the poor (ibid).

Vegetarianism was widely practiced in China—particularly after Buddhism entered China around the first and second centuries CE (Simoons 1991). As pointed out by Wang (2019, 15), it was only with Emperor Wu of the Liang (464–549 CE) that meat eating and alcohol drinking was forbidden among "religious professionals with state power." Before that it was not mandatory— albeit highly recommended—for a Buddhist to desist from meat and alcohol. Confucianists had no general opposition to meat eating and slaughtering, but

Daoists were advised to abstain from meat, although for different reasons than the Buddhists. Where Buddhists abstained due to respect for animal life, Daoists held that "the many gods sustaining one's body dislike the odor of flesh, and that if one eats it they may escape, thereby shortening one's life" (Simoons 1991, 32). Although Confucianism included compassion for animal life, both Confucius and Mencius ate meat sparingly. They also advocated animal sacrifice, if it was done right (ibid.). Both pigs and dogs were mentioned by Mencius as "perfectly respectable meat animals" (Huang 2000, 58), and Confucius advocated abstention from meat in fasting periods or during mourning periods, which could last up to three years (Sterckx 2011).

In Chinese history, as elsewhere, animals had multiple functions apart from providing the service of "meat"; they also "provided draft power, used household wastes, and provided manure to fertilize cropland" (Bai et al. 2018, 2). According to a study from the 1940s, 75 percent of domesticated animals in China were "work animals, compared to 10 percent in the U.S." (Simoons 1991, 295). We can assume that the remaining 25 percent was food for humans, given that for farmers in 1920s, only 2 percent of calorie intake came from meat (ibid., 293). If this figure has been relatively stable over time, it means that domesticated animals were more helpful in producing plant foods to be eaten by humans than in providing direct meat.

The pig has had an especially central role in China: most households would raise at least one or two pigs per year and were more valuable alive than dead because they ate wastes that no one could eat and produced valuable manure (Schneider 2017). As pointed out by Lander, Schneider, and Brunson (2020, 7), "Given how rarely common people ate pigs, they might not have considered them worth the effort of raising if they had not also provided other services, namely, cleaning up waste and producing fertilizer." Farmers often fed food leftovers and agricultural by-products to their pigs, who in turn provided useful manure for their, typically, cereal-intensive farming. The pig has been one of the most important domesticated animals, and it has continued to be significant throughout Chinese history until today (Simoons 1991, 296). In the Yellow River and Yangtze River valleys, pigs started taking an increasingly important role in agricultural societies about 7,000 years ago (Lander, Schneider, & Brunson 2020). About 6,000 years ago, pigs became dietary staples in the Yellow River valley, and in other regions of China it took several millennia more (ibid.). The centrality of the pig can, for instance, be seen through the Chinese character for "home," which shows a pig under a roof (*jiā* 家). It often survived on table scraps and leftovers, and in several places in China "pigs were actually quartered in the family garbage pit and regularly fed human excreta and garbage" (Simoons 1991, 296). Thus, the pig transformed inedible wastes into valuable manure, and, in the end, would end up as human food itself.

The period immediately after the Communist Party came to power was dominated by hunger, and meat in 1970s represented about 6 percent of calorie intake (Smil 2004, 89). This changed abruptly from the opening up era starting in 1978 with the privatization of farming and Deng Xiaoping's policy of "letting peasants produce what they can do best" (ibid., 95). According to Smil (2004, 208), from 1978 when Deng Xiaoping consolidated his power, in less than five years he "turned the world's most communalized, rigidly planned and badly underperforming agricultural system into tens of millions of small private enterprises." As agriculture became modernized in the 1980s, leveraged by heavy government subsidies, kitchen wastes and food losses were transformed from a value provided by the pigs to an environmental burden that would contaminate the soil (Bai et al. 2018, 4). For instance, in 2010, agriculture was a larger source of water pollution than industry (Schneider 2017).

It appears today that traditional values of frugality, moderation, vegetarianism, and reduced food waste have been particularly under pressure in conjunction with rapid industrialization and intensification of food production—and meat in particular. One impact of China's large-scale industrialization of pork production in the past 30 years has been that smaller farms and households no longer keep their own pigs. Ninety-eight percent of pork farms in China raise fewer than 50 pigs, but they produce only one-third of the pork—the rest is produced by centralized industrial scale farms (Wang 2020). Meat changed from being a luxury to eat once per year, to something eaten several times per day for a billion people today (Bai et al. 2018). Alongside the increased industrialization of meat there has also been a shift in the meaning and presence of meat in the everyday life of the average Chinese person. It can be argued that China is a particularly interesting case precisely because the squeeze between traditional and modern values is more prominent than in Western countries—as explained earlier. It is nevertheless the case that reducing waste and consumption are integrated in understandings of sustainability among Chinese people (Liu et al. 2019), and this might indeed be a returning trend in contemporary China. In the next section we delve further into the details of contemporary meat use in China.

MEAT IN CONTEMPORARY CHINA

The story of contemporary meat eating in China cannot be distinguished from the massive increase in overall standards of living experienced since the reform and opening up after Deng Xiaoping came to power in 1978 (Liu et al. 2009). At that point, most Chinese people had grown accustomed to never having enough food to eat. As Yasuda (2018, 46) puts it, "The specter of famine has long haunted the collective memory of the Chinese people." The failed Great Leap Forward from 1959 to 1961 led to mass starvation (ibid.). The period during the Cultural Revolution from 1968 to 1978 was not much better in terms of availability of food (Smil 2004), but after the Cultural Revolution followed something akin to an agricultural revolution. Due to the fear that starvation would lead to massive social unrest, ensuring that enough food was supplied for the masses was central to Deng Xiaoping's efforts after 1978 (Yasuda 2018). Between 1979 and 1995 agricultural production increased on average 6.5 percent annually, and China was at that point already self-sufficient in major agricultural products (Yasuda 2018).

The Chinese Communist Party (CCP) is known to have a sophisticated governance apparatus consisting of a mix of top-down and bottom-up approaches that very often achieve what it sets out to do using experimentation, centralization, and visions of the future as planning tools (e.g., Korsnes 2014, 2016). The Chinese government is currently advising citizens to eat less meat through updated dietary guidelines (Harvey 2016), and there can be no doubt that the CCP has the tools and clout to carry out a reduction in meat—but the trick lies in making it acceptable by industry, citizens, and local governments alike. The large inequality existing in China implies that there are still large portions of the population, that are still rural, who would need to improve the quality of their diets. A recent study showed, for instance, that if all Chinese would follow the 2016 dietary guidelines, GHG emissions would increase by 7.5 percent (He et al. 2019). This means that there still might be time to shift the diets of those who are still not urban and middle-incomers toward a less meat-intense, more sustainable and healthy diet as, for example, suggested by the 2019 EAT-Lancet report (Willet et al. 2019).

A central government instrument to guide nutritional intake in China is the Chinese Dietary Guideline, published for the first time in 1989, then updated in 1997, 2007, and 2016. Lei and Shimokawa (2020) compared these and found that each revised guideline was updated according to Chinese people's changes in consumption habits as well as nutritional requirements. Whereas the 1997 guidelines for the first time provided recommendations about meat and dairy consumption, where for meat the advice was an appropriate consumption of lean meat, and to reduce the amount of fatty meat for people in urban areas, while for milk it was recommended to "consume milk, beans or dairy or bean products frequently" (ibid., p. 2), the 2016 version also encouraged soybean as an alternative to meat proteins (ibid.). Nevertheless, as shown by Lei and Shimokawa (2020), Chinese people have not been following the official nutrition recommendations. Largely, between 1991 and 2011, people increasingly overconsumed meat, and increasingly underconsumed vegetables compared to the guidelines (ibid). It appears that the considerable support given to the animal-based food industry by the Chinese government is directly at odds with the recommendation to reduce meat consumption. Apart from an encouragement by Xi Jinping in 2020 to reduce food waste, no concrete steps have been taken to reduce meat consumption after the new dietary guidelines were published (Reid 2021).

The correlation between increased income and increased meat consumption has been documented by several studies (e.g. Liu et al. 2009; Lei and Shimokawa 2020). Higher income also appears to be correlated to a larger increase in meat consumed away from home compared to that eaten at home, in line with overall global trends (Bai et al. 2020). In turn, both increased income and eating away from home are associated with larger plate waste (Xu et al. 2020). What is more, waste is generally larger in urban areas: in Shanghai about 12 percent of all food supplies are wasted, against only 2 percent in rural China (Gu et al. 2019). Understanding the interrelations of dining out, increased income, urbanization and how this leads to increased meat consumption as well as increased food waste is therefore important. Nevertheless, as also argued by Hansen (2018) in Vietnam, we believe that reducing the analysis to a binary understanding of low-high income or an urban-rural scale is masking some of the nuances behind why meat increasingly has become interweaved with "modern" life in China. As, for instance, shown by Rinkinen et al. (2017) in a study of cold chains in Hanoi and Bangkok, urban food supply is situated in a larger context influenced by global systems of food production, with mass produced and distributed foods, supermarkets, the necessity of certain technologies such as a fridge, as well as changing concepts of freshness, quality, and safety. Although rapid changes in the composition of Chinese meals is largely an urban and middle-class phenomenon, there are numerous aspects to how it has come about. In addition to the rising trend of eating out (Ma et al. 2006; Min et al. 2015), there have been increases in eating fast food (Zhang et al. 2014), and in buying food via online platforms (Liu et al. 2019; Liu and Chen 2019). More recently, a focus on the relations between meat consumption and health (Li et al. 2020) has induced a trend of eating less meat (Browne et al. 2017; Reid 2021). Takeaway food has undergone rapid changes in the the past few years. Services such as Meituan and ele.me deliver food, groceries, and other items to people's homes, often at lower prices than restaurants and shops (Chen et al. 2019). Such changes are strongly connected to symbolic aspects of social status and position, and can have adverse effects on personal health (Maimaiti et al. 2018).

There is a growing fashion of eating vegetarian food in Chinese communities (see, e.g., Reid 2021), but this trend is still considered to be marginal. Moreover, eating less meat might not necessarily be linked with environmental and social ethics nor the Buddhist and other Chinese traditions of meat avoidance. Rather, this meatless lifestyle appears to be linked to health, food safety, bodily ethics, and modern/international lifestyle choices (Klein 2013, 2017; Neo 2016). The everyday discourse about meat consumption is transformed from the traditional thinking about wealth, well-off, and higher social status (in Chinese literature, officials and political elites are conventionally called "meat eaters") to the rethinking of health (rather than "ethic" in many developed countries). For example, for Chinese urban consumers, green or organic food consumption often refers to a healthy eating behavior (Klein 2013, 2017). The official discourse of meat in China is today largely about how to produce pork and other types of meat safely and sustainably to feed the large Chinese population with stable prices, in order to maintain the social stability. In other words, meat eating is not much concerned with the environmental aspect of sustainability but the political-economic one.

The changes in Chinese people's meat consumption can also be seen in relation to the nationwide anxieties shifting from a concern for food security (i.e., having enough to eat) to food safety (having safe and healthy food). The focus on mass production of agricultural products during the 1980s and 1990s puts considerations for food safety lower on the list of priorities (Yasuda 2018). In order to boost production, high levels of chemicals such as pesticides and antibiotics were used (ibid.), which not only increased chemical pollution to both agricultural land and freshwater supplies but also made food unsafe (Jen and Chen 2017). A study of 60 specialized "household pig farms," a term used for domestic farming based on production for sale, rather than for self-consumption (see Schneider 2017), for more information), from 2012 found that only a bit more than half of the households complied with food safety laws (Yasuda 2018). Moreover, the industrialization of food production in the past few decades have increased the excessive use of food additives and food fraud, which have become major concerns for food safety in China (Jen and Chen 2017).

The collective fear of unsafe food has spread among Chinese consumers in the past few decades, which has brought about social anxieties and trust panic and has triggered preferences of buying imported food in Chinese society. In a Chinese context, Gong and Jackson (2012) indicate in their research on (grand)parenting practices, after the 2008 infant milk powder scandal in China, that the unsafe food environment undermined Chinese (grand)parents' trust in domestic infant formula and encouraged their high loyalty to foreign (imported) brands. This anxiety of food has an impact on both local and imported meat consumption as well. Some recent studies have demonstrated that Chinese urban consumers are willing to pay more for food safety claims, animal welfare practice information, and officially approved organic/green food certification associated with meat products and prefer imported than domestic beef (see, for example, Ortega et al. 2016; Loebnitz and Aschemann-Witzel 2016; Wang et al. 2018). These food safety concerns have pushed the Chinese government to reform and strengthen food safety standards, laws, and regulations (such as the release of Food Hygiene Standard and Food Quality Standard in 2005 and the revision of Chinese Food Safety Law released in 2015) at both national and provincial levels in recent years (Jen and Chen 2017).

According to Shimokawa (2015), the environmental problems caused by agriculture gains little attention in Chinese societies, making it harder to suggest changes to current agricultural practices. China has also been found to lack mechanisms that provide environmental feedbacks institutionally and politically (ibid.). We would argue that a deeper understanding of the way in which meat is connected to interrelated cultural (e.g., status), practical (e.g., dining out), and technological (e.g., ordering food via online platforms, or using fridges) factors could enable an analysis of the wider factors that have led to meat becoming embedded in a variety of eating practices in China. What is more, it is useful to understand how the way in which meat production has become increasingly industrialized and intensified has contributed to the increase in meat consumption, for instance, through international fast-food chains such as McDonalds or Kentucky Fried Chicken (KFC) (Liu et al. 2009; Yuan et al. 2019).

The first KFC opened in Beijing in 1987, and since then KFC has opened more than 5,000 restaurants in 1,100 Chinese cities—making it the largest fast-food chain in China (businessinsider.com 2019). In 2013 there was an estimated total of two million fast-food restaurants in China (Wang et al. 2016). One study has found that—apart from increased income and urbanization—such a massive and quick growth involved shifting habits of eating at home to eating out, direct marketing strategies by the fast-food industry, as well as improvements in fast-food supply chains and franchising systems (Wang et al. 2016). One factor explaining the rapid growth of fast-food chains in China was lifestyle changes including faster daily life paces (ibid.). Such lifestyle changes would, for instance, allow for combining eating out with friends and family with other activities such as shopping or going to the movies.

The increase of fast-food chains, which in many ways have made Chinese foodways more similar to European and American ones, appears to correlate with increased meat consumption (Yuan et al. 2019). This increase in eating fast food necessarily also must have been combined with increased and adequate supply of meat. This has been described by Schneider (2017, 93) as China's industrial meat regime, with a capitalist industrial livestock production where "large-scale operations (. . .) manage a majority of the production, processing, distribution, and sale of pigs and pork" at the expense of smallholder farmers. Much of this industrial production is based on a con-centrated animal feeding operation (CAFO) involving imports of soybeans and other crops from abroad (see also Stølen, this volume), with fundamental changes for the connection between production and consumption (Schneider 2017). Weis (2013, 8) described the changes rather poetically in this way, referring to the overall global trend of what he terms a "meatification" process:

> Its landscapes can be likened to islands of concentrated livestock within seas of grain and oilseed monocultures, with soaring populations of a few livestock spe-cies reared in high densities, disarticulated from the surrounding fields. These islands of concentrated livestock and seas of monocultures are then rearticulated by heavy flows of crops such as corn/maize, barley, sorghum, soybeans, and rapeseed/canola cycling through animals. This disarticulation and rearticulation is mediated by an array of technologies, inputs, and large corporations, and marked by the loss of large volumes of usable nutrition.

The shift toward eating more packaged and processed food is also a relatively recent phenomenon in China, and it has led to increased risk of overweight among children and teenagers (Zhou et al. 2015). A recent study found that 46 percent of adults and 15 percent of children are obese or over-weight in China (Wang et al. 2019). This change is strongly connected to a retail revolution with a boom of supermarkets and retail stores, which made ultra-processed food readily available (Zhou et al. 2015). Before the 1980s, most of the provision was centrally distributed and controlled by state-owned enterprises (Hu et al. 2004). This changed as agriculture was increasingly liberalized and private retail was legalized (ibid). The supermarket boom started in the early 1990s and was directly connected to China's agricultural development making food available for more people (Hu et al. 2004). These supermarket chains were not only Chinese, but also foreign brands such as Carrefour and Walmart. Over time, supermarkets took over a large share of not only staple foods, but also fresh meats typically sold in wet markets (Hu et al. 2004; Wang et al. 2018). All in all, therefore, the rapid growth of meat consumption can be better understood through the lens of a "system of provision" (Fine 2002), which has contributed to reduced prices, increased availability, and changed diets and concepts of freshness and quality toward a different, more fast-tracked and meat-intense practice. In other words, the close entanglement and coevolution of demand with supply for meat products show how not only urbanization or increased income can explain meat has come to serve new needs for China's population.

If only urbanization and income levels were explanatory factors of increased meat consumption, a suggestion of a way forward for reduced and more sustainable meat consumption would be limited to reduced urbanization and reduced income. However, we believe that the way in which meat has become entangled with the performance of certain eating, cooking, and shopping practices in Chinese cities can be altered through a careful unweaving, or a "disembedding," of certain elements connected to a variety of meat-related food practices. For instance, as shown through the growing presence of decentralized, community-supported agriculture in China, ideas and enactments of "safe, healthy, and local food" are spreading quickly (Yasuda 2018). In this way, the multiple food safety scandals that have occurred in China could move meat-related food practices toward less large-scale intensified to more local solutions built on socialized trust in knowing where the meat comes from. Such a start would not be enough, however, to break free from the grip of fast-food, fast lifestyles, a deeply entrenched meat industry supporting an elevated status of meat that has underpinned and reinforced demand for meat in China during the past 40 years.

CONCLUDING THOUGHTS

Growing crops and raising livestock have major environmental and climatic consequences on Earth's biophysical conditions. In the Confucian order, properly conducted farming was seen as the foundation of society—and a central pillar was for humans and animals to get along harmoniously (Bray 2018). The peasant was once important for the Chinese Communist Party's ascent to power—as, for instance, told through the tale of the Long March—but those who produce most of China's food today are not peasants but employees in large agro-industrial complexes (Schneider 2017; Schwoob 2018). China has seen an explosion in the amount of animal products as part of meals. Between 1980 and 2010 annual per capita meat consumption increased four times, with poultry and pork increasing especially rapidly (Bai et al. 2018). China is now the world's largest producer of livestock products and produces and consumes half of the world's total pig meat (Weis 2013). As much as 65 percent of grain produced is fed to animals, and more than half of all agricultural pollution is connected to livestock (Gu et al. 2019). Plant-based diets cause fewer negative environmental effects than animal-source foods, and it is estimated that GHG emissions from agriculture can be reduced by as much as 80 percent by 2050 if we would switch to more plant-based diets (Willett et al. 2019, 472).

In this chapter, we started with an exploration of how meat has figured in Chinese food and eating practices in history, and then moved on to look at the same in present-day China. One facet that would be interesting to explore further is the relatively common claim that the Chinese in history were so-called "involuntary vegetarians," implying that people "had a virtually meatless diet not by choice but because of poverty" (Wang 2019, 15). To be sure, as elaborated on in the first part of this chapter, Buddhism, Daoism, and Confucianism all advocated restraint with regards to meat eating—but they did not ask every believer to avoid meat. If the tenet posited in this chapter is true, namely that modern-day fast-food and production-side actors among others have increased meat consumption considerably through a reduction in prices and through host of other means, then a question remains: How much meat would a "regular" Chinese meat eater eat, if meat was produced locally, ethically, and sustainably? Such a counterfactual question is of course impossible to answer, but it is very likely that the amount of meat consumption would be lower than today. It is also very likely that people would be satisfied with such a lower amount. Nevertheless, it is today's dreams that define current needs and wants, as illustrated by the statement of this man who grew up in Liaoning Province in the 1970s: "When I was a boy, my dream was to eat meat. Today I can eat meat for breakfast, lunch, and dinner if I want to . . . this is progress" (Schneider 2017, 91).

This discussion of what can be considered "enough" and what is "too much" meat consumption also has repercussions for China's current industrial meat complex. In fact, issues such as the ASF, and most likely also Covid-19, have led to increased preference for large-scale producers because they are thought to have better safety and infection control routines:

> These highly decentralized farms make government oversight difficult. There is also enormous pressure for these farms to keep up with the market price for pork, and to maintain steady production. The government was finding [ASF] a convenient excuse to eradicate these small farms, making way for centralized, industrial-scale operations. (Wang 2020, Kindle Loc. 858)

The embeddedness of industrial solutions for China's food production mean that moving away from large-scale intensified agriculture appears difficult. Nevertheless, changing urban foodways (such as the popularity of eating out, consuming takeaway food, buying imported food, and the fashion of vegetarianism) and the recent outbreaks of viral respiratory diseases of zoonotic origin (such as SARS in 2002 and the current Covid-19 pandemic) bring new meanings and values of (reduced) meat consumption. The recent food scandals brought about by the industrialization and commercialization of food systems have increased a public concern for food safety in urban China. This collective anxiety of food safety issues has triggered both a popular trend of (over)consuming imported meat from supermarkets or via e-commerce platforms, and a social movement to slower, more organic, smaller-scale food production.

The nationwide concern for food safety brings about another feature of the meat-eating discourse in China as highlighted in this chapter: health. Compared to Western countries where the meat-eating discourse is dominated by issues relating to animal ethics and environmental sustainability, the Chinese focus appears to be on the health impact of meat eating. For instance, being vegetarian or eating less meat refers to a healthier dietary choice; avoiding eating wild animals is believed to be a way to prevent the spread of zoonotic virus. However, this concern for health issues is not leading to a distinction between Western voluntary and ethical foodways and Chinese health-oriented food culture. Rather, both interpretations of meat cultures are entangled with the global trend of constructing an alternative food system aimed at reducing the social and environmental problems generated by the current industrialized food systems. This avenue is still marginal, but shifting meanings via embracing ethical consumption, environmental sustainability, health and safety risks, animal welfare, fair trade, labor conditions, and human rights combined have the potential to contribute to transforming and reducing demand for meat in China.

REFERENCES

Bai, Junfei, James L. Seale Jr, and Thomas I. Wahl. 2020. "Meat Demand in China: To Include or Not to Include Meat Away from Home?" *Australian Journal of Agricultural and Resource Economics* 64 (1): 150–170.

Bai, Zhaohai, Wenqi Ma, Lin Ma, Gerard L. Velthof, Zhibiao Wei, Petr Havlík, Oene Oenema, Michael RF Lee, and Fusuo Zhang. 2018. "China's Livestock Transition: Driving Forces, Impacts, and Consequences." *Science Advances* 4 (7): eaar8534.

Bray, Francesca. 2018. "Ch. 6. Where Did the Animals Go? Presence and Absence of Livestock in Chinese Agricultural Treatises." In *Animals through Chinese History: Earliest Times to 1911*, edited by Roel Sterckx, Martina Siebert and Dagmar Schäfer. Cambridge University Press.

Browne, Alison L., Josephine Mylan and Zhu Di. 2017. "On the 'Meat Edge'? Meat Consumption and Reduction in Middle Class Urban China." Accessed December 2, 2017. https://discoversociety.org/2017/12/06/on-the-meat-edge-meat-consumpti on-and-reduction-in-middle-class-urban-china/.

Businessinsider.com. 2019. "KFC is by Far the Most Popular Fast Food Chain in China and It's Nothing Like the US Brand—Here's What It's Like." *Harrison Jacobs*, Mar 8, 2019. Accessed December 5, 2020. https://www.businessinsider.co m/most-popular-fast-food-chain-in-china-kfc-photos-2018-4 .

Chang, Kwang-Chih (Ed.). 1977. *Food in Chinese Culture. Anthropological and Historical Perspectives*. New Haven and London: Yale University Press.

Chen, Lulu, David Ramli and Peter Elstrom. 2019. "The World's Greatest Delivery Empire." March 28, 2019. https://www.bloomberg.com/features/2019-meituan-ch ina-delivery-empire/.

Dunne, Daisy. 2020. "Interactive: What is the Climate Impact of Eating Meat and Dairy?." September 14, 2020. https://interactive.carbonbrief.org/what-is-the-climate-impact-of-eating-meat-and-dairy/.

Fao.org. 2020. "ASF Situation in Asia Update." Accessed February 20, 2021. http://www.fao.org/ag/againfo/programmes/en/empres/ASF/situation_update.html

Fine, Ben. 2002. *The World of Consumption: The Material and Cultural Revisited.* London: Routledge.

Ft.com. 2020. "How Swine Fever is Reshaping the Global Meat Trade." January 11, 2021. https://www.ft.com/content/42f2170a-20e8-11ea-b8a1-584213ee7b2b.

Gong, Qian, and Peter Jackson. 2012. "Consuming Anxiety? Parenting Practices in China after the Infant Formula Scandal." *Food, Culture & Society* 15 (4): 557–578.

Gu, Baojing, Xiaoling Zhang, Xuemei Bai, Bojie Fu, and Deli Chen. 2019. *Four Steps to Food Security for Swelling Cities.* Nature Publishing Group.

Hansen, Arve. 2018. "Meat Consumption and Capitalist Development: The Meatification of Food Provision and Practice in Vietnam." *Geoforum* 93 (July): 57–68. https://doi.org/10.1016/j.geoforum.2018.05.008.

Harvey, Chelsea. 2016. "China is Encouraging Its Citizens to Eat Less Meat—and that Could be a Big Win for the Climate." Accessed January 2, 2019. https://www.washingtonpost.com/news/energy-environment/wp/2016/05/27/china-is-encouraging-its-citizens-to-eat-less-meat-and-that-could-be-a-big-win-for-the-climate/

He, Pan, Giovanni Baiocchi, Kuishuang Feng, Klaus Hubacek, and Yang Yu. 2019. "Environmental Impacts of Dietary Quality Improvement in China." *Journal of Environmental Management* 240: 518–526.

Hu, Dinghuan, Thomas Reardon, Scott Rozelle, Peter Timmer, and Honglin Wang. 2004. "The Emergence of Supermarkets with Chinese Characteristics: Challenges and Opportunities for China's Agricultural Development." *Development Policy Review* 22 (5): 557–586.

Huang, Hsing-Tsung. 2000. *Science and Civilisation in China, Volume 6, Biology and Biological Technology, Part V: Fermentations and Food Science.* Cambridge, UK: Cambridge University Press.

Jackson, Tim 2017. *Prosperity Without Growth: Foundations for the Economy of Tomorrow* (2nd ed.). Abingdon, Oxon: Routledge.

Jen, Joseph J., and Junshi Chen (Eds.). 2017. *Food Safety in China.* Oxford: Wiley Blackwell.

Klein, Jakob A. 2013. "Everyday Approaches to Food Safety in Kunming." *The China Quarterly* 214: 376–393.

Klein, Jakob A. 2017. "Buddhist Vegetarian Restaurants and the Changing Meanings of Meat in Urban China." *Ethnos* 82 (2): 252–276.

Korsnes, Marius. 2014. "Fragmentation, Centralisation and Policy Learning: An Example from China's Wind Industry." *Journal of Current Chinese Affairs* 43 (3): 175–205.

Korsnes, Marius. 2016. "Ambition and Ambiguity: Expectations and Imaginaries Developing Offshore Wind in China." *Technological Forecasting and Social Change* 107: 50–58.

Laborde, David, Will Martin, Johan Swinnen, and Rob Vos. 2020. "COVID-19 Risks to Global Food Security." *Science* 369 (6503): 500–502.

Lander, Brian, Mindi Schneider, and Katherine Brunson. 2020. "A History of Pigs in China: From Curious Omnivores to Industrial Pork." *The Journal of Asian Studies* 79 (4): 865–889.

Lei, Lei, and Satoru Shimokawa. 2020. "Promoting Dietary Guidelines and Environmental Sustainability in China." *China Economic Review* 59: 101087.

Li, Jie, Jun Justin Li, Xiaoru Xie, Xiaomei Cai, Jian Huang, Xuemei Tian, and Hong Zhu. 2020. "Game Consumption and the 2019 Novel Coronavirus." *The Lancet Infectious Diseases* 20 (3): 275–276.

Liu, Chen, and Jiaxi Chen. 2019. "Consuming Takeaway Food: Convenience, Waste and Chinese Young People's Urban Lifestyle." *Journal of Consumer Culture*, 1469540519882487.

Liu, Chen, Gill Valentine, Robert M. Vanderbeck, Katie McQuaid, and Kristina Diprose. 2019. "Placing 'Sustainability' in Context: Narratives of Sustainable Consumption in Nanjing, China." *Social & Cultural Geography* 20 (9): 1307–1324.

Liu, Hongbo, Kevin A. Parton, Zhang-Yue Zhou, and Rod Cox. 2009. "At-Home Meat Consumption in China: An Empirical Study." *Australian Journal of Agricultural and Resource Economics* 53 (4): 485–501.

Loebnitz, Natascha, and Jessica Aschemann-Witzel. 2016. "Communicating Organic Food Quality in China: Consumer Perceptions of Organic Products and the Effect of Environmental Value Priming." *Food Quality and Preference* 50: 102–108.

Ma, Hengyun, Jikun Huang, Frank Fuller, and Scott Rozelle. 2006. "Getting Rich and Eating out: Consumption of Food Away from Home in Urban China." *Canadian Journal of Agricultural Economics/Revue Canadienne d'agroeconomie* 54 (1): 101–119.

Maimaiti, Mayila, Xueyin Zhao, Menghan Jia, Yuan Ru, and Shankuan Zhu. 2018. "How We Eat Determines What We Become: Opportunities and Challenges Brought by Food Delivery Industry in a Changing World in China." *European Journal of Clinical Nutrition* 72 (9): 1282–1286.

Myers, Samuel S., Matthew R. Smith, Sarah Guth, Christopher D. Golden, Bapu Vaitla, Nathaniel D. Mueller, Alan D. Dangour, and Peter Huybers. 2017a. "Climate Change and Global Food Systems: Potential Impacts on Food Security and Undernutrition." *Annual Review of Public Health* 38 (1): 259–277.

Nam, Ki-Chang, Cheorun Jo, and Mooha Lee. 2010. "Meat Products and Consumption Culture in the East." *Meat Science* 86 (1): 95–102.

Neo, Harvey. 2016. "Ethical Consumption, Meaningful Substitution and the Challenges of Vegetarianism Advocacy." *The Geographical Journal* 182 (2): 201–212.

Neo, Harvey, and Jody Emel. 2017. *Geographies of Meat: Politics, Economy and Culture*. Taylor & Francis.

Ortega, David L., Soo Jeong Hong, H. Holly Wang, and Laping Wu. 2016. "Emerging Markets for Imported Beef in China: Results from a Consumer Choice Experiment in Beijing." *Meat Science* 121: 317–323.

Raworth, Kate. 2017. *Doughnut Economics: Seven Ways to Think like a 21st-Century Economist*. Chelsea Green Publishing.

Reid, Crystal. 2021. "China's Appetite for Meat Fades as Vegan Revolution Takes Hold." March 9, 2021. https://www.theguardian.com/world/2021/mar/09/chinas-appetite-for-meat-fades-as-vegan-revolution-takes-hold.

Schneider, Mindi. 2011. *Feeding China's Pigs: Implications for the Environment, China's Smallholder Farmers and Food Security. ISS Staff Group 4: Rural Development, Environment and Population.* Institute for Agriculture and Trade Policy. Retrieved from http://hdl.handle.net/1765/51021

Schneider, Mindi. 2017. "Wasting the Rural: Meat, Manure, and the Politics of Agro-Industrialization in Contemporary China." *Geoforum* 78: 89–97.

Schwoob, Marie-Hélène. 2018. *Food Security and the Modernisation Pathway in China.* Springer.

Shi, M. I. N., Jun-fei Bai, James Seale Jr, and Thomas Wahl. 2015. "Demographics, Societal Aging, and Meat Consumption in China." *Journal of Integrative Agriculture* 14 (6): 995–1007.

Shimokawa, Satoru. 2015. "Sustainable Meat Consumption in China." *Journal of Integrative Agriculture* 14 (6): 1023–1032.

Simoons, Frederick J. 1991. *Food in China. A Cultural and Historical Inquiry.* Boca Raton, London, New York: CRC Press.

Smil, Vaclav. 2004. *China's Past, China's Future: Energy, Food, Environment.* New York & London: RoutledgeCurzon.

Smith, Richard. J. 2015. *The Qing Dynasty and Traditional Chinese Culture.* London: Rowman & Littlefield.

Spence, Jonathan. 1977. "Ch'ing." In *Food in Chinese Culture. Anthropological and Historical Perspectives*, edited by Kwang-Chih Chang, 259–295. New Haven and London: Yale University Press.

Sterckx, Roel. 2011. *Food, Sacrifice, and Sagehood in Early China.* Cambridge: Cambridge University Press.

Sterckx, Roel. 2019. *Chinese Thought: From Confucius to Cook Ding.* Penguin Books. E-book.

Wallace, Rob. 2016. *Big Farms Make Big Flu: Dispatches on Influenza, Agribusiness, and the Nature of Science.* NYU Press.

Wang, H. Holly, Junhong Chen, Junfei Bai, and John Lai. 2018. "Meat Packaging, Preservation, and Marketing Implications: Consumer Preferences in an Emerging Economy." *Meat Science* 145: 300–307.

Wang, Jianhua, Jiaye Ge, and Yuting Ma. 2018. "Urban Chinese Consumers' Willingness to Pay for Pork with Certified Labels: A Discrete Choice Experiment." *Sustainability* 10 (3): 603.

Wang, Youfa, Liang Wang, Hong Xue, and Weidong Qu. 2016. "A Review of the Growth of the Fast Food Industry in China and Its Potential Impact on Obesity." *International Journal of Environmental Research and Public Health* 13 (11): 1112.

Wang, Youfa, Hong Xue, Mingxiao Sun, Xinya Zhu, Li Zhao, and Yuexin Yang. 2019. "Prevention and Control of Obesity in China." *The Lancet Global Health* 7 (9): e1166–e1167.

Wang, Xiaowei. 2020. *Blockchain Chicken Farm.* Farrar, Straus and Giroux. Kindle.

Wang, Yahong. 2019. "Vegetarians in Modern Beijing: Food, Identity and Body Techniques in Everyday Experience." PhD Diss., University of Glasgow.

Weis, Tony. 2013. *The Ecological Hoofprint: The Global Burden of Industrial Livestock.* London and New York: Zed Books Ltd.

Wertz, S. K. 2007. "The Five Flavors and Taoism: Lao Tzu's Verse Twelve." *Asian Philosophy* 17 (3): 251261.

Willett, Walter, Johan Rockström, Brent Loken, Marco Springmann, Tim Lang, Sonja Vermeulen, Tara Garnett, David Tilman, Fabrice DeClerck, and Amanda Wood. 2019. "Food in the Anthropocene: The EAT–Lancet Commission on Healthy Diets from Sustainable Food Systems." *The Lancet* 393 (10170): 447–492.

Wilhite, Harold. 2016. *The Political Economy of Low Carbon Transformation: Breaking the Habits of Capitalism*. Oxfordshire: Routledge.

Xu, Zhigang, Zongli Zhang, Haiyan Liu, Funing Zhong, Junfei Bai, and Shengkui Cheng. 2020. "Food-Away-from-Home Plate Waste in China: Preference for Variety and Quantity." *Food Policy* 97: 101918.

Yasuda, John K. 2017. *On Feeding the Masses*. Cambridge University Press.

Yuan, Ming, James Lawrence Seale Jr, Thomas Wahl, and Junfei Bai. 2019. "The Changing Dietary Patterns and Health Issues in China." *China Agricultural Economic Review* 11 (1): 143–159.

Zhang, Hong, Liu, Fang and He, Zhongwei. 2020. "Analysis and Countermeasures on China's Pork Price Fluctuation Under African Swine Fever." *Agricultural Outlook* 16 (7), (张红,刘芳,何忠伟. 2020. 非洲猪瘟下中国猪肉价格波动分析与对策.农业展望 16 (7)).

Zhang, Min, Weiping Wu, Lei Yao, Ye Bai, and Guo Xiong. 2014. "Transnational Practices in Urban China: Spatiality and Localization of Western Fast Food Chains." *Habitat International* 43: 22–31.

Zhou, Yijing, Shufa Du, Chang Su, Bing Zhang, Huijun Wang, and Barry M. Popkin. 2015. "The Food Retail Revolution in China and Its Association with Diet and Health." *Food Policy* 55: 92–100.

Chapter 6

Eating a Capitalist Transformation

Economic Development, Culinary Hybridization, and Changing Meat Cultures in Vietnam

Arve Hansen

INTRODUCTION

Vietnamese food has gained significant attention and acclaim internationally over the past decades.[1] Recognized as both healthy and tasty—and much thanks to dishes like pho and *banh mi*—Vietnamese food is now available in most corners of the world, served in everything from inexpensive restaurants through hip food trucks to haute cuisine establishments. Vietnamese food culture is rich and diverse, including food from 54 different ethnic groups and several distinct culinary regions. Only a fraction of this is included in the international version of Vietnamese food, and most dishes are largely unknown outside national borders. Some of these dishes, including, for example, duck fetus, dog meat, snake meat, or different kinds of wild meat and meat from rare animal species, also represent a significant part of the food culture, although they are rarely represented in tourist brochures. Vietnam is home to a wide diversity of meat cultures, enabled by a rich fauna and developed through a long and complex history, including periods of severe food shortage.

These meat cultures are however changing. First of all, Vietnam has seen some of the fastest increases in per capita meat consumption in the world in recent decades as diets have increasingly been "meatified" (Weis 2013; Hansen 2018). As late as the 1980s, meat was a luxury only consumed on special occasions. Indeed, in 1990, the average Vietnamese consumer still ate only 12 kilograms of meat a year, or about a fifth of the average meat consumption in OECD countries the same year. By 2017, the average Vietnamese consumer ate 53.2 kilograms of meat every year, a staggering

440 percent increase, and now at almost four-fifths of the OECD average (OECD 2021).[2] Importantly, these numbers only contain internationally common types of meat (beef, poultry, pork, and mutton), hence excluding, for example, common types of meat in Vietnam like frog or the significant dog meat consumption in northern parts of the country.[3]

These changes are closely connected to the fact that Vietnam has been home to one of the fastest growing economies globally the past few decades (Bekkevold et al. 2020). The shift from the planned economy during the earlier days of the Communist regime to the current hybrid-capitalist "socialist market economy" has involved remarkable improvements in living standards and the development of a consumer society (Hansen 2020). As part of larger economic and societal changes, Vietnam has seen several food transformations. First and foremost, Vietnamese eat much more food overall than they used to, an unsurprising fact taking into account the many millions of Vietnamese who have escaped poverty in this period (Marzin and Michaud 2016). Although in many ways a great success story of improved nutrition, obesity and nutrition-related diseases are increasingly replacing undernutrition as central health challenges (Raneri et al. 2019), while food safety replaces food security as a central concern among consumers and policymakers alike (Ehlert and Faltmann 2019). In terms of meat, although the average Vietnamese consumer still eats less meat than the average consumer in OECD countries, they eat much meat compared to the average consumer in other countries in Southeast Asia, and much meat relative to average income in a global comparative perspective (see Hansen 2018). For example, the average person in Thailand, an upper middle-income country with three times the GDP per capita of Vietnam (World Bank 2021), consumes less than half the quantity of meat annually compared to in Vietnam (OECD 2021).

Beyond the increase in the amount of meat consumed, Vietnamese meat cultures are changing in terms of what kind of meat is eaten, how it is eaten, and how and where the animals are raised and slaughtered. In Vietnam, like in China (see Korsnes and Liu this volume), pork has been and still is the main type of meat consumed. Indeed, pork is central to the point that the Vietnamese word for meat, *thit*, without further specification, implies pork. However, while pork consumption has seen very rapid increase since *doi moi*, the consumption of chicken and beef has grown much faster (OECD 2021). As I return to below, quite different changes take place among some segments of the urban middle classes, where there are clear tendencies toward "demeatification." The Vietnamese government is also sensitive toward outside perceptions in its struggles to create "rich, civilized, and beautiful cities" (see Endres 2019) and attract tourists, something that recently led to a proposed—but yet to be implemented—ban on dog meat in central areas of Hanoi (see Lampard 2021). In summary, meat-related food practices in Vietnam are undergoing complex and often contradictory changes. This chapter seeks to unveil some of this complexity, revisiting how and why meat consumption has increased so rapidly in Vietnam and analyzing how and why meat cultures change.

There is a general correlation between income and meat consumption. In essence, people eat more meat as they get wealthier (Sans and Combris 2015; MacLachlan 2015). However, this fact masks the significant variation in changes in meat consumption as countries grow more affluent (see Hansen and Syse, this volume). Existing research has shown how increasing meat consumption in developing countries is driven by a complex set of factors including urbanization, increasing income, expanding middle classes, and globalization (see Milford et al. 2019; Lange 2016). Many scholars have also pointed toward high meat consumption as a typical "Western" dietary trait, and in a much cited article, Pingali (2007) claimed that meat increases in Asia is part of an overall "Westernization" of diets caused by increased global interconnectedness. It would be easy to make a similar point about Vietnam, with the expansion of supermarkets, Western fast-food chains, and Western-style steak houses (see Hansen and Jakobsen 2020a). But as is argued in this chapter, the "Westernization thesis" exaggerates foreign influences on local food practices, demands a clear Western-centric gaze, and is blind to most of the daily food practices in Vietnam and how deeply embedded food cultures are in society. It also, I argue, demands that we treat capitalism as a Western phenomenon, which is a rather unhelpful proposition. Instead, I argue a more accurate explanation and description is found in cultural and culinary hybridization alongside the social, material, and political co-creation of demand within the expansion of capitalism. Inspired by the concept of "variegated capitalism"—which highlights how capitalism takes different shapes in different cultural and institutional settings yet always follows the same underlying logics (Peck and Theodore 2007)—I analyze how the capitalist transformation of food and meat systems opens for contextually distinct food cultures within structural-institutional homogenization (see also Ram 2004).

Following some notes on the "eating ethnography" that this chapter draws on, I start by looking into the supply and provisioning of meat in Vietnam, seeing these as forming the background for changing meat cultures in the country. I then zoom in on meat eating, focusing particularly on the increasing popularity of eating out (Hansen 2018), a trend generally associated with dietary changes (see Lange 2016).

EATING ETHNOGRAPHY

This chapter primarily draws on fieldwork on changes in food provision and practice in Vietnam in 2017 and 2018, with a follow-up visit in 2019. Based in Hanoi, I conducted more than 50 interviews, half of which were with members of middle-class households and the rest including government officials, agribusiness representatives, food system experts, representatives of abattoirs, speciality food producers, farmers, owners of restaurants and street food kitchens, and market vendors. The discussions I had with these interviewees on food and food systems represent the core of the knowledge on which the chapter draws. However, from an epistemological starting point valuing contextual sensitivity and grounded research, I have in addition sought to as far as possible live the practices I study. Since I am particularly interested in understanding the intersection between systems of provision, foodscapes, and everyday practices, I focused on where people buy and eat their food. This meant shopping at markets and supermarkets, but also eating at all sorts of outlets frequented by the middle classes. Since the Hanoian middle classes are so diverse, this included street kitchens, inexpensive restaurants, fast-food outlets, food courts at shopping malls, and high-end restaurants. Importantly, I also draw on knowledge from 10 years of doing research in and on Vietnam, with food and food culture central interests from the very beginning, although until recent years these interests were an addition to rather than an integral part of my research. My knowledge of food in Vietnam is built on a very large number of informal food conversations, many meals in the homes of friends and colleagues all over Vietnam, countless work lunches in office canteens, as well as an estimated 2,000 meals at restaurant and street food joints. A disclaimer is that although my approach to food culture is to eat what those around me eat and always eat what I am served, I have so far managed, to my knowledge at least, to avoid threatened species and dog meat. The latter is itself interesting. Rationally, I do not see a big difference in eating pigs and eating dogs. I am not even particularly fond of dogs. But I still seek to avoid eating them as long as I can, something that is not particularly difficult. The point is that I see this as a good example of the deep embeddedness and embodiment of food cultures in taste, and of how consumer preferences are shaped by much more than individual choice and rational decisions. I am digressing, but this does take us to the meat of the chapter, starting at the uneven geographies of meat.

THE UNEVEN GEOGRAPHIES OF MEAT

Meat is a broad food category, including a wide range of animals and farming practices, slaughter methods, production and provisioning processes, food cultures, and eating practices. Overall, as pointed out earlier, there is clear empirical evidence for the fact that meat consumption overall increases with economic growth and increased affluence. *How* and *how much* it changes and *what* kind of meat is consumed, however, differs considerably depending on context (Milford et al. 2019). For example, parts of Central Asia, most notably Mongolia, stand out with very high levels of per capita sheep meat consumption. Chicken is increasing in most parts of the world (see Hansen, Jakobsen, and Wethal, this volume), but no country eats more chicken per person than Israel. Australia and New Zealand, together with Northern and Southern America, stand out globally with high levels of beef consumption per capita. East and Southeast Asia are at the opposite end of the spectrum, with low levels of per capita beef consumption. However, although behind many European countries in per capita terms, East Asia stands out with very high levels of overall pork consumption. Indeed, China alone eats roughly half of all pork in the world every year.[4]

Meat cultures differ significantly also within Vietnam, between regions, ethnic groups, classes, genders, and generations. For example, some meat practices, like consuming he-goat meat and jungle meat, come with perceived fertility- or virility-enhancing qualities, are often served with strong alcohol, and are therefore "hyper-masculine" (Avieli 2019). And while going for a meal of pork offal congee (*chao long*), often served with pork blood, remains popular, I was often told that the youth now consider such practices old-fashioned. Furthermore, while both old and young for different reasons (mainly religion, health, or social distinction, but also politics, see Avieli 2014) may wish to limit their meat consumption, as I discuss later, adhering to a strictly vegetarian or vegan diet is more popular among younger generations. While pork and chicken are common across all income groups, and while there can be considerable prestige in adhering to a vegetarian diet (Avieli 2014), the richest also eat imported beef accompanied by imported wine, something that easily costs close to a monthly salary of a worker. In addition, many among those who can afford it purchase organic meat or meat from foreign, particularly Japanese, supermarkets, driven by widespread food quality concerns in the country (Ehlert and Faltmann 2019). New and alternative networks for acquiring "clean" (*sach*) food, including meat, directly from the countryside have also emerged (Faltmann 2019).

As stated in the introduction, Vietnamese eat much more meat than before. Statistics clearly show this trend (figure 6.1), although the fact that there are no statistics for internationally less common types of meat like frog, dog, snake, or wild boar means that Vietnamese meat consumption levels are significantly understated in these statistics.

That said, as figure 6.1 shows, since 2017 there has been some decrease in the consumption of beef and a significant slump in the consumption of pork. The former can at least partly be explained by disruptions in the Indian buffalo sector (see Jakobsen and Nielsen this volume), the main source of imports of beef (from buffalo), while the latter is mainly due to dramatic

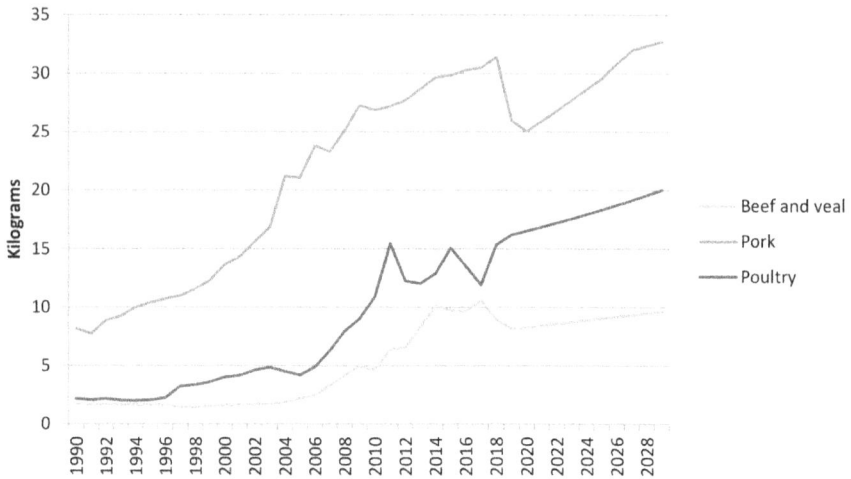

Figure 6.1   Meat Consumption Per Capita, 1990–2019, with Projections to 2029.

disruptions to domestic meat supply, as well as a certain increased skepticism among consumers, following the outbreak of the African Swine Fever (ASF) since 2018 which led to the death and culling of about six million pigs, or 20 percent of the total pig population (FAO 2021; OECD/FAO 2020). Poultry consumption has seen ups and downs due to repeated outbreaks of the avian flu, while the disruptions to pork supply recently caused a rapid increase in poultry consumption. While all forms of meat consumption are projected to gradually pick up again (figure 6.1), these disruptions, including the Covid-19 pandemic (see Hansen and Jakobsen 2020b), could possibly also have deep impacts on meat cultures. At least they have severely impacted an entire industry that until recently had seen very rapid growth, which in turn has led to dramatic increases in meat imports.

PROVISIONING MEAT

Agriculture has in different ways always been a central part of Vietnam's development, from the politics of resistance by the Viet Minh through the grossly underperforming farmer collectives of the planned economy to the rapid growth in output and the rapid decline in poverty levels following market reforms (see Cole and Ingalls 2020). Indeed, although urbanization and industrialization tend to steal the headlines, and although agriculture's share of GDP has declined from more than 40 percent in the late 1980s to about 14 percent in 2019, still almost two-thirds of the Vietnamese population are registered as living in rural areas and more than a third have agriculture as their main occupation[5] (World

Bank 2021). The agricultural sector has remained predominantly small-scale (see Rigg et al. 2016), although the government has long aimed to upscale, modernize, and industrialize agricultural production (Cesaro 2016).

The growth in output in Vietnam's agricultural sector overall has been dramatic (see Marzin and Michaud 2016). This includes the livestock sector, which represents an increasingly large share of total agricultural production (Hansen 2018). To take the year of reforms as a starting point, annual domestic beef production grew more than threefold from 135.980 tonnes in 1986 to 449.767 tonnes in 2019. Pig meat production increased from 625.000 tonnes in 1986 to 3.816.414 tonnes in 2018, a more than sixfold increase, before the dramatic drop from 2019 due to the impact of ASF. The fastest growing sector, in Vietnam as in the world on average (see Hansen, Jakobsen, and Wethal, this volume), is poultry. Poultry production increased eightfold from 132.900 tonnes to 1.089.111 tonnes, after very rapid increases in particularly chicken production since the early 2000s (FAOSTAT 2021).

The Vietnamese government has supported the livestock sector through a variety of support programs (OECD 2015) and has targeted further growth in the sector. Vietnam operates with 10-year plans, and the government's development strategy for 2021 to 2030 for the livestock sector aims for it to both meet domestic demand and increase exports. Indeed, Vietnam aims to export as much as 25 percent of pork products and 15 percent to 20 percent of poultry products (*Vietnam News* 2020). The industry has picked up production again after the dramatic impact of ASF, and for 2021 targets 5 percent to 6 percent growth (*Vietnam Plus* 2021). As for agriculture overall this includes industrialization, upscaling, and farm specialization (Cesaro 2016), as well as attracting large capital from home and abroad. Many changes are already taking place within the smallholder structure, as many smallholders serve as contract farmers for large domestic and regional corporations, and many smallholders, with the help of international organizations and Vietnamese authorities, have introduced a range of changes to make production more efficient and produce higher quality meat (see Stür et al. 2013).

Vietnam's livestock sector is increasingly integrated in a larger "Asian meat complex" through both intraregional and interregional trade and investment flows (Jakobsen and Hansen 2020). Indeed, as much as 60 percent of the raw materials used for animal feed are now imported (Cesaro 2016). This is increasingly the case for meat as well, as domestic supply is struggling to keep up with demand.

Imports

While Vietnam is normally self-sufficient in pork, poultry and beef demand has by far outgrown domestic supply. Indeed, by 2020, as much as 70 percent of the beef consumed was either from imported cattle or imported meat (*Vietnam Plus* 2020), while the past decade has seen significant poultry imports. The amount has varied considerably year on year, including an all-time high of 818 thousand tonnes in 2011.While Vietnam imported 328 thousand tonnes of poultry in 2019, mainly from Hong Kong and the United States (Chatham House 2021), new outbreaks of the avian flu will likely lead to more imports.[6]

The domestic sector is struggling to compete with the often significantly cheaper imported products. This is now also the case for pork, after the African swine flu crisis led to rapid increases in imports of pork too (Euromeatnews 2020), although the domestic pork industry is rapidly picking up again. The Covid-19 pandemic in turn affected both supply and demand, although interestingly the import of cattle from Australia grew rapidly during the Covid-19 situation, possibly due to restrictions on imports from Thailand, Cambodia, and Laos (Meat and Livestock Australia 2020). Indeed, and interestingly, one of the largest international flows of meat in the world take form of buffalo meat from India to Vietnam, but little is known about the consumption side of this trade, perhaps because much of it continues on to China (Jakobsen and Hansen 2020).

The point here is to show that the changes in Vietnam's consumption of meat are fed by and made possible by both domestic production and the opening of Vietnam's borders to meat from abroad. It should be noted that such trade includes much informal trade with neighboring countries that goes under the radar in statistics. In addition, there are structural changes along entire livestock supply chains in Vietnam that affect consumption and meat cultures.

Structural Changes

Farming in Vietnam has, as stated earlier, remained mostly small-scale, but the government is clear in its intent to scale up the sector in order to contribute to economic growth, to produce safe food for the domestic market, and for exporters to meet the strict requirements of, for example, European countries. This is already visible in the form of large domestic and international corporations increasingly investing in the sector, including global giants like Cargill, powerful regional corporations like CP and Japfa, and a range of big and small domestic enterprises (see *Vietnam Plus* 2021). CP Vietnam is the domestic subsidiary of Thailand's largest company and one the world's largest meat and feed corporations, the Charoen Pokphand Group (for more on their role in the feed industry, see Cole 2020). CP Vietnam's export-only poultry complex in Binh Phuoc province in the south of the country is set to produce and process 100 million chickens annually by 2023, making it the largest chicken farm in Southeast Asia (The Poultry Site 2020; *Vietnam Plus* 2021). The feed industry is increasingly dominated by imports and regional and global capital, small-scale neighborhood slaughtering in urban areas has been replaced by larger abattoirs outside the cities, and while individual traders on motorbikes delivering meat to wet markets remain the norm, they are increasingly replaced by large company trucks delivering meat to restaurants and supermarkets. I witnessed this in 2017 when I visited one of Hanoi's largest pig abattoirs (see figure 6.2). The compound housing the abattoir was divided into 24 smaller lots, 23 of which were operated by small family enterprises. Traders on motorbikes bought entire pig carcasses, while a separate area in the middle of the compound was designated for trade in offal. The 24th lot looked similar to the rest, but was larger and had trucks picking up the carcasses. Above the lot was a sign showing that this lot belonged to CP Vietnam. While this more industrialized version of the meat system was a minority in this abattoir, there are good reasons to believe that this represents an image of both the likely and—at least for the government—desired future of Vietnamese meat production.

The latter is important. Vietnam has been considered a latecomer to the global process of supermarketization (Reardon and Timmer 2007), but following Vietnam's entry to the WTO, regional and national supermarket

Figure 6.2   Traders and Pig Carcasses on Motorbikes.

brands are increasingly important actors in urban foodscapes. This is an intended strategy by the government (Wertheim-Heck et al. 2015). For example, in Hanoi, the authorities have aimed specifically at rapidly increasing the number of convenience stores (Vietnam Investment Review 2019). And the private sector seems ready to live up to this goal, with both foreign and domestic actors investing heavily in the Vietnamese food sector. The powerful domestic conglomerate Vingroup alone plans to have 4,000 convenience stores nationwide (Vietnam Investment Review 2018). That said, traditional wet markets do remain the most important source of food for the majority of urban Vietnamese, particularly among the poorer segments of the population (Wertheim-Heck et al. 2019).

Supermarkets are not just different spaces for acquiring food, they represent an often radically different way of providing food from farm to fork, including the consolidation of power and profit in the hands of corporations. As Hansen and Jakobsen (2020a) argue, they represent new "meatscapes," changing how meat is sourced, traded, and sold, and how consumers encounter and purchase meat. Supermarket shopping is known to increase the consumption of processed food (Boysen et al. 2019; Demmler et al. 2018). This is highly visible in Vietnam, where supermarkets display a wide range of meat products not available elsewhere and in sharp contrast to the "warm" meat sold in markets (figure 6.3).

That said, the capitalist expansion in food retail also has variegated outcomes and the many supermarkets also have large fresh meat sections that

Figure 6.3   Meat at a Hanoi Supermarket (left) and a Hanoi Market Vendor (right).

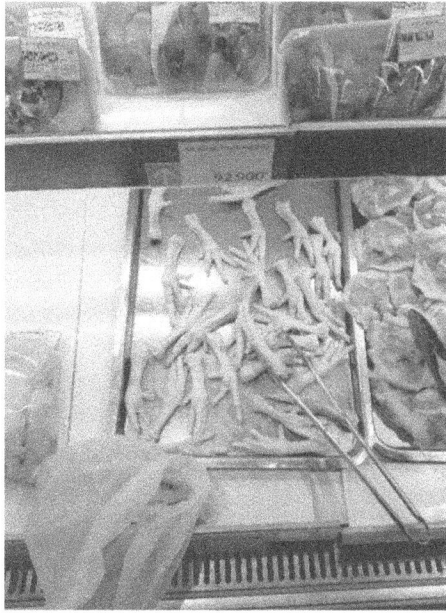

Figure 6.4   "Fresh" Chicken Feet at a Hanoi Supermarket.

include types of meat popular in street markets, such as chicken feet (see figure 6.4). But their "cold chains" (Rinkinen et al. 2017) enable international trade in frozen meat. This is rather novel in Vietnam, where the dominant meat culture values fresh and "warm" meat. Besides, most local markets cannot provide frozen meat, due to the cooling infrastructure required. The frozen meat in Vietnamese supermarkets often come from the large meat industries of, for example, Brazil, Canada, and the United States, and is often significantly cheaper than locally sourced meat. Processed meat and frozen meat are more mobile, and the distance this creates between the animals killed and the consumers may contribute to further altering the overall meat culture in Vietnam. At least it represents a significant movement away from "traditional" practices of fresh meat shopping a strong valuation of locally sourced food.

MEATIFYING FOOD PRACTICES: EATING
OUT AND CULINARY HYBRIDIZATION

The "meatification of diets" (Weis 2013) takes place through complex processes where production and consumption, supply and demand, are co-shaped by capital, policymakers, and everyday practices (Hansen 2018). The juncture between these are the "meatscapes" where consumers encounter and acquire meat. Markets and supermarkets play important parts, but so do the many outlets that allow people to consume meat away from home. Vietnamese cities are characterized by a plethora of food venues of all sizes and shapes, from the smallest food shacks to large, high-end restaurants. Eating out is deeply embedded in everyday practices in Vietnam, particularly eating at street kitchens (see Hansen, 2021):

> You have meat, and the broth is already balanced because you have 6-7 different spices. You have ginger, star anise, cinnamon, onions, ginger, and they put all the *pho* spices into the beef broth. And it's so good and really flavorful and it helps with digestion. They grill all this and then they put it back into the broth. Without it, it is not really delicious. That's why it's always more delicious outside, because you have to cook the broth for 7-8 hours. That's why we only do one dish, because it takes so much time to prepare. And they do it over night, so the broth is so good. But for the family, no one is going to spend 7 or 8 hours on the heating, electricity and everything and you spend a lot of time cleaning and preparing, but it's not as good. (Interview, March 2017)

Discussing food in a beautiful old villa in Hanoi's French Quarter, Hien, a young, middle-class woman, and her mother are explaining the allure of street food. They have their regular places they go to, as every Hanoian would, Hien explains. And they go there often. Eating out is an essential part of everyday life for many Hanoians. Indeed, many of the middle-class households I interviewed would eat out several times a day, enabled by a rich street food scene serving affordable, healthy, and tasty food, in turn enabled by a very large precariat of low-paid migrant workers (see also Hansen, 2021). It is part of the rhythms and geographies of mundane practices, for those who can afford it.

Most street food kitchens serve more or less "traditional" Vietnamese food. Meat forms a part of a wide range of what are considered "traditional" Vietnamese dishes, although this is probably due to alterations over time rather than a true reflection of what daily diets historically have involved for most Vietnamese (see Peters 2012). Vietnamese foodscapes are in general more meat-intensive, and so is traditional food. Today, the street food scene involves a range of different types of meat, often with generous servings. While, for example, frog hot pot is a Hanoi classic and duck is highly popular, pork is still the most common type of meat. Pho, the famous and highly popular breakfast dish that Hien discusses earlier, is in many ways odd, since it is made with beef. And many would ardently claim that it has to be made with beef, although the chicken version is also highly popular. Importantly, you do not just get "beef," you get to choose from a wide variety of animal parts and ways of preparing them. The origins

of pho are disputed. It is widely considered Vietnam's national dish, but
Peters (2010) argues convincingly for it being a Chinese Vietnamese hybrid
with a specifically colonial history. Beef broths were certainly uncommon in both countries, as indeed was any beef that was not from buffalo.
But the French colonizers in Vietnam wanted beef,[7] and indeed imported
cattle, often from France, to meet the demand (Peters 2012). But most of
the butchers were Vietnamese and Chinese,[8] as were indeed the servants
buying the meat and the cooks preparing it. This, according to Peters, is
the likely background for the beef broth of pho. As she puts it, "Networks
of Chinese and Vietnamese who butchered meat for the French or cooked
their meals probably diverted beef remnants to street soup vendors, whose
numbers increased with the rapid onset of colonial urbanization" (Peters
2010, 160). This is an interesting case of culinary transformations through
the encounter of different food cultures. Indeed, food is constantly changing and hybridizing. Also street food is constantly in motion, with new
versions emerging. My personal favorite example of food globalization in
Vietnamese foodscapes is the *banh mi döner kebab* (figure 6.5). Adopted by
hawker stalls in different parts of Vietnam, this meta-hybrid sees the *banh
mi*—a French Vietnamese culinary hybrid—meet *döner kebab*—a Turkish
German culinary hybrid. The result bears little resemblance with any of the
originals, but the Vietnameseness of the dish is firmly underlined by the fact
that it is usually served with pork, which of course is not the case for the
typical Turkish-inspired döner.

A Balancing Act: Foreign Food and Local Meat Cultures

Returning to the quote by Hien earlier, she starts out saying that when buying
pho in the streets, the broth has already been balanced. This can be interpreted
in different ways. It could simply have meant that the taste is good because of
the good balance of spices. But what Hien was talking about here runs much
deeper than that. Balance is a crucial part of culinary practices in Vietnam
and relates to the important role played by the opposing energies of *am* (yin)
and *duong* (yang) in dominant Vietnamese belief systems. Most people in
Vietnam today, particularly among the younger population, would not usually
speak of these energies directly, nor how they affect culinary practices. But
most would know that different types of food are "hot" and "cold," although
not necessarily knowing that these qualities are originally determined by
cosmological theory. Still, in a culinary culture where "anything edible is
essentially or potentially a medicine and vice versa" (Avieli 2012, 223),
people do engage with the practical implications of this theory. As I have
often experienced, and as Avieli (2012) explains, all dishes and ingredients,
as well as all seasoning and cooking techniques, have heating and cooling

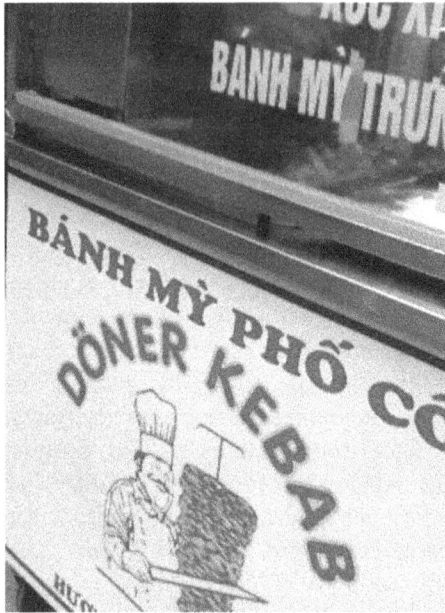

Figure 6.5   *Banh mi döner kebab.*

qualities. Thus, in order to maintain physical and emotional harmony, dishes must be balanced, both through the setup of the meal and by the use of herbs and other ingredients. To take one example, beef should be accompanied by ginger. My friends and colleagues would not necessarily be able to explain why this is the case, but they would argue that it is a necessity. And most would have at least some knowledge of how to create balance in and through food. This is a typical example of the complexity and the embodiment and naturalization of food culture, which is an important part of why continuity always accompanies change in the processes of hybridization that take place when different food cultures meet.

In a typical Vietnamese meal, steamed rice forms the center of the meal, accompanied by side dishes. The latter should be balanced, and include greens, boiled soup (*canh*), fish sauce (*nuoc mam*) and a "dry" (*kho*) dish, often meat or fish (Avieli 2012). The traditional meal is eaten together, with the dishes on the table and everyone eating from small bowls, adding first rice, then other ingredients. However, the principles of the balanced meal are often kept also in food spaces where one eats alone, such as in my office canteen (figure 6.6).

Foreign food practices challenge these deeply embedded ways of eating, although a certain balance is often achieved through ordering additional rice

Figure 6.6   The Five Elements.

to almost any kind of meal. One of the most obvious changes in Vietnamese urban foodscapes the past decade come in the form of food franchises. The most famous global fast-food chains are there. Kentucky Fried Chicken was first and established its first outlets in the country as early as 1997. Burger King and McDonald's came a lot later. As did a variety of East Asian franchise, like Lotteria from Korea and Jollibee from the Philippines. In addition, a wide range of Vietnamese franchises have popped up, many of them owned by large corporations. Many of these food spaces come with very different scripts for cooking and eating than what has been the norm in the past. Similar to supermarkets in relation to traditional markets, the standardization that these franchises develop and depend on require very different infrastructure than street kitchens. In many cases this involves imported meat, exemplified by McDonald's Vietnam that on its opening advertised with 100 percent imported meat. Importantly, they also tend to only serve the standard meat types, pork, beef, and chicken.

These franchises do not necessarily lead to an overall Westernization of diets. Usually, they are just one part of a diverse diet that for the vast majority of Vietnamese consumers would be dominated by typically Vietnamese dishes, including rice. In addition, these franchises tend to adapt to local taste buds (Watson 2006), and many of them would indeed serve rice meals in Vietnam. Still, they do contribute to the globalization of more meat-intense ways of eating, and are part of what is known as "nutrition transition" toward more fatty, sugary, and processed food. They also contribute significantly to the standardization of meat cultures, from farm to fork. This is part and parcel of a capitalist diet, where corporate interests across food systems are part of simultaneously expanding and limiting the options available to consumers (Hansen and Jakobsen 2020a; Wilk 2018; Otero 2018). In other words, the variegated expansion of capitalism (Peck and Theodore 2007) leads to a structural-institutional homogenization of food and meat (Ram 2004). This process clearly influences local meat practices and cultures, but in turn takes different shapes in the encounter with these practices and cultures. Eating a rice lunch at McDonald's or Burger King in Hanoi or Ho Chi Minh City is an obvious example, while eating street food made with industrially produced meat is a less obvious example of the same overall process.

At the higher end, Japanese and Korean style barbecue restaurants are particularly popular, and represent an upmarket version of popular street food practices where food is barbecued directly on the guests' table. These tend to be highly meat-intensive, and from my observations and interviews often use much imported meat (see Hansen 2018). Most of these are owned by Vietnamese capital, and represent examples of a bourgeoning market for upper middle-class food spaces. Another central trend here is the rapidly expanding number of steak houses. These obviously represent the epitome of meat-centrality, and again mainly use imported meat.

However, also vegetarian foodscapes are expanding rapidly. While a few years ago vegetarian restaurants meant Buddhist restaurant, there is now a large variety of places, including at the highest end. These places are often highly popular, and are able to benefit from a "traditional" food culture strongly inspired by Buddhist thinking (see Peters 2012). Although the Vietnamese take on this is mainly to avoid meat on certain days or at certain times of the month, few would be strangers to eating a vegetarian meal. Furthermore, reducing meat consumption is widely considered as healthy in Vietnam. However, reducing meat consumption is something quite different from not eating any meat at all. Thus, the growing vegetarian trend visible among urban middle classes tends to be restricted to the younger segments of the population. Many of them are struggling to explain their vegetarianism to their families. And interestingly, almost all the vegetarians I have talked to, including Buddhist devotees, said they would eat meat when served at family meals. This practice has many explanations, including respect for food, family, and elders, as well as different takes on Buddhist thought when it comes to food norms and social relations. It serves as an example of the complexity of food culture, and supports research in other countries on the social challenges encountered by so-called "meat reducers" (Mylan 2018). Anyways, this trend toward demeatification is highly interesting and underresearched, and could potentially, as in China (see Korsnes and Liu, this volume), partly counter the expected further increase in meat consumption as Vietnam grows richer.

CHANGING MEAT CULTURES

Vietnam's foodscapes have undergone radical changes the past decades. This chapter has discussed how these changes have contributed to changing meat cultures. Although also characterized by continuation, and although any claims of "Westernization" must disregard deeply embedded food cultures, Vietnam's capitalist transformation has brought along rapid meatification and a tendency toward a standardization of meat cultures. That said, Vietnamese food cultures remain mainly inspired by "traditional" foodways, including the need to balance meals according to *am duong* (yin and yang) principles and a rich diversity of dishes and ingredients. Still, the changes in "meat-scapes," particularly supermarkets and new middle-class food spaces, bring along highly different scripts and practices for producing, trading, and eating meat. The ongoing industrialization of the domestic livestock sector, combined with the opening for imports, have enabled the dramatic meatification of Vietnamese diets. But these changes have taken place gradually through everyday food practices and foodscapes. As meat has become the norm in most meals, and as more meat-intensive practices are becoming normalized, meat consumption is expected to continue increasing. The extent to which this increase will mainly involve industrial meat, or also alternative forms of meat, remains to be seen. The same goes for whether the increasing popularity of vegetarian food trends could challenge further meatification.

NOTES

1. Big thanks to my colleagues and field assistants in Vietnam and to Nguyen Le, Jostein Jakobsen, and Karen Lykke Syse for excellent input to earlier versions of this chapter.

2. Note that there are many inaccuracies with such data, since they, for example, do not separate between meat being eaten or wasted. Furthermore, the main international data use different forms of measurement and thus vary considerably. The OECD database, on which these data are based, measures meat consumption in thousand tonnes of carcass weight (except for poultry expressed as ready to cook weight) and in kilograms of retail weight per capita.

3. Although dog meat is consumed all over Vietnam, it is considerably more common in the north (see also Avieli 2011). No reliable data for dog meat consumption are available. Animal rights advocacy groups have claimed as many as five million dogs are slaughtered for consumption every year, but these numbers have never been verified (see VnExpress 2016).

4. All of the above assertions are based on FAOSTAT numbers

5. Employment in agriculture has declined from 70.7 percent in 1991 to 36.2 percent in 2020, while 80 percent of the population lived in rural areas in the late 1980s

versus 63.3 percent in 2019 (World Bank 2021). These numbers should be used with caution, though, as many of these people live in urban areas and work in other sectors parts of the year (see Rigg, Salamanca, and Thompson 2016).

6. At the time of writing, the latest major outbreak was in February 2021.

7. Vietnam was part of French Indochina from 1884 (earlier for southern parts of the country) until their defeat against Viet Minh in 1954. The leftovers of colonial rule take many forms, not least in food and drinks such as *banh mi* (bread), *bit tet* (steak), *ca phe* (coffee), and *bia* (beer).

8. As an interesting sidenote, Peters (2012) explains that many French butchers had sought to establish butcheries to meet the demand for proper French cuts of meat. However, most of them went out of business as the French living in Vietnam rarely bought their own meat, and the Vietnamese and Chinese servants preferred local butchers.

REFERENCES

Avieli, Nir. 2011. "Dog Meat Politics in a Vietnamese Town." *Ethnology* 50 (1): 59–78.

———. 2012. *Rice Talks: Food and Community in a Vietnamese Town*. Bloomington: Indiana University Press.

———. 2014. "Vegetarian Ethics and Politics in Late-Socialist Vietnam." In *Ethical Eating in the Postsocialist and Socialist World*, edited by Yuson Jung, Jakob A. Klen and Melissa L. Caldwell. Berkeley: University of California Press, 144–166.

———. 2019. "Forbidden from the Heart: Flexible Food Taboos, Ambiguous Culinary Transgressions, and Cultural Intimacy in Hoi An, Vietnam." In *Food Anxiety in Globalising Vietnam*, edited by Judith Ehlert and Nora Katharina Faltmann, 77–103. Singapore: Springer Singapore. https://doi.org/10.1007/978-98 1-13-0743-0_3.

Bekkevold, Jo Inge, Arve Hansen, and Kristen Nordhaug. 2020. "Introducing the Socialist Market Economy." In *The Socialist Market Economy in Asia: Development in China, Vietnam and Laos*, edited by Arve Hansen, Jo Inge Bekkevold, and Kristen Nordhaug, 3–25. Singapore: Springer Singapore. https://doi.org/10.1007/978-981-15-6248-8_1.

Boysen, Ole, Kirsten Boysen-Urban, Harvey Bradford, and Jean Balié. 2019. "Taxing Highly Processed Foods: What Could Be the Impacts on Obesity and Underweight in Sub-Saharan Africa?" *World Development* 119 (July): 55–67. https://doi.org/10 .1016/j.worlddev.2019.03.006.

Cesaro, Jean-Daniel. 2016. *Une Croissance sans Limite ? : Vers Une Nouvelle Géographie de l'élevage Au Vietnam*. http://www.theses.fr/2016PA100131/d ocument.

Chatham House. 2021. *Meat Trade Data: Poultry Imports to Vietnam*. https://resourc etrade.earth/?year=2019&importer=704&category=81&units=weight&autozoom=1.

Cole, Robert, and Micah L. Ingalls. 2020. "Rural Revolutions: Socialist, Market and Sustainable Development of the Countryside in Vietnam and Laos." In *The*

Socialist Market Economy in Asia: Development in China, Vietnam and Laos, edited by Arve Hansen, Jo Inge Bekkevold, and Kristen Nordhaug, 167–194. Singapore: Springer Singapore. https://doi.org/10.1007/978-981-15-6248-8_6.

Demmler, Kathrin M., Olivier Ecker, and Matin Qaim. 2018. "Supermarket Shopping and Nutritional Outcomes: A Panel Data Analysis for Urban Kenya." *World Development* 102 (February): 292–303. https://doi.org/10.1016/j.worlddev.2017.07.018.

Ehlert, Judith, and Nora Katharina Faltmann. 2019. "Food Anxiety: Ambivalences Around Body and Identity, Food Safety, and Security." In *Food Anxiety in Globalising Vietnam*, edited by Judith Ehlert and Nora Katharina Faltmann, 1–40. Singapore: Springer Singapore. https://doi.org/10.1007/978-981-13-0743-0_1.

Endres, Kirsten W. 2019. "Traders versus the State: Negotiating Urban Renewal in Lào Cai City, Vietnam." *City & Society* 31 (3): 341–364. https://doi.org/10.1111/ciso.12193.

EuroMeatNews. 2020. "Vietnam Increases Meat Imports at a Record Pace." *EuroMeatNews.* April 29, 2020. https://euromeatnews.com/Article-Vietnam-increases-meat-imports-at-a-record-pace/3819.

Faltmann, Nora Katharina. 2019. "Between Food Safety Concerns and Responsibilisation: Organic Food Consumption in Ho Chi Minh City." In *Food Anxiety in Globalising Vietnam*, edited by Judith Ehlert and Nora Katharina Faltmann, 167–204. Singapore: Springer Singapore. https://doi.org/10.1007/978-981-13-0743-0_6.

FAO. 2021. *ASF Situation in Asia & Pacific Update.* http://www.fao.org/ag/againfo/programmes/en/empres/ASF/situation_update.html

FAOSTAT. 2021. *FAOSTAT Data.* http://www.fao.org/faostat/en/#data

Hansen, Arve. 2018. "Meat Consumption and Capitalist Development: The Meatification of Food Provision and Practice in Vietnam." *Geoforum* 93 (July): 57–68. https://doi.org/10.1016/j.geoforum.2018.05.008.

———. 2020. "Consumer Socialism: Consumption, Development and the New Middle Classes in China and Vietnam." In *The Socialist Market Economy in Asia: Development in China, Vietnam and Laos*, edited by Arve Hansen, Jo Inge Bekkevold, and Kristen Nordhaug, 221–243. Singapore: Springer Singapore. https://doi.org/10.1007/978-981-15-6248-8_8.

———. 2021. "Negotiating Unsustainable Food Transformations: Development, Middle Classes and Everyday Food Practices in Vietnam". European Journal of Development Research. https://doi.org/10.1057/s41287-021-00429-6.

Hansen, Arve, and Jostein Jakobsen. 2020a. "Meatification and Everyday Geographies of Consumption in Vietnam and China." *Geografiska Annaler: Series B, Human Geography* 102 (1): 21–39. https://doi.org/10.1080/04353684.2019.1709217.

Hansen, Arve and Jakobsen, Jostein. 2020b. "COVID-19 and the Asian Meat Complex." *East Asia Forum.* September 29, 2020. https://www.eastasiaforum.org/2020/09/29/covid-19-and-the-asian-meat-complex/.

Jakobsen, Jostein, and Arve Hansen. 2020. "Geographies of Meatification: An Emerging Asian Meat Complex." *Globalizations* 17 (1): 93–109. https://doi.org/10.1080/14747731.2019.1614723.

Lampard, Ashley. 2021. "What Happened to Hanoi's Dog Meat Ban?" *Southeast Asia Globe*. February 5, 2021. https://southeastasiaglobe.com/hanois-dog-meat-ban/.

Lange, Helmut. 2016. "Same, Same – but Different: On Increasing Meat Consumption in the Global South." In *Food Consumption in the City: Practices and Patterns in Urban Asia and the Pacific*, edited by M. Sahakian, C. Saloma, and S. Erkman, 23–46. London: Routledge.

MacLachlan, Ian. 2015. "Evolution of a Revolution: Meat Consumption and Livestock Production in the Developing World." In *Political Ecologies of Meat*, edited by Jody Emel and Harvey Neo. London: Routledge.

Marzin, Jacques and Agnalys Michaud. 2016. "Evolution of rural development strategies and policies: Lessons from Vietnam." Doccument de travail ART-Dev. 2016–5. https://agritrop.cirad.fr/582603/1/Marzin%20Michaud%202016%20Rural%20development%20strategies%20Vietnam%20def.pdf.

Meat and Livestock Australia. 2020. *Stalling Market Demand Impacts Live Cattle Export Prices*. April 30, 20. https://www.mla.com.au/prices-markets/market-news/2020/stalling-market-demand-impacts-live-cattle-export-prices/

Milford, Anna Birgitte, Chantal Le Mouël, Benjamin Leon Bodirsky, and Susanne Rolinski. 2019. "Drivers of Meat Consumption." *Appetite* 141 (October): 104313. https://doi.org/10.1016/j.appet.2019.06.005.

Mylan, Josephine. 2018. "Sustainable Consumption in Everyday Life: A Qualitative Study of UK Consumer Experiences of Meat Reduction." *Sustainability* 10 (7): 2307. https://doi.org/10.3390/su10072307.

OECD. 2021. *Meat Consumption (Indicator)*. doi: 10.1787/fa290fd0-en (Accessed on January 19, 2021).

OECD. 2015. *Agricultural Policies in Viet Nam 2015*. Paris: OECD Publishing. http://dx.doi.org/10.1787/9789264235151-en.

OECD/FAO. 2020. *OECD-FAO Agricultural Outlook 2020–2029*. Rome: FAO and Paris: OECD Publishing. https://doi.org/10.1787/1112c23b-en.

Otero, Gerardo. 2018. *The Neoliberal Diet: Healthy Profits, Unhealthy People*. 1st ed. Austin: University of Texas Press.

Peck, Jamie, and Nik Theodore. 2007. "Variegated Capitalism." *Progress in Human Geography* 31 (6): 731–772. https://doi.org/10.1177/0309132507083505.

Peters, Erica J. 2010. "Defusing Phở: Soup Stories and Ethnic Erasures, 1919–2009." *Contemporary French and Francophone Studies* 14 (2): 159–167. https://doi.org/10.1080/17409291003644255.

———. 2012. *Appetites and Aspirations in Vietnam: Food and Drink in the Long Nineteenth Century*. Lanham, MD: AltaMira Press.

Pingali, Prabhu. 2007. "Westernization of Asian Diets and the Transformation of Food Systems: Implications for Research and Policy." *Food Policy* 32 (3): 281–298. https://doi.org/10.1016/j.foodpol.2006.08.001.

Ram, Uri. 2004. "Glocommodification: How the Global Consumes the Local - McDonald's in Israel." *Current Sociology* 52 (1): 11–31. https://doi.org/10.1177/0011392104039311.

Raneri, Jessica E., Gina Kennedy, Trang Nguyen, Sidrig Wertheim-Heck, Ha Do, and Phuong Hong Nguyen. 2019. *Determining Key Research Areas for Healthier Diets and Sustainable Food Systems in Viet Nam.* Washington, DC: International Food Policy Research Institute. https://doi.org/10.2499/p15738coll2.133433.

Reardon, Thomas and C. Peter Timmer. 2007. "The Supermarket Revolution with Asian Characteristics." In *Reasserting the Rural Development Agenda: Lessons Learned and Emerging Challenges in Asia,* edited by Arsenio M. Balisacan and Nobuhiko Fuwa. Singapore: ISEAS Publishing.

Rigg, Jonathan, Albert Salamanca, and Eric C. Thompson. 2016. "The Puzzle of East and Southeast Asia's Persistent Smallholder." *Journal of Rural Studies* 43 (February): 118–133. https://doi.org/10.1016/j.jrurstud.2015.11.003.

Rinkinen, Jenny, Elizabeth Shove, and Mattijs Smits. 2019. "Cold Chains in Hanoi and Bangkok: Changing Systems of Provision and Practice." *Journal of Consumer Culture* 19 (3): 379–397. https://doi.org/10.1177/1469540517717783.

Robert Cole. 2019. "Across the Mountain Tracks: Global Agri-Food Networks and Agrarian Change in Laos' Northeast Borderlands." September.

Sans, P., and P. Combris. 2015. "World Meat Consumption Patterns: An Overview of the Last Fifty Years (1961–2011)." *61st International Congress of Meat Science and Technology (61st ICoMST), 23-28 August 2015, Clermont Ferrand, France* 109 (November): 106–111. https://doi.org/10.1016/j.meatsci.2015.05.012.

Stür, Werner, Truong Tan Khanh, and Alan Duncan. 2013. "Transformation of Smallholder Beef Cattle Production in Vietnam." *International Journal of Agricultural Sustainability* 11 (4): 363–381. https://doi.org/10.1080/14735903.2013.779074.

The Poultry Site. 2020. *Largest Poultry Farm in Southeast Asia Opens in Vietnam.* https://www.thepoultrysite.com/news/2020/12/largest-poultry-farm-in-southeast-asia-opens-in-vietnam

Vietnam Investment Review. 2018. *117 VinMart+ Stores to be Launched Per Day.* December 30, 2018. https://www.vir.com.vn/117-vinmart-stores-to-be-launched-per-day-64857.html

Vietnam Investment Review. 2019. *Convenience Stores Have Strong Development in the Future.* April 01, 2019. https://www.vir.com.vn/convenience-stores-have-strong-development-in-the-future-66784.html.

Vietnam News. 2020. *Domestic Livestock Industry Set New Development Targets.* October 29, 20. https://vietnamnews.vn/economy/803995/domestic-livestock-industry-set-new-development-targets.html

Vietnam Plus. 2020. https://en.vietnamplus.vn/imported-beef-grabs-70-percent-of-market-share/194071.vnp

Vietnam Plus. 2021. *Livestock Industry Targets Production Growth of 6 Percent.* January 08, 21. https://en.vietnamplus.vn/livestock-industry-targets-production-growth-of-6-percent/194455.vnp

VnExpress. 2016. *Vietnam Kills at Least 5 Million Dogs a Year, Mostly in Brutal Ways.* October 14, 2016. https://e.vnexpress.net/news/travel-life/vietnam-kills-at-least-5-million-dogs-a-year-mostly-in-brutal-ways-3483313.html

Watson, James L., ed. 2006. *Golden Arches East: McDonald's in East Asia.* 2nd ed. Stanford, CA: Stanford University Press.

Weis, Anthony John. 2013. *The Ecological Hoofprint: The Global Burden of Industrial Livestock.* London: Zed Books.

Wertheim-Heck, Sigrid C. O., Sietze Vellema, and Gert Spaargaren. 2015. "Food Safety and Urban Food Markets in Vietnam: The Need for Flexible and Customized Retail Modernization Policies." *Food Policy* 54 (July): 95–106. https://doi.org/10.1 016/j.foodpol.2015.05.002.

Wertheim-Heck, Sigrid, Jessica Evelyn Raneri, and Peter Oosterveer. 2019. "Food Safety and Nutrition for Low-Income Urbanites: Exploring a Social Justice Dilemma in Consumption Policy." *Environment and Urbanization* 31 (2): 397–420. https://doi.org/10.1177/0956247819858019.

Wilk, Richard. 2018. "Global Junk: Who is to Blame for the Obesity Epidemic?" *Revista de Administração de Empresas* 58 (3): 332–336. https://doi.org/10.1590/s 0034-759020180311.

World Bank. 2021. *World Development Indicators.* https://data.worldbank.org/.

Chapter 7

Bovine Contradictions

The Politics of (De)meatification and Hindutva Hegemony in Neoliberal India

Jostein Jakobsen and Kenneth Bo Nielsen

The focus of this chapter is India's apparently paradoxical relationship with beef. In the stereotypical popular perception, India is the land of holy cows, revered by the nation's vegetarian Hindu majority. At the same time, but perhaps lesser known to the world, India is also a world-leading exporter of beef—overwhelmingly in the form of buffalo meat, commonly known as carabeef—accounting for as much as 20 percent of global exports. In this chapter, we seek to move beyond the mere recognition of this as an apparent paradox to argue that while the coexistence of these two trends may indeed appear paradoxical, they are conjoined in uneasy tension within the broader hegemonic project of India's Hindu nationalist government, led by the Bharatiya Janata Party (BJP) and Prime Minister Narendra Modi. This hegemonic project is centered on the twin ideological agenda of Hindu nationalism that seeks to turn India into a Hindu majoritarian state (Chatterji et al. 2019; Nilsen, Nielsen and Vaidya 2022), and neoliberal economic policies that seek to create new spaces for capitalist accumulation. Meat and bovine bodies are, we argue, crucial sites where this contradictory hegemonic project plays out. On the one hand, promoting cow protectionism and vegetarianism furthers the Hindu nationalist project by consolidating the image of India as first and foremost a Hindu nation and relegates non-Hindus to the status of denizens. On the other hand, the meatification of Indian agricultural exports and their integration into global value chains and regional "meat complexes" furthers the opening of the Indian agrarian economy, spurring capitalist accumulation by integration with growing transnational markets.

We proceed as follows. First, we outline our approach to hegemony and the conceptual framework for our analysis of the politics of (de)meatification in neoliberal India. Thereafter, we explore cow vigilantism, Hindu national-ism, and the workings of the violence of demeatification. We then turn to the political economy of meat and the agro-industrial neoliberalization it partakes in. With both elements to the bovine contradiction described, we lay out pre-liminary thoughts on its current negotiation and its implications for the Hindu nationalist hegemonic project.

HEGEMONY IN NEOLIBERAL INDIA

Hegemonic processes concern the ways in which consent to a dominant order is educed and maintained. According to Gramsci (1998, 239), hegemonic processes are mediated in and through what he refers to as "the integral state," that is, the fusion of political and civil society, which weaves its institutions, discourses, and technologies of rule into the fabric of the everyday life of subaltern groups. This in turn makes it possible for dominant social groups to educe their consent. However, this process is a gradual and contentious one; the Gramscian notion of hegemony does not entail stability but is instead always fragile, subject to negotiations and rife with contradictions (Hall 2011, 727–728).

 Combining this view of hegemony with an examination of the logics of state power, Poulantzas (1978) discusses the state as "a relationship of forces, or more precisely the material condensation of such a relationship among classes and class fractions" (ibid., 128, emphasis removed). This relation-ship, Poulantzas emphasizes, is necessarily strained, frequently conflictual, giving rise to series of "internal contradictions within the State" (ibid., 131, emphasis removed). In what follows, we will argue for taking "bovine con-tradictions," that is, the tensions between the economic and cultural aspects of Modi's hegemonic Hindutva project, as these play out within the realm of bovine meat, as a lens into the internal contradictions of the neoliberal Indian state. To proceed along these lines, we contextualize the uneven and tension-fraught nature of neoliberal hegemony in contemporary India.

 In economic terms, the growth model pursued by all Indian governments since the gradual opening of the economy, commonly seen as taking off in 1991, has been starkly uneven. Indeed, the highly skewed pattern of devel-opment, generating stark social and economic inequities of "poverty amid plenty" (Kohli 2012), has been widely recognized (see, for example, Dreze and Sen 2014). While the neoliberalization of the Indian state and economy has been restrained and incomplete—only properly gaining in pace and intensity from the mid-2000s—the overall thrust has been toward opening to private capital of ever more sectors, creating avenues for accumulation for corporate and dominant class interests, representing both domestic and international capital (see, for example, Chatterjee 2008). This has placed evident pressure on Indian governments to negotiate the required consent to a regime that produces stark inequality in the context of competitive democratic politics. The compromises that result from such negotiations have, as Ahmed and Chatterjee (2016, 332) argue, revealed the "contradiction of the simultaneous production of neoliberal and welfare policy." The period of Congress-led governmental coalitions from 2004 to 2014 are especially important in this regard insofar as they placed a marked focus on establishing ambitious welfare programs in employment, food security, and education, while also remaining committed to liberalizing economic reforms (see Nilsen and Nielsen 2016). With the coming to power of Modi's assertive Hindu nationalist government, however, we have seen a departure from the inclusive neoliberalism of the prior coalition.

To clarify what the BJP's hegemonic project is about, we turn to Palshikar's (2019) work on the BJP's strategy for crafting a new hegemony. According to Palshikar, the Modi regime seeks the support of corporate interests for its neoliberal *economic* agenda by convincing the corporate classes that this agenda will be implemented vigorously irrespective of its Hindu chauvinist *sociopolitical* agenda. At the same time, the BJP seeks approval for its *sociopolitical* agenda from the larger public by linking it directly to the *economic* agenda: the ordinary citizen is thus sought to be convinced that their economic well-being is primarily a function of a strong nation and that, therefore, the hurdles in becoming a strong nation—in this rendering explicitly defined as a "Hindu nation"—need to be overcome. The "hurdles" in question include "pampered religious minorities," "anti-national elements," "seditious liberal intellectuals," and so on. To sustain this hegemonic project, Modi's ability to bring together the middle classes and corporate interests becomes crucial. As Palshikar writes, "Modi emerges as the extraordinary leader because of skilfully marrying an aggressive corporatized economy with an assertive majoritarian politics" (Palshikar 2019, 114). Other scholars have likened this "aggressive corporatized economy" to a form of "expedited neoliberalism" (Desai 2016) that promises quick returns on investments, business-friendly policies, and overall pro-capital economic measures, to the benefit of dominant class interests. Among the many initiatives where this is visible, Prime Minister Modi's flagship "Make in India" program (Chacko 2018) that we return to later is, with its emphasis on ease of doing business indicators and FDI inflows, probably the most well-known.

However, it cannot be taken for granted that the marriage between an aggressive corporatized economy and an assertive Hindu majoritarian politics will always be a harmonious one. Indeed, the contradiction between the economic and sociopolitical aspects of Modi's hegemonic project becomes particularly visible, we argue, in the context of bovine politics and economics.

Here we argue that the Hindu nationalist ideology of cow-veneration and its violent enforcement stands in a tension-fraught relation to the neoliberal search for new spaces for capital accumulation, in this case in the form of meat exports as a lucrative business. The latter forms, we suggest following Gramsci (1998), an economic "essential" that even Hindutva cultural politics struggles to "touch"—although, as we shall see, this particular economic "essential" does not come away unscathed from the current negotiation of India's bovine contradiction.

COW VIGILANTISM AND HINDU NATIONALISM

For the purpose of the discussions that follow, an important distinction can be made between cows, which are considered sacred by many Hindus, and buffalos, which are often considered merely as an economic (and sometimes even demonic) animal (Hardy 2019). Similarly, the slaughter of cows is illegal in a large number of Indian states, while the slaughter of buffalos is not criminalized to the same extent. Hence, it is the cow that is mostly in the news, particularly because of the increasing vigilante violence around its protection. The buffalo, in contrast, is not accorded similar "protection" and receives less attention in the discourse around bovine politics, despite its crucial role as the source of carabeef for exports. Yet in the domain of meat and diets these distinctions are often blurred, particularly when we examine topics such as vegetarianism and cattle slaughter as they are articulated within the hegemonic Hindu nationalist project.

The caricature image of India as an overwhelmingly vegetarian country populated by cow-worshipping, otherworldly Hindus who practice nonviolence toward all living creatures is a well-established one. Although in no small measure a product of the colonial Orientalist imagination, this perceived "Hindu ethic" that is thus made to define India as a whole has over the past decades acquired ever more positive connotations. Not only are cow-veneration and vegetarianism widely read as benign aspects of India's cultural heritage. At the current conjuncture, where the accelerating meatification of global diets is a cause for concern and where large-scale environmental destruction calls for more sustainable ways of living, they can be said to constitute important components in India's soft power arsenal, alongside postcolonial democracy, yoga, and Bollywood. Yet within India, buffalos, cows, meat, diets, and vegetarianism are intensely politicized and contested issues (Staples 2019).

Whereas Hindu nationalists and fundamentalists see vegetarianism and cow-veneration as millennia-old cultural traditions that define Hinduism as a religious practice, secular historians argue that the elevation of the cow to sacred status for *all* Hindus is a more recently invented and historically contested tradition. A case in point is historian D. N. Jha's book *The Myth of the Holy Cow*. Published in 2002, the book is probably the most well-known effort at exploding the long-held myth of an unbroken history of Hindu vegetarianism and cow reverence. In this book, Jha outlines substantial textual evidence of ritual killing, eating, and sacrifice of allegedly "holy" cows throughout Hindu history. Jha thus shows how cow meat was part of early Indian nonvegetarian dietary traditions. In India, the book caused controversy even before it was published. As excerpts were posted on the Internet and picked up by newspapers, the book was canceled by the publisher, burned by religious activists, and called "sheer blasphemy" by a spokesman for the Hindu nationalist World Hindu Council (VHP). Death threats were made (Eakin 2002).

The history of cow protectionism as a political tactic is of a relatively recent date and can be traced back to the latter half of the nineteenth century when it was deployed to assert Hindu identity and unify diverse castes and communities (Freitag 1980). In the colonial context, the cow was an eminently useful symbol for highlighting and politicizing the perceived differences between Muslims (who ate it) and Hindus (who revered it), and for moving this difference into the domain of public agitation. During the 1880s cow protection societies, or *gaurakshini sabhas*, were formed and were particularly active in North India. These societies petitioned the colonial government and fought legal battles in the name of the cow, but also organized processions that led to deadly communal clashes between Hindus and Muslims (Metcalf and Metcalf 1998, 150–155). Among Hindu nationalists, this "rallying round the cow" (Pandey 1981) was to produce a shared sense of Hindu identity and unity, with India's Muslim minority cast as the antagonistic "other." It was through the cow that community, nation, and religion were conjoined, and by referring to the cow as "mother," Hindu nationalists sought to evoke the same imagery as the term "Mother India": symbolic purity and virtue that must be protected at all costs from those who threaten the Hindu nation (Gittinger 2017).

Although *The Myth of the Holy Cow* is first and foremost a historical study, Jha also observes—with a certain understatement—that "the killing of cattle seems to have emerged again and again as a troublesome issue on the Indian political scene even in independent India" (Jha 2002, 19). Indeed, just five years after India had become an independent nation, the Hindu nationalist organization, the Rashtriya Swayamsevak Sangh (RSS), collected upward of 17 million signatures on a petition that demanded a national ban on cow slaughter. This was the RSS's first mass public agitation after independence, and cow protection and a national ban on cow slaughter have remained core issues with the RSS ever since, even if it currently advocates "a more nuanced approach" (Andersen and Damle 2019, 176). In the early 1950s, the Bharatiya Jana Sangh, the forerunner of the BJP, similarly made cow protection one of its core elements and, in the mid-1960s, the RSS spearheaded a "great all-party campaign" for the protection of the cow that eventually attempted to storm the Indian parliament to pressure legislators to criminalize cow slaughter in the entire country (Copland 2014). While cow protectionism has thus largely been associated with the Hindu right, it was also widely endorsed by the secular Congress party, and many Congress-ruled states have passed laws restricting or banning the slaughter of cattle.

In the decade leading up to the publication of Jha's book, cow protection gradually became less important within the RSS and BJP as priorities shifted toward economic growth and liberalization. However, it remained a core issue with other organizations within the larger Hindu nationalist movement, and in recent years it has assumed an unprecedented centrality to Indian politics. Since 2014, when Prime Minister Modi came to power fronting an aggressive Hindu nationalist ruling bloc, bovines make almost daily headlines. On the one hand, ever-stricter laws are passed to ostensibly "protect the cow" while, on the other hand, vigilante groups aggressively punish those who do not sufficiently respect the cow. We look at these two aspects of contemporary cow protection politics in turn.

Legislating for the Cow

Cow protection is under article 48 of the Indian Constitution a state subject within India's federal system, meaning that there is no central law on this question that applies to the whole country. Rather, India has "a patchwork of state laws on cow protection, ranging from no bans to total prohibition" (Andersen and Damle 2019, 177). Nonetheless, some form of cow protection now exists in a large majority of India's states and Union Territories. Three quarters of the states banning cow slaughter make it a cognizable offence (alongside rape, murder, and theft), while in half it is a non-bailable offence (alongside sedition, counterfeiting, and trafficking). Modi is known to favor a national ban on cow slaughter (ibid., 179), and while such a national ban has so far not materialized, state-level legislative changes have systematically made the slaughter of cows or even the sale and possession of cow beef illegal in ever-larger parts of the country under Modi's tenure (Jaffrelot 2019, 59). Modi's home state of Gujarat, for instance, in 2017, amended an act from 1954 that criminalized cow slaughter, transportation of cows for slaughter, and the possession of beef, to extend the maximum sentence for cow slaughter to life imprisonment. Other BJP-controlled states such as Maharashtra and Haryana have also toughened cow protection legislation by criminalizing beef consumption in 2015. The former has imposed a total ban on the slaughter of all cattle (bulls and bullocks included) and has completely banned all transport of cattle out of the state (Ramdas 2017). In Haryana, the state police has set up a so-called cow task force (Jaffrelot 2019, 62). And Uttar Pradesh, under the hard-liner Hindu nationalist chief minister Yogi Adityanath, recently imposed unprecedentedly strict legal punishments for various offences ranging from cow slaughter to "endangering the life of cows" by, for example, not providing them food and water.

Cow Vigilantism

Enhanced legal protection for the cow and higher sentences for offenders have gone hand in hand with a steep rise in cow protection vigilantism as gangs of predominantly armed young men affiliated with a broad spectrum of Hindu nationalist organizations have taken it upon themselves to protect the cow, either as a sacred duty or for personal gain, or both. These vigilante groups are not part of the state apparatus, but form part of the new power structure under the BJP qua their ideological and sometimes organizational closeness to the party in power. This includes the Akhil Bharatiya Vidyarthi Parishad, the student wing of the RSS, which has been involved in several violent attacks on student associations over beef eating within university campuses, as we return to later (Ilaiah Shepherd 2019). They roam the roads and abattoirs in search of culprits transporting cows for slaughter, or track down people claimed to have killed cows, frequently determined to beat, maim, or kill people, and Muslims in particular. Their operations are often based on, and stoke, rumors about water buffalo traders and handlers—which is a perfectly legal trade—illegally transporting cows for slaughter. As Patel (2018) argues, such violent "Islamophobic gastronomy" as a way of adjudicating over citizenship is becoming increasingly widespread not just in India, but in authoritarian populist regimes across the globe.

As described by Jaffrelot (2019, 59), North India was between 2015 and 2017 "the theatre of a series of lynchings of Muslims, following a near identical pattern each time: the Muslims accused of cattle smuggling or consuming beef were attacked and, in dozens of cases, died of their wounds." In one tragic case, a Muslim in Uttar Pradesh was accused of killing a cow 30 years earlier and was beaten to death (Manor 2019, 122). Muslim cattle transporters have become favorite targets for these self-appointed cow protectors, who often work in close conjunction with the police. Indeed, cow vigilantes increasingly operate with the blessing of the state and BJP MLAs, MPs, and ministers, who even, sometimes, openly garland them (Anderson and Jaffrelot 2018). In contrast, Hindu cattle and cattle transporters are generally spared (Jaffrelot 2019, 60), thus underlining the crucial role of anti-Muslim sentiments in contemporary cow vigilantism. Yet Dalits, the formerly untouchable castes, have also been targeted by such groups. In one much-publicized incident, seven Dalits were thrashed and urinated upon in Prime Minister Modi's home state of Gujarat for performing their traditional occupation, namely skinning cows (Manor 2019, 123). All in all, in early 2019, Human Rights Watch reported that 44 people had been killed since 2015 and 280 people injured in vigilante attacks against cattle traders across the country. Sadly, these numbers fall far short of capturing the full extent of the violence and atrocities of contemporary cow vigilantism. Nor do they capture how vigilante violence is increasingly conjoined with more insidious scientific technologies including "beef detection kits" and "water buffalo detection kits." While these are ostensibly designed to prevent vigilante attacks, they in effect multiply the ways bovine bodies are involved in the surveillance and disciplining of certain populations (Parikh and Miller 2019).

Toward a Hindu Rashtra

Legal cow protectionism and violent vigilantism play crucial roles within the larger hegemonic project of the BJP and affiliated Hindu nationalist organizations. They "partake of a new formation of the state, the formation of a *de facto* if not a *de jure* Hindu *rashtra*" (Jaffrelot 2019, 65) through unofficial and often violent forms of social and moral regulation that unfold with tacit or overt endorsement by the state. It is far from an uncontested project, and it has been resisted most dramatically through "beef festivals" organized in different parts of India, on campuses by university students, and in public spaces in cities by political parties. Dalits, and especially Dalit student groups, have been at the forefront of organizing such festivals as a way of asserting a counter-hegemonic Dalit identity, in opposition to the deeply Brahmanical version of Hinduism promoted by Hindu nationalist organizations (Natrajan 2018). And yet, the BJP's hegemonic project currently remains on a strong footing in the sociopolitical domain. As Bruckert (2019, 310) argues, "In this cultural battle to impart specific significations to meat, Hindu nationalists seem to have taken the upper hand" by combining law and vigilante violence with occasional allusions to globally resonant "secular repertoires such as environmentalism, prevention of cruelty to animals, morality or hygiene to command their religious agenda."

In our discussion so far, we have located the question of cow protection and meat eating within a politics of religious difference, focusing on the assertive Hindu majoritarianism that seeks to transform India into a Hindu *rashtra* by establishing a fundamental difference between cow-revering Hindus and beef-eating Muslims. This is a recurring theme within much of the scholarly literature that focuses on the symbolic and physical contestations centered on meat eating and their entailments for the future of the country as a "Hindu nation." And yet, such careful analysis of presumed religious motives behind cow protection and vigilantism should not lead us to neglect economic arguments, not merely within cow protectionist politics as recently pointed out by Adcock and Govindrajan (2019), but also in the larger political economy of meat. To foreground the economic dimension, we now shift the attention toward the ways in which beef and bovine bodies function as central nodes to the contradictions of neoliberalization in contemporary India (Ahmed and Chatterjee 2016) or, more precisely, the contradictions of the Hindu nationalist hegemonic project spearheaded by Modi.

THE POLITICAL ECONOMY OF MEAT

As argued earlier, the surge in violent attention to beef eating under Modi's rule takes place in an uneasy coexistence with another surge, namely, in beef exports. In 2015, India emerged as the world's largest exporter of beef—overwhelmingly from buffaloes—and the meat industry has continued increasing. In this sense, the geographer Tony Weis's (2013) concept of "meatification" can help shed light on the Indian scene. Although meat has not moved to the center of Indian diets, Indian agricultural production has become increasingly structured according to the capitalist logics of the "industrial grain-oilseed-livestock complex" centered on the human consumption of meat—even if that consumption mostly happens outside of India, or is centered on poultry (Jakobsen 2020). To the extent that we can speak of an Indian meatification, then, it is thus crucially tied to international markets in meat products where regional Asian importers are important (Jakobsen and Hansen 2020). At the same time, India is in fact the world's second fastest growing market for processed meat and poultry (Das 2017), and this also contributes to the growth in the Indian meat industry.

Opening agrarian India for increased export orientation is part and parcel of the assertive neoliberal economic policies of the Modi government, and although the rapid growth in beef exports began under the earlier dispensation, they have stabilized at a high level under Modi, both in terms of value and quantity (see figure 7.1).

Yet while the *economic* process of meatification thus aligns well with government policies and priorities, it finds itself conjoined in a contradictory relationship with the *sociopolitical* project of cow protectionism and vigilantism that is equally central to the Hindu nationalist hegemonic project.

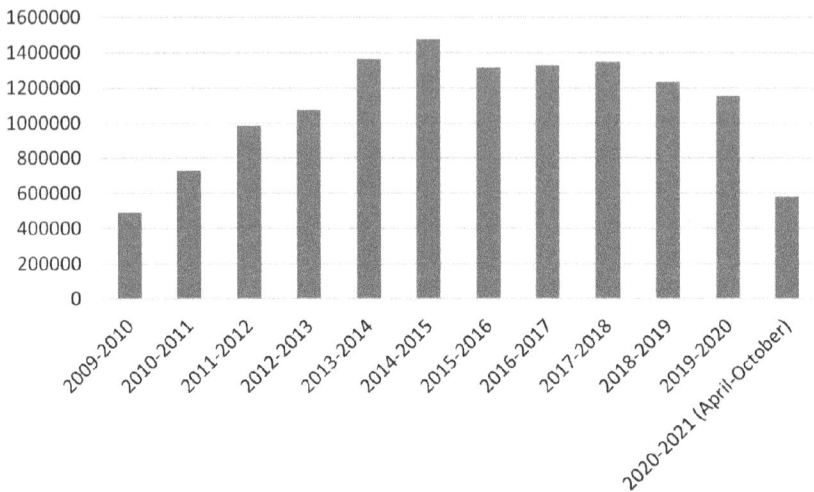

Figure 7.1   India Buffalo Meat Exports (Quantity in Tonnes [MT]).

Moderate Meatification at Home

By global standards, meat consumption remains very low in India compared to other middle-income countries (Jakobsen and Hansen 2020). This notwithstanding, absolute vegetarianism also remains much more limited than what is commonly assumed. A recent scholarly assessment of existing large-scale surveys of household consumption patterns concludes that "characterizing India as a vegetarian land is a gross misrepresentation of reality: the vegetarian population of India is at best 31%, and realistically less than 20%" (Natrajan and Jacob 2018, 63). A large share of India's population thus does eat meat, and this population is not limited to Muslims, Christians, and Dalits. The situation is thus one where a large proportion of the population consumes meat, but in relatively small quantities or irregularly.

In spite of this limited growth in meat consumption, some researchers maintain that India nonetheless increasingly fits with the "livestock revolution" narrative, involving dietary shifts and diversification in developing countries experiencing economic growth (see Hansen, Jakobsen, and Wethal, this volume). While this shift is much less evident in meat consumption in India than in countries such as China and Brazil, it is clearly seen in the "near doubling of aggregate milk consumption as food in India between the early 1980s and the late 1990s" (Khan and Bidabadi 2004, 107). This massive increase in domestic milk consumption was the outcome of the so-called Operation Flood, a government program that transformed India from a milk-deficit country to the world's largest milk producer in less than three decades

(Scholten 2010). This points to a significant livestock sector, estimated to employ as much as 20 million people.

India's livestock economy is described as largely decentralized, involving small herds reared, grazed, and utilized by smallholder farmers rather than industrialized operations. An assessment from 2009 held that "with both bovines and smaller animals, the sector is dominated by largely non-intensive 'domestic' rearing, where feeding only in stalls is rare" (Dorin and Landy 2009, 134). Due to the politically contentious nature of cattle slaughtering, numbers from the 1990s held abattoirs in the country to be overwhelmingly "small, unlicensed units" with only around 25 units "relatively large" and "geared to the export market" (Dorin and Landy 2009, 136).[1]

Meat Exports

The political economy of bovine meat in India is not, then, based primarily on domestic meatification of diets—although that too is a factor—but is rather closely tied to export markets. Emerging out of the country's decentralized and smallholder-based livestock system, the past decade or two has witnessed an astonishing rise of meat exports based on beef overwhelmingly from buffalo which elide the legal restrictions imposed on cow slaughter. Even more specifically, according to a U.S. Department of Agriculture report, India's export meat sector is largely based on culled dairy animals, predominantly reared by smallholder farmers before being sold to traders and, then, exporters (Landes et al. 2016; FICCI 2013). This indicates a close link between dairy and industrial scale killings of bovine animals—both buffaloes and cows—yet largely ignored by cow protection legislation (Narayan 2019). While unable to compete with advanced industrial livestock operations, the report states, "Indian exports are meeting demand in the fastest growing segment of the world beef market, primarily among low- and middle-income countries in Asia and the Middle East" (Landes et al. 2016). Among these countries, Vietnam is by far the largest market for Indian beef, which, with an export flow at 1.8 billion USD in 2018, comprised the third largest single trade flow in meat globally.[2] As we will see, India's exports to Vietnam are known to flow further into China—a country that does not allow import of Indian buffalo meat (see Jakobsen and Hansen 2020)—meaning that Vietnam connects India to one of the world's largest markets in meat.

India's rise as a meat export powerhouse appears to have been most pronounced from 2008 to 2014, when export volumes expanded by 17 percent annually (Landes et al. 2016; see figure 7.1) and the country emerged as the foremost beef exporter globally. A rare report into the conditions of India's surging meat industry comments that this period also saw governmental efforts at strengthening the export industry, including by India's National Meat and Poultry Processing Board, established in 2009, which held that "as the country's livestock industry is changing, India attempts to become a key player in the global meat market" (cited in Brighter Green 2020, 2). During the past decades, buffalo meat production in India has increased significantly, with numbers from the UN's Food and Agriculture Organization showing a 54.1 percent increase in buffalo meat production in India from 1990 to 2018 (see figure 7.2).

This surge has been accompanied by a significant restructuring of the export-oriented part of the livestock industry. Departing from the unorganized picture of the 1990s, the period of the meat export boom sees exporters arising as key actors in the political economy of meat. The USDA report details "49 registered export-oriented buffalo slaughter and processing facilities in the country, along with 39 facilities that handle only processing and 11 that handle only slaughter" (Landes et al. 2016). This indicates a highly concentrated industry with a limited number of players. Concentration is witnessed geographically by a few Indian states dominating the industry—Uttar Pradesh as the most prominent by far, followed by Maharashtra, Andhra Pradesh/ Telangana, and Punjab (Landes et al. 2016). This geographical clustering by states may even gloss over an even more concentrated form of clustering as the industry is in fact most concentrated in a few cities alone, with Mumbai and New Delhi dominating the scene to the extent that these two cities, combined, reportedly account for 66 percent of the revenue in the industry (Export Genius 2017). Concentration also appears in ownership, leading one commentator to hold that India's meat export industry is "owned by just a

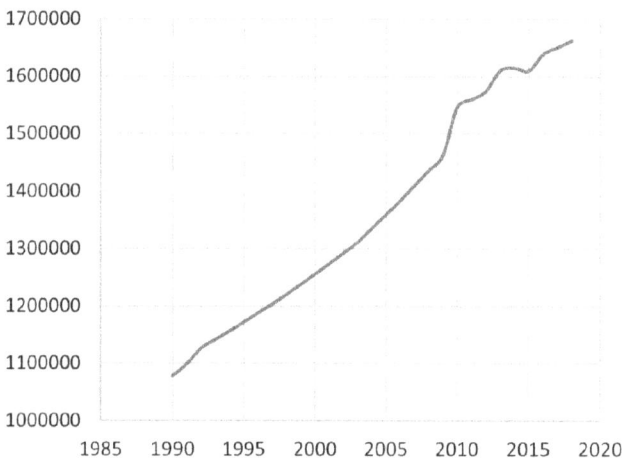

Figure 7.2   India Buffalo Meat Production (Tonnes).

clutch of people" (Anand 2014). However, hard facts about the industry are hard to find, no doubt related to the controversial nature of beef in the Indian polity. From the data that is available, we find that Mumbai-based Allanasons Private Limited is considered the leading company in the industry. A rare newspaper report describing this actor writes,

Fauzan Alavi, a Director with Allanasons, said that in both years [2014–2015 and 2015–2016] the company exported around Rs 10,000 crore of buffalo meat. Total exports are around Rs 25,700 crore, which means that Allanasons exports more than a third of India's buffalo meat. (Dhara 2017)

Relations between Modi's government and this surging industry are, as we can expect, strained and contradictory. Indeed, in his 2014 electoral campaign, Modi's discourse featured the meat industry as a villain, lambasting the incumbent Congress-led government for allowing a "Pink Revolution" in meat in breach with "Hindu" values. "This country wants a Green Revolution," Modi said at an election rally, adding that,

But those at the centre want a Pink Revolution. Do you know what it means? When animals are slaughtered, the colour of their flesh is pink. Animals are being slaughtered and taken out of the country. The government in Delhi is giving subsides to those who are carrying out this slaughter. (Kumar 2014)

The most striking contradiction involved here is of course the fact that the meat industry, as noted earlier, continued growing despite the rise in violent vigilantism and legislative crackdowns that followed after Modi's win in 2014. Political opponents and commentators in the country have repeatedly pointed to this as proof of Modi's "double standards," including by way of speculations about the alleged involvement of BJP politicians in the meat industry in BJP-controlled states (Press Trust of India 2018). Indeed, in 2015 newspapers circulated proof that subsidiaries of Allanasons had donated some INR 2.5 crores to BJP for the 2014 election campaign (Dhawan 2015). Given the opaque and enigmatic ways in which money flows in Indian politics (Kapur and Vaishnav 2018), this indicates the existence of larger unreported transactions.

The contradictory relationship between Modi and the meat industry has been evident in other domains too. In the symbolic domain, Modi's government has recognized and even rewarded Allanasons for "outstanding export performance," and for its overall contributions to the food sector during Modi's tenure. And, in the policy domain—according to an RTI response by the Union Ministry of Food Processing Industries—the government subsidy for slaughterhouses actually increased by 33 percent during Modi's first term in power, in spite of his earlier strong criticism of his predecessor's excessive subsidies to the industry (Sharma 2019). This increase in subsidies came under the central government–run scheme of the National Mission for Food Processing, introduced in 2014, aiming to upgrade and modernize slaughtering facilities in the country, as part of a broader thrust toward modernizing supply chains for ease of capital flows in agro-industrial sectors, with an emphasis on food processing including meat. This, we would argue, resonates with the broad "Make in India" agenda of Modi's government, where "ease of doing business" is central, including in streamlining and upgrading processing, facilities, and value chains across different sectors of the economy. India's food processing sector was indeed in 2019 recognized by the USDA (2019) as a "sunrise sector" with great potential for capital investment.

The rapidly growing export orientation of Indian agriculture thus maintains its pace (Jena 2019), with a new federal agricultural export policy formulated in 2018 seeking to double agricultural exports by 2022 (Government of India 2018). While promoted as a contributor to realizing the Modi government's expressed aim of doubling farmers' income, the policy stresses the need for opening for increased private investments in production and processing, and for upgrading and intensifying integrated supply chains.[3] Whereas the export policy has been criticized by leading actors in the meat export sector for ignoring livestock (James 2018), the Agriculture Export Policy pinpoints "meat" as one of 10 commodities with "very high potential," even as it refrains from specifying what "meat" would mean (Government of India 2018). The policy is also focused heavily on supply chain upgrading, including renewed emphasis on processing, infrastructure, logistics, cold storage, and so on, by attracting private investments in combination with increased state involvement in agro-processing. These are all elements of an agro-industrial reform that would arguably benefit meat exports.

Currently, the clearest indicator of continuing meat export expansion under Modi is the concerted efforts at agreements with China for direct imports of bovine meat from India, thus gaining access to the massive Chinese market directly and not by way of the mentioned Vietnamese proxy. These efforts at trade agreements with China have been ongoing since 2014, described by an (anonymous) leading government official as being a "top priority" for Modi's government (Mathew 2017). Modi's government has concentrated its efforts also on controlling foot and mouth disease in the livestock herd, in order to fulfill the strict Chinese regulations. Indeed, this effort was described in newspapers as one of the first actions taken by Modi's second government in 2019 (Pandey 2019). However, in late 2019, crackdowns in China on trade of buffalo from Vietnam put this lucrative business at risk, ostensibly leading to speculations on the Indian side about shifting toward Indonesia as a possible step-in market (Parija 2019). Brazil has also emerged as a new potential collaborator. In early 2020—just prior to the Covid-19 crisis, which presumably has put these ambitions on hold—the Indian Industry Association invited the Brazilian government to be the country partner for the "India Food Expo 2020." President Bolsonaro led a delegation from the Brazilian meat, poultry, and processed food sector to Delhi, with the primary aim of promoting trade ties between India and Brazil in these sectors (KNN India 2020). As a final indication of the continuing drive toward export expansion, we note how leading industry representatives during the height of the Covid-19 crisis formulated goals of stepping into meet emerging shortages due to global slump in meat production.

CONCLUDING DISCUSSION: NEGOTIATING BOVINE CONTRADICTIONS

In this chapter we have analyzed how India's bovine contradiction is expressive of deeper contradictions within the broader hegemonic project of India's Hindu nationalist government. This hegemonic project is centered on the twin ideological agenda of Hindu nationalism and Hindu majoritarian statecraft, and neoliberal economic policies that seek to create new spaces for capitalist accumulation. Meat and bovine bodies are, we have argued, crucial sites where this contradictory hegemonic project plays out. On the one hand, the Hindu nationalist component of this hegemonic project is furthered through a mix of legal and extralegal cow protection measures, while, on the other, the meatification of Indian agricultural exports and their integration into global value chains further the neoliberalization of the Indian agrarian economy. In short, this bovine contradiction lays bare the tensions between the economic and cultural aspects of Modi's hegemonic Hindutva project, as well as the deeper internal contradictions of the neoliberal Indian state.

One way in which this tension between the two pillars of the broader hegemonic project has been negotiated has been the "Modi-RSS power-sharing pact" under which "Modi's undisputed writ runs through major areas like the economy, commerce, foreign affairs and security [while] the RSS gets a free hand in determining the social, cultural and educational agenda" (Kanungo 2019, 134). Yet it is clear that the two agendas of the broader hegemonic project cannot always be pursued in relatively splendid isolation, and that they sometimes—and sometimes violently—collide and clash. The Hindu nationalist sociopolitical project that relies on cow protectionism and vigilantism has, for example, had very direct economic repercussions for at least parts of the meat industry. There has been a clampdown on the cattle trade, and the targeted violence of vigilante groups has instilled fear among cattle transporters, including the legal transportation of buffalo. And bans on transport and the slaughter of cattle mean that farmers can no longer sell their aged milk-yielding cattle as animal markets collapse. Selling cattle once the lactation or reproductive age is over usually recovers 30 percent to 40 percent of the cost of a new milk-yielding animal, and the inability to recover this amount leads to economic hardship among farmers and additional problems of stray cattle that destroy crops (Alavi 2018). Surveillance, violence, and fear have thus lead to a breakdown in supply chains and animal markets, as well as in other sectors involved in the livestock economy such as leather and dairy. Such effects are perhaps most acutely felt in the informal parts of the industry, yet the slump in industry growth since Modi's rise to power (see figure 7.1) indicates repercussions for the broader industry.

The large northern state of Uttar Pradesh, India's top meat producer, is an illustrative case in point. In 2015, the National Green Tribunal had ordered all slaughterhouses running without requisite permits to be shut. But only in 2017 did a newly elected BJP state government use the ruling as a pretext to target the meat industry by ordering action against slaughterhouses and meat sellers operating without valid licenses and violating environmental and health rules. The closure affected the slaughterhouses directly, but also meat sellers and farmers, as well as related industries such as leather, dairy, and transportation. As a result, the informal market comprising butchers, meat suppliers, and all those trading in animal by-products took a severe economic hit. The economic consequences of cow vigilantism—as well as the accompanying legislation protecting the cow—are thus significant, and in many respects hinder the ongoing meatification of Indian agriculture. At the same time, while this has also hit the formal market of large, export-oriented actors that run mechanized and well-equipped slaughterhouses and have all the required permits, these could nonetheless continue to operate legally. This has led to speculations that the crackdown on the cattle trade would in fact skew the market in favor of big actors operating at scale, and expand the market for its frozen meat products (Moudgil 2017) in a context in which buffalo meat for domestic consumption is otherwise overwhelmingly based on the production of fresh meat (Ramdas 2017b).

Yet, while vigilante violence and legislative change have hit the meat industry with a certain force, it is not the case that rampant vigilantism rules the day. Rather, we find that the RSS which controls the sociocultural agenda is aware of the contradiction and has adopted "a more nuanced approach to a policy which threatens the lucrative multibillion-dollar beef and leather industries" (Andersen and Damle 2019, 176). The restraint—whether self-imposed or not—put on RSS forces may also be seen in the context of the broader contradiction between neoliberal expediency and majoritarian authoritarianism, where Hindu nationalist forces are well-aware that violence and political instability is generally off-putting to (foreign) investors

(Chaudhary et al. 2020). This, we suggest, may be interpreted as signs of the limits to which the economic "essential" may be touched, even in a context where all parties have to make certain "sacrifices."

NOTES

1. The poultry sector is an exception from this pattern, with steep growth, factory farming, and strong corporate agribusiness influence emerging over the past decades (Dorin and Landy 2009, 138; Brighter Green 2012; see also Jakobsen 2020). To the extent that India shows any clear signs of meatifying its diets, poultry is key as the foremost meat eaten (beef from buffalo being second).

2. Data from https://resourcetrade.earth.

3. Predictably enough, the export policy has been criticized by civil society activists for being "anti-farmer" in its ambition of increasing the integration of the country's agricultural sector with globalized capital, something that, critics hold, evidently does not benefit small farmers (see, for example, Pal 2018).

REFERENCES

Adcock, Cassie and Radhika Govindrajan. 2019. "Bovine Politics in South Asia: Rethinking Religion, Law and Ethics." *South Asia: Journal of South Asian Studies* 42 (6): 1095–1107. DOI: 10.1080/00856401.2019.1681726

Ahmed, Waquar and Ipsita Chatterjee. 2016. "Antinomies of the Indian State." In *The Palgrave Handbook of Critical International Political Economy*, edited by Alan Cafruny, Leila Simona Talani and Gonzalo Pozo Martin, 331–349. London: Palgrave Macmillan.

Alavi, Fauzan. 2018. "India Should Leverage Its Livestock Treasure Beyond Milk." *The Indian Express*, July 5. https://indianexpress.com/article/india/india-should-leverage-its-livestock-treasure-beyond-milk-5246101/.

Andersen, Walter and Shridhar D. Damle. 2019. *Messengers of Hindu Nationalism: How the RSS Reshaped India*. London: Hurst and Company.

Brighter Green. 2012. "Veg or Non-Veg? India at the Crossroads." Report available at https://www.brightergreen.org/files/india_bg_pp_2011.pdf

Bruckert, Michaël. 2019. "The Politicization of Beef and Meat in Contemporary India: Protecting Animals and Alienating Minorities." In *Culinary Nationalism in Asia*, edited by Michelle T. King, 150–169. London: Bloomsbury.

Chacko, Priya. 2018. "The Right Turn in India: Authoritarianism, Populism and Neoliberalisation." *Journal of Contemporary Asia* 48 (4): 541–565. DOI: 10.1080/00472336.2018.1446546

Chatterjee, Partha. 2008. "Democracy and Economic Transformation in India." *Economic and Political Weekly* 42 (16): 53–62.

Chatterji, Angana P., Thomas Blom Hansen and Christophe Jaffrelot, eds. 2019. *Majoritarian State: How Hindu Nationalism is Changing India*. London: Hurst & Co.

Chaudhary, Archana, Selcuk Gokoluk and Ronojoy Mazumdar. 2020. "Deadly Delhi Riots have Foreign Investors Rethinking about India's Attractiveness." *The Print*, March 5. https://theprint.in/economy/deadly-delhi-riots-have-foreign-investors-rethinking-about-indias-attractiveness/375892/

Copland, Ian. 2014. "History in Flux: Indira Gandhi and the 'Great All-Party Campaign' for the Protection of the Cow, 1966–8." *Journal of Contemporary History* 49 (2): 410–439.

Das, Sharmila. 2017. "India is Second Fastest Growing Processed Meat and Poultry Market: Report." *RetailTech*, April 24. https://retail.economictimes.indiatimes.com/news/food-entertainment/food-services/india-is-second-fastest-growing-processed-meat-and-poultry-market-report/58346229

Desai, Radhika. 2016. "The Slow-Motion Counterrevolution: Developmental Contradictions and the Emergence of Neoliberalism." In *Social Movements and the State in India: Deepening Democracy?*, edited by Kenneth Bo Nielsen and Alf Gunvald Nilsen, 25–51. London: Palgrave Macmillan.

Dhara, Tushar. 2017. "India's Biggest Buff Meat Exporter Gets Govt Award for 'Outstanding Performance'." *News18*, June 14. https://www.news18.com/news/india/indias-biggest-buff-meat-exporter-gets-govt-award-for-outstanding-performance-1432427.html

Dhawan, Himanshi. 2015. "BJP Got Rs. 2.50 cr in Donations from Firms Exporting Buffalo Meat." *The Times of India*, December 16. https://timesofindia.indiatimes.com/india/BJP-got-Rs-2-50-cr-in-donations-from-firms-exporting-buffalo-meat/articleshow/50195323.cms

Dorin, Bruno and Frederic Landy. 2009. *Agriculture and Food in India: A Half-century Review from Independence to Globalization*. New Delhi: Manohar.

Drèze, Jean and Amartya Sen. 2013. *An Uncertain Glory: India and Its Contradictions*. Princeton: Princeton University Press.

Eakin, Emily. 2002. "Holy Cow a Myth? An Indian Finds the Kick is Real." *The New York Times,* August 17. https://www.nytimes.com/2002/08/17/books/holy-cow-a-myth-an-indian-finds-the-kick-is-real.html.

Export Genius. 2017. "Top Beef Exporters in India: Report on Beef and Other Meat Exporters." *Export Genius Blog.* https://www.exportgenius.in/blog/top-beef-exporters-in-india-report-on-beef-and-other-meat-exporters-22.php

Freitag, Sandria B. 1980. "Sacred Symbol as Mobilizing Ideology: The North Indian Search for a 'Hindu' Community." *Comparative Studies in Society and History* 22 (4): 597–625.

Government of India. 2018. *Agriculture Export Policy*. New Delhi.

Gramsci, Antonio. 1998. *Selections from the Prison Notebooks*. London: Lawrence & Wishart.

Hall, Stuart. 2011. "The Neo-Liberal Revolution." *Cultural Studies* 25 (6): 705–728. doi: 10.1080/09502386.2011.619886

Hardy, Kathryn C. 2019. "Provinzialising the Cow: Buffalo-Human Relationships." *South Asia* 42 (6): 1156–1172.

Ilaiah Shepherd, Kancha. 2019. "Freedom to Eat." *Caravan Magazine*, November 01. https://caravanmagazine.in/reportage/fight-beef-democratic-right.

Jaffrelot, Cristophe. 2019. "A *De Facto* Ethnic Democracy? Obliterating and Targeting the Other, Hindu Vigilantes, and the Ethno-State." In *Majoritarian State: How Hindu Nationalism is Changing India,* edited by Angana P. Chatterji, Thomas Blom Hansen and Christophe Jaffrelot. Oxford: Oxford University Press, 41–67 .

Jakobsen, Jostein. 2020. "The Maize Frontier in Rural South India: Exploring the Everyday Dynamics of the Contemporary Food Regime." *Journal of Agrarian Change* 20 (1): 137–162.

Jakobsen, Jostein and Arve Hansen. 2020. "Geographies of Meatification: An Emerging Asian Meat Complex." *Globalizations* 17 (1): 93–109. DOI: 10.1080/14747731.2019.1614723

James, Nandana. 2018. "Buffalo Meat Exports Take A Hiding Without Policy Support, Need Hand-Holding by Government." *The Hindu Business Line*, December 07. https://www.thehindubusinessline.com/economy/agri-business/10-billion-potential-of-buffalo-exports-will-be-affected-if-govt-doesnt-hand-hold-on-policy-side/article25691779.ece

Jena, Pragyansini. 2019. "India's Agricultural Exports Climb to Record High." *Medium.com*, February 25. https://medium.com/@pragyansini.dairykart/indias-agricultural-exports-climb-to-record-high-b6c196525a39.

Jha, Dwijendra Narayan. 2002. *The Myth of the Holy Cow*. London: Verso.

Kanungo, Pralay. 2019. "Sangh and Sarkar: The RSS Power Centre Shifts from Nagpur to New Delhi." In *Majoritarian State: How Hindu Nationalism is Changing India*, edited by Angana P. Chatterji, Thomas Blom Hansen and Christophe Jaffrelot. Oxford: Oxford University Press, 133–149 .

Khan, Akram A., and Farhad Shirani Bidabadi. 2004. "Livestock Revolution in India: Its Impact and Policy Response." *South Asia Research* 24 (2): 99–122. https://doi.org/10.1177/0262728004047907

KNN India. 2020. "IIA Invites Brazil to be Country Partner for 'India Food Expo 2020'." *KNN India*, January 25. https://knnindia.co.in/news/newsdetails/global/iia-invites-brazil-to-be-country-partner-for-india-food-expo-2020

Kohli, Atul. 2012. *Poverty Amid Plenty in the New India*. Cambridge; New York: Cambridge University Press.

Kumar, Roshan. 2014. "Modi Targets 'Pink Revolution'." *The Telegraph*, April 03. https://www.telegraphindia.com/india/modi-targets-pink-revolution/cid/191376

Landes, Maurice, Alex Melton, and Seanicaa Edwards. 2016. "From Where the Buffalo Roam: India's Beef Exports." United States Department of Agriculture. https://www.ers.usda.gov/publications/pub-details/?pubid=37673

Manor, James. 2019. "Can Modi and the BJP Achieve and Sustain Hegemony?" In *Majoritarian State: How Hindu Nationalism is Changing India*, edited by Chatterji, Angana P., Thomas Blom Hansen and Christophe Jaffrelot. Oxford: Oxford University Press, 133–149.

Mathew, Liz. 2017. "China Finally Agrees to Import Buffalo Meat from India." *The Indian Express*, January 16. https://indianexpress.com/article/business/business-others/china-finally-agrees-to-import-buffalo-meat-from-india-4476301/

Moudgil, Manu. 2017. "UP's Slaughterhouse Crackdown: Butchers, Farmers, Traders Hit, Big Businesses Gain." *Indiaspend*, July 15. https://archive.indiaspen

d.com/cover-story/ups-slaughterhouse-crackdown-butchers-farmers-traders-hit-b
ig-businesses-gain-92135

Narayanan, Yamini. 2019. "Jugaad and Informality as Drivers of India's Cow
Slaughter Economy." *Environment and Planning A: Economy and Space* 51 (7):
1516–1535.

Natrajan, Balmurli, and Suraj Jacob. 2018. "'Provincialising' Vegetarianism: Putting
Indian Food Habits in Their Place." *Economic and Political Weekly* 53 (9):
54–64.

Nilsen, Alf Gunvald and Kenneth Bo Nielsen. 2016. "Social Movements, State
Formation and Democracy in India: An Introduction." In *Social Movements and
the State in India: Deepening Democracy?*, edited by Kenneth Bo Nielsen and Alf
Gunvald Nilsen, 1–23. London: Palgrave Macmillan.

Nilsen, Alf Gunvald, Kenneth Bo Nielsen and Anand Vaidya. 2022. "Theorizing
Law, Social Movements and State Formation in India." *Comparative Studies of
South Asia, Africa and the Middle East.*

Pal, Sumedha. 2018. "PMO Gives Go-Ahead to Anti-Farmer Agriculture Export
Policy." *News Click*, October 05. https://www.newsclick.in/pmo-gives-go-ahead-a
nti-farmer-agriculture-export-policy

Palshikar, Suhas. 2019. "Toward Hegemony: The BJP beyond Electoral Dominance."
In *Majoritarian State: How Hindu Nationalism is Changing India,* edited by
Angana P. Chatterji, Thomas Blom Hansen and Christophe Jaffrelot, 101–116.
Oxford: Oxford University Press.

Parija, Pratik. 2019. "China's Crackdown on Illegal Meat Puts India's \$2-bn Trade at
Risk." *Business Standard*, December 09. https://www.business-standard.com/articl
e/economy-policy/china-s-crackdown-on-illegal-meat-puts-india-s-2-bn-trade-at-ri
sk-119120900078_1.html

Parija, Pratik and Shruti Srivastava. 2020. "Top Buffalo Meat Shipper India Keen to
Fill Global Shortage." *Bloomberg Quint*, May 08. https://www.bloombergquint.
com/global-economics/top-buffalo-meat-shipper-india-keen-to-fill-global-shortage

Parikh, Aparna and Clara Miller. 2019. "Holy Cow! Beef Ban, Political Technologies,
and Brahmanical Supremacy in Modi's India." *ACME: An International Journal
for Critical Geographies* 18 (4): 835–874. https://acme-journal.org/index.php/
acme/article/view/1758.

Patel, Raj. 2018. "Islamophobia Gastronomica – On the Food Police, Rural Populism
and Killing." *OpenIndia*, February 26. https://www.opendemocracy.net/openIndia/
raj-patel/islamophobia-gastronomica-on-food-police-rural-populism-and-killing

Poulantzas, Nicos. 1978. *State, Power, Socialism.* London: New Left Review
Editions.

Press Trust of India. 2018. "Beef Export Flourishing under PM Modi's Regime."
Deccan Herald, March 31. https://www.deccanherald.com/content/667682/beef-
export-flourishing-pm-modis.html

Ramdas, Sagari R. 2017a. "The Beef Ban Effect: Stray Cattle, Broken Markets
and Boom Time for Buffaloes." *The Wire*, April 26. https://thewire.in/politics/
beef-ban-cattle-market

Ramdas, Sagari R. 2017b. "The Sordid Truth About the BJP's Drive Against Meat in UP." *The Wire*, April 08. https://thewire.in/politics/up-illegal-meat-bjp

Scholten, Bruce A. 2010. *India's White Revolution: Operation Flood, Food Aid and Development*. London: IB Tauris.

Sharma, Madhur. 2019. "Modi Slammed UPA for Subsidising Slaughterhouses, But His Govt Gave Them 33% More Money." *The Print*, December 05. https://theprin t.in/india/governance/modi-slammed-upa-for-subsidising-slaughterhouses-but-his -govt-gave-them-33-more-money/329800/

Staples, James. 2019. "Blurring Bovine Boundaries: Cow Politics and the Everyday in South India." *South Asia: Journal of South Asian Studies* 42 (6): 1125–1140.

USDA. 2014. "India's Agricultural Exports Climb to Record High." https://www.fas .usda.gov/data/india-s-agricultural-exports-climb-record-high

USDA. 2019. "India's Food Processing Sector: A Sunrise Sector." https://apps.fas .usda.gov/newgainapi/api/report/downloadreportbyfilename?filename=Food%20P rocessing%20Ingredients_New%20Delhi_India_5-7-2019.pdf

Weis, Tony. 2013. *The Ecological Hoofprint: The Global Burden of Industrial Livestock*. New York and London: Zed Books.

Chapter 8

Reconnecting Life and Death in the British Alternative Halal Meat Movement

Hibba Mazhary

INTRODUCTION AND BACKGROUND

Halal meat is a particularly valuable sector to explore within the growing global meat industry as it constitutes an increasing share of worldwide meat production. The global halal meat market is worth $150 billion a year and is fast growing (Bergeaud-Blackler 2007). The UK presents an important site of halal consumption, where British Muslims consume 20 percent of the country's lamb despite constituting less than 5 percent of the population (EBLEX 2013). They are also reported to eat more meat overall per capita than the national average (Stannard and Clarke 2020). On the production side, 3 percent of cattle, 22 percent of chickens, and 71 percent of sheep killed in the UK are slaughtered using a halal method (including stun and non-stun) (Food Standards Agency 2019).

Halal slaughter in Britain was initially characterized by very informal networks of slaughter; early Muslim settlers in Britain from the mid-twentieth century onward would buy livestock from farms and slaughter them personally (Lever 2018). The first halal certification body in the UK, the Halal Food Authority (HFA), which accepts preslaughter stunning, emerged in 1994, carrying out inspections of slaughterhouses and granting licenses (Lever 2018). This was followed by the more orthodox Halal Monitoring Committee (HMC) in 2003, who advocated for non-stun slaughter and stressed the religiously dubious nature of stunned meat (Lever 2018). Since then, there has been a proliferation of other agencies and labels, and there is currently no national standard for halal meat in the UK; Bergeaud-Blackler (2015, 122) suggests that states are unwilling to set up these standards as they do not want to embody "this ultimate role of controller" concerning a religious issue.

"Halal" refers to what is permissible under Islamic law, but more specifically halal slaughter involves a single incision using a sharp knife across the animal's throat, severing the carotid arteries, esophagus, and trachea without separating the head from the body (Masri 1989). This must be carried out while uttering a specific prayer and blood must be drained from the animal. At the intersection of food, faith, and ethics, halal meat is an enduring site of public scrutiny and contestation. The topic of halal draws attention to the everyday encounter between religion and secular modernity; conflicts regarding secularization, animal rights, and morality are increasingly being "waged on the terrain of beef, chicken, lamb and veal" (Mukherjee 2014, 25). Halal meat controversies are frequent in the UK, such as the phenomenon of "halal hysteria" in 2014, where fast-food chains such as PizzaExpress were accused of secretly selling halal meat, prompting a media investigation into different supermarkets and chains (Sommers 2014). Around this time there was also a petition initiated by the British Veterinary Association calling for an end to non-stun slaughter, leading to a parliamentary debate on the subject (Downing 2015).

The main contention in these controversies is whether halal meat is obtained through stun or non-stun slaughter (Lever et al. 2010); stunning, when an animal is rendered unconscious before slaughter (by various methods), is generally perceived to be more humane than its non-stun counterpart. Non-stun slaughter is currently banned in a number of European countries including Denmark, Sweden, and Iceland (Grumett 2015) and has similarly been prohibited in Norway (Bjørkdahl and Syse, this volume). More recently, several regions of Belgium have introduced laws for mandatory pre-stunning (BBC 2020). Religious ritual slaughter is exempted from the UK's non-stun slaughter ban, as seen in the 1974 Slaughterhouse Act (Bergeaud-Blackler 2015) and the 1995 Welfare of Animals (Slaughter or Killing) Regulations (Barclay 2011), dating back to the 1933 Slaughter of Animals Act (Downing 2015). Although the majority of halal meat is stunned before slaughter—84 percent of poultry, 75 percent of cattle, and 63 percent of sheep (Food Standards Agency 2015)—it is the smaller non-stun proportion that provokes much debate. The Farm Animal Welfare Council (2003, 36) advised the British government to repeal the exemption, arguing that in non-stun slaughter the necessary conditions of "pre-slaughter handling facilities that minimise stress and induction to a period of unconsciousness without distress" are not satisfactorily met. Faith communities have however responded to this by arguing that non-stun slaughter, if carried out correctly, is more humane (Lever 2018).

This study examines how such debates are reflected in the alternative British halal meat movement. While dominant meat cultures in high-income countries are often characterized by increasing intensification and the distancing of consumers from the sites of meat production (Serpell 1986), countercultures have also emerged in an attempt to resist and reverse such processes. This chapter examines the alternative halal meat movement, as such a countercultural movement, one that seeks to resist growth and rising consumption and to reconnect consumers with spaces of food production. Having gained popularity in the past decade, this movement is character- ized by higher-welfare standards, free-range and/or organic certification, and small-scale operations, although it still remains a niche movement. Offering a fresh perspective on explorations of alternative food networks (AFNs), which are often white, middle-class spaces, this study focuses on an ethnically diverse and financially disadvantaged religious minority community (Muslim Council of Britain 2015).

This chapter draws upon fieldwork in 2015 on three different farms (Honest Produce, the Organic Halal Company [OHC], and Halal Pastures) prominent in the alternative industry.[1] Methods used include 6 in-depth semi-structured interviews with halal farmers and environmental campaigners, short group interviews with a total of 20 customers from 1 alternative halal farm, 2 days of participant observation at one farm's open event, and textual and visual analysis of literature distributed by the farms. The farms were selected due to their free-range and/or organic standards and their marketing of "ethical" and "higher-welfare" meat. Interviews were transcribed and then analyzed using inductive codes emerging from the data. All participant and company names used throughout are pseudonyms. After a review of halal consumption in the geographical and wider literature, this chapter explores how consumers seek to reconnect with spaces of halal meat production as part of this coun- tercultural alternative movement. As this often also involves a reconnection with animal death, the chapter subsequently focuses on spaces and practices of killing. The final section examines the entanglement of sacred and secular motivations of producers and consumers for this reconnection.

SITUATING HALAL CONSUMPTION

Halal meat consumption has been widely explored within anthropology (Bergeaud-Blackler 2007, 2015; Fischer 2011), as well as in human geog- raphy (Isakjee and Carroll 2019; Lever 2018, 2020; Miele 2013, 2016). However, this work has largely focused on the conventional halal meat indus- try while its alternative counterpart has been relatively neglected by popular media and academic discourse, with the exception of Istasse's (2015) study on the Dutch "Green Halal" movement and Robinson's (2014) on the Taqwa Muslim food cooperative in the United States. This chapter draws upon the geographies of religion, food, and animals to frame the topic of halal meat.

Discussions of ethical consumerism within food geographies are linked with discussions of animal death within animal geographies, as well as with questions in geographies of religion and ethics about the interface between the sacred and the secular. Placing halal meat as a topic of geographical and political ecological enquiry draws attention to how space is negotiated in sites of slaughter and instilled with sacred meaning and to how halal consumption is inscribed upon different scales, most significantly on the scale of the body (Isakjee and Carroll 2019).

Within the geographies of food literature, Cook et al. (2004) draw upon Harvey's (1990) call to de-fetishize commodities and to make connections between producers and consumers by following the routes of "things," a journey that reveals material and human relationships and power relations. Examples of studies following supply chains include Watts's (2004) work on hogs, and Hughes's (2000) study on cut flowers. Scholars have observed that food systems in affluent societies are characterized by consumers' disconnection from spheres of production, involving both a "cartographical and cognitive" distance (Eden et al. 2008, 1045), where consumers are increasingly alienated and deskilled regarding food production (Kneen 1993).

This consumer disconnection is particularly endemic to meat production. For example, Serpell (1986) argues that the concealment of abattoirs in remote rural locations acts as a "distancing device" from animal death. Close encounters with animal death, such as through urban slaughter (Blecha and Davis 2014), therefore often provoke visceral reactions. Fitzgerald (2010) traces a "social history of the slaughterhouse," beginning in the eighteenth century where animal slaughter moved away from city centers out of public view as it was seen to contravene ideals of hygiene and propriety (Philo 1998; Burt 2006). This marked the beginning of a formalization and centralization of slaughter. As well as physical concealment, consumers are detached from animals killed for food through a set of "broader tacit embodied practices" (Evans and Miele 2012, 6) such as de-animalized presentation of meat in shops (Herzog 2010; Syse and Bjørkdahl 2021) and euphemistic vocabulary (Serpell 1986). Stewart and Cole (2009) observe how children's media and toys obfuscate the act of killing animals for food, and Bekoff (2002) similarly points out that many children do not reconcile the hamburgers and bacon sandwiches that they consume with the image of the cows and pigs that must die to create their meal (Volden and Wethal, this volume).

Distancing of animal death is not uniform and is often more pronounced in high-income countries. For example, Kunst and Palacios Haugestad's (2018, 356) psychological study that randomly showed consumers in the United States and Ecuador a pork roast with the head present or absent found that U.S. consumers, who were "less exposed to unprocessed meat on a daily basis," were more disturbed by the intact head. Moreover, Parry and Potts

(2010) observe the emerging Western countertrend of the "New Carnivore" movement, which includes chefs killing animals on TV and journalists like Michael Pollan (2006) trying to reinsert animals and slaughter into meat consumption, "not as a deterrent to flesh consumption, but as an incentive" (Parry and Potts 2010, 382). This "traditional cruelty" (Parry 2009) evokes "meat nostalgia" (Syse 2017) for past animal rearing practices. This illustrates the complex and nonlinear nature of distancing from animal death. Halal slaughter is a generative angle from which to explore this distancing as it represents one of the few instances where "slaughter comes into view" in the secular West (Lever 2018, 889).

Authors in food geography have also devoted much attention to efforts to reconnect with food production and resist changing food cultures, such as locavorism, vegetarianism, and organic farming (Bell and Valentine 1997; Guthman 2004), focusing on AFNs. AFNs "reconvene trust between food producers and consumers" and "redistribute value . . . against the logic of bulk commodity production" (Whatmore et al. 2003, 389) and consist of more localized and traceable food systems (Goodman et al. 2010). Major themes in the AFN literature include trust (Whatmore et al. 2003) and anxiety (Guthman 2009). One concern voiced in AFN research is that such networks fail to engage a diverse range of consumers (Guthman 2011). Abrahams (2008) highlights the need for AFN coordinators to think beyond the archetypal profile of consumers as white, middle-class professionals (Goodman and Goodman 2008). Ramirez (2014, 749) similarly aims to "de-center the white actor as the presumed practitioner of community food work" by bringing marginalized communities to the forefront in decision-making in community food projects. Work in political ecology has likewise acknowledged that alternative food spaces are often racially homogenous (Hayes-Conroy and Hayes-Conroy 2013). Through its focus on the ethical halal movement, this chapter contributes to this "de-centering" by expanding the set of actors that are perceived to occupy AFN spaces. Halal meat consumers also offer interesting insights due to their navigation of multiple complementary or conflicting ethical codes, both sacred and secular, and how they emphasize spiritual motivations to reconnect with food production.

Animal death for the sake of food is justified by a "logic of sacrifice," in which humans have the exclusive capacity to be "murdered" whereas animals cannot be "murdered" and are merely "killable." The death of animals is instead given the label "sacrifice," where animals "can be killed and thus ingested symbolically and materially" (Haraway 2008, 78–79). Haraway makes a brief reference to "secular and religious humanism" upholding this notion of sacrifice, yet there is scope for further examining how religious ideology intersects with this "logic of sacrifice." The topic of halal is a suitable lens to consider this because it encompasses animal death and religious motivation. Halal slaughter, with its set rituals, also presents a break from the process of decline in ritualization surrounding animal slaughter in the last century (Bjørkdahl and Syse, this volume). Ritualized animal slaughter for food therefore provides a fertile site of crossover between the sacred and the secular.

Halal slaughter is located at the intersection of two significant cultural shifts, with the rise of industrialization of food production and countermovements, on the one hand, and the increasingly blurry lines between the sacred and the secular, on the other. In the past few decades, religion has become a popular subject of social and cultural geography research (Kong 2010). Studies on Islam and Muslims in particular have emerged in geography, with scholarship being attentive to topics of faith and gender in transnational contexts (Dwyer 2000; Hopkins 2007). Scholars of religious geographies have been particularly concerned with the interface between the sacred and the secular. The secular is becoming "less obviously secular" (Heelas 1998, 3), and there is increasingly an overlap between the religious and nonreligious (Ivakhiv 2003, 2006; Maddrell 2009). For instance, Bartkowski and Swearingen (1997) draw attention to how environmentalist movements can become imbued with religious ideas of purity and justice. The merging of the religious and the secular has also been explored in veiling practices of Turkish Muslim women (Gökarıksel 2009) and in the UK's Scout Movement (Mills 2012). Ritual slaughter and meat consumption exemplify how the sacred is branching out into "unofficially sacred" spaces (Kong 2001) such as abattoirs, butchers, and supermarkets. Similarly, Mukherjee (2014) points to how mainstream fast-food corporations such as McDonald's and Kentucky Fried Chicken are beginning to offer halal-certified products, with gastronomy increasingly becoming a site of sacred/secular conflict. This interface between the sacred and the secular is also highlighted by Fischer (2011, 69), who observes that "modern forms of halal consumption . . . challenge and reconfigure what are often considered separate secular realms of state, government, and politics, on the one hand, and the intimacy of religious life and expression, on the other." This chapter explores how the "unofficially sacred" spaces of the farm and the slaughterhouse become imbued with religious meaning, first examining spaces of reconnection with food production, before turning to reconnection with animal death and finally to sacred and secular motivations for this reconnection.

SPACES OF RECONNECTION: ANIMAL LIVES

I begin by focusing on the ways in which consumers in the alternative British halal meat movement seek to reconnect with spaces of food production.

These encounters are modulated through the interplay of (mis)trust, anxiety, hope, and reassurance. The mainstream halal certification market is characterized by prevalent distrust and the continued "demand for further guarantees" (Bergeaud-Blackler 2015, 107). Almas (1989) discusses how, in an individualistic risk society, anxiety regarding food is mostly directed at the level of the individual consumer, who must take responsibility for their food choices. Risk is highly embedded in food, with Stassart and Whatmore (2003, 450) arguing that risk in food is both a property of consumer alienation from production and the "metabolic intimacies between human and nonhuman bodies" when we ingest food. Consequently, consumers are cautious to put their trust in food producers. Many of the customers interviewed at the Honest Produce open day were disillusioned with the conventional halal meat industry and expressed doubt regarding its integrity, acted as an impetus to seek alternatives:

"The current British halal industry is questionable and there is a lack of awareness about animal welfare." (Customer 7)

"The question of where the animal came from, how it lived, how it was killed, well, there's a big question mark on that question." (Customer 13)

Stakeholders in the mainstream halal industry appear keen to emphasize the ostensible traceability of their system, with the HFA, one of the two main British halal certification agencies, assuring consumers in a promotional booklet that "all meat we certify is under strict inspection and monitoring," and that "we take animal welfare very seriously." Despite this, customers at Honest Produce seemed disenchanted with this and wanted more tangible evidence of care of animals. Similarly, the owners of Halal Pastures were disillusioned with the lack of traceability in the mainstream halal sphere and stated this dissatisfaction prompted them to initially set up their business in alternative halal farming. This disillusionment with the mainstream industry likewise acted as an impetus for consumers to seek alternatives.

In response to this heightened anxiety and mistrust regarding animal welfare standards of mainstream halal meat, the pioneers of the alternative halal movement attempt to establish trust and reassure customers of their commitment to ethical living conditions. They do this by stressing their distinctiveness from conventional halal food producers.

This emphasis on difference is conveyed by the signage at the Honest Produce open day (figure 8.1). Below a list of meal choices is a circled Arabic phrase reading *Halalan tayyiban*, which is a conscious redesign of the circular Arabic "halal" symbol on the doors of mainstream halal food establishments such as fast-food outlets. The nod toward mainstream halal is

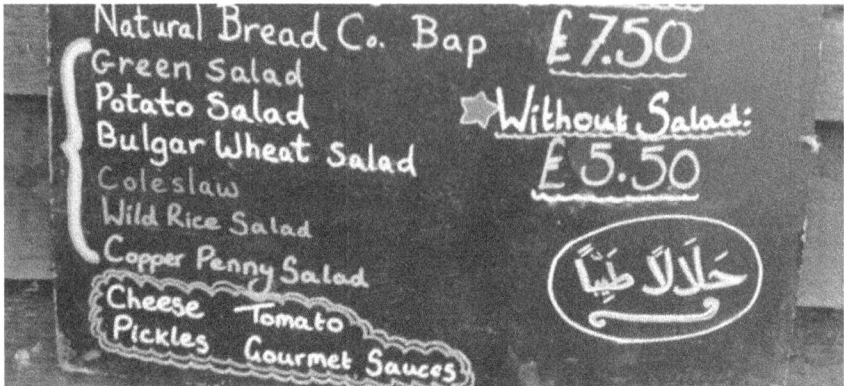

Figure 8.1   Farm Café Sign Advertising Burgers at an Honest Produce Open Day.

accompanied by the extra guarantee of *tayyib*, which demonstrates how the organization actively seeks to stress its uniqueness and its perceived superiority in terms of wholesome and trustworthy food production. *Tayyib* is an Islamic concept translating to lawful and good, and is taken by members of the alternative halal movement to mean wholesome food produced in sustainable and high-welfare conditions. The co-owner of Halal Pastures expressed her understanding of the term:

> *Tayyib* encompasses how the animal is treated and raised. It's the respect towards the animal, it's the rights of the animal. I have a responsibility to the creation of God. It's very similar to the term "organic" and the guidelines put down. You can't have halal without *tayyib*.

Food producers in the alternative halal meat sector also establish their difference by drawing upon the fears that consumers have about the mainstream industry. Blay-Palmer and Donald (2008) argue that fear is a defining element of AFNs; this is created and codified in advertising and literature in the alternative network by using fear-based descriptors. Figure 8.2 shows a poster that customers perused while queuing for the barbecue lunch provided at the Honest Produce open day. The poster employs numerous fear-based descriptors in relation to mainstream halal food production, referring to the existence of "metallic iron," "bleach," and "a toxic cocktail of . . . chemicals." This creation of unease is, however, offset by hope created in the form of positive assurances that the lunch customers are about to consume is "ethically reared" and "quality, natural, healthy food." This poster therefore exemplifies the common interplay of fear and hope in the communication between food producers and consumers in AFNs (Blay-Palmer and Donald 2008).

Cheaper burgers use:

- CHEAP FLOUR in the buns, with all the bran and germ removed... along with 70 percent of the nutrients.
- A TOXIC COCKTAIL of around 12 different chemicals under the name of "flour improves"
- METALLIC IRON (which is not digestible)
- BLEACH to make it nice and white.

- CHEAP CUTS OF MEAT, with very little "real" meat but plenty of connective tissues, blood vessels, peripheral nerves, adipose tissue, cartilage and bone.
- "OTHER MEATS" in a beef or lamb burger. Studies showed up to 29 percent horse or pork in some beef burgers (including halal ones!).
- A LOT OF WATER...on average 49 percent! Little of this is from the meat and is actually added (coated in fat molecules).
- Cheap FILLERS soy, rusk and whatever else they can get away with.

Our produce is ethically reared and produced using the finest ingredients. Along with fresh buns from the 'Natural Bread Company' and the healthy home-made salads we are providing you with quality natural healthy food.

We admit we cannot compete on price. Would you really expect us to try?

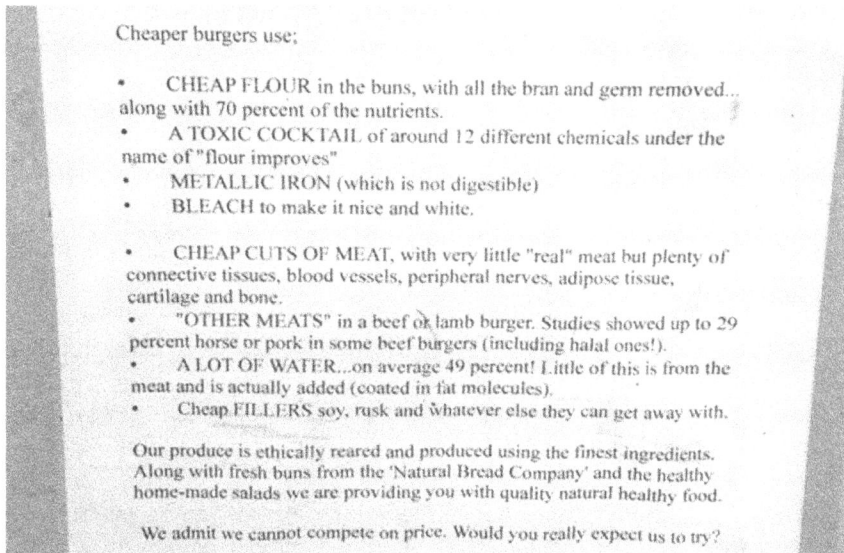

Figure 8.2   Poster at Honest Produce Open Day Café.

Traceability and visibility also help to create hope and assuage anxiety for consumers when they are able to directly reconnect with the spaces of rearing and killing of the animals they eat. Customers at the Honest Produce open day were particularly interested in the spaces of animal rearing, and throughout the tour they were able to inspect the chicken enclosures and paddocks, as well as the hills where the lambs grazed. They posed detailed questions such as what method was used to thatch the farmhouse, how the compostable toilets worked, as well as what the animals ate and where they roamed. This proximity builds consumer trust and erodes demand for external certification. Honest Produce and the OHC chose not to be certified by the UK's two main halal certifying bodies (HMC and HFA). Instead, they relied on personal contact to establish relations of trust, as conveyed by the statement on Honest Produce's website that "our guarantee is a very personal one which our customers are educated enough to appreciate through their direct contact with us." This echoes Eden et al.'s (2008, 1050) description of the concept of "face work," where connecting with individuals in sites of food production is "necessary to re-embed faceless systems, such as food production, and anchor trust."

Reconnection with spaces of halal meat production was therefore prompted by mistrust of the mainstream industry. Food producers within the alternative halal movement employed "techniques of visibility" (Miele 2011, 2079) and harnessed entangled emotions of hope and anxiety to communicate their standards of animal welfare and their dissimilarity from the conventional halal market. This emphasis on traceability reassured their customers, who were drawn to the opportunity of accessing detailed information about the spaces of rearing of the animals they consumed.

SPACES OF KILLING: ANIMAL DEATH

A significant part of reconnection with spaces of food production is reconnection with spaces of animal death. This section explores how animals were killed in the alternative halal meat farms and what meanings were attached to these moments of slaughter. First, death was regarded as a disproportionate fixation by pioneers of the alternative halal movement. The owners of Honest Produce pointed to a preoccupation with death in the halal meat industry. Discussions in media and policy spheres regarding the sector are usually framed by the idea of death (Frazer 2015; Harvey 2010), centering on how, when, and at whose hands the animal dies. Alternative farm proprietors contended that there should equally be a focus on spaces of living and rearing, as these constitute a more significant portion of the animals' existence.

Animals in this movement were slaughtered in close proximity to their place of rearing, as well as in the vicinity of the living spaces of their human killers, arguably making the act of killing more immediate. The farms studied placed an emphasis upon localized networks of slaughter. Honest Produce slaughtered their sheep and cattle in an abattoir approximately seven kilometers away, and all three establishments slaughtered their chickens onsite. Owners of the farms take pride in this proximity; one of the proprietors of Halal Pastures stated that

> we worked hard to get our own abattoir, years and years of struggle, and now we don't have to drive four to five hours anymore to transport our chickens, it's just a hundred metres away. We fought hard for it and, you know, it was worth it.

This is in contrast with the conventional meat industry where slaughterhouses are in isolated, concealed locations (Serpell 1986) and where the space of the isolated abattoir is a material manifestation of the emotional and physical distance humans try to create between themselves and animals (Smith 2002). Customers of Halal Pastures and the OHC were invited to visit the farms and view the abattoirs in which slaughter takes place. This is in contrast to the trend of "distancing" sites of killing from the consumer, and thus perhaps necessitates more of a confrontation with the "moral difficulties associated with using and killing animals" (Blecha and Davis 2014, 69) than in the mainstream halal meat industry, challenging "unreflective meat-eating"

(Syse 2017). Gillespie (2011) however takes issue with the idea of "humane" slaughter in small-scale facilities by arguing that although it may involve better animal welfare, it still fails to stop slaughter in itself.

The proximity of the abattoirs from the farms represents an uncommon (in the highly industrialized UK context) closeness to the act of killing animals for food. Proximity to the spaces of killing exposed both slaughterers and consumers to the highly emotional, affective dimension of the slaughter process. The farmers in the alternative halal industry made emotional connections with their animals, interacting with them on a close spatial and temporal scale (Riley 2011), and it was a painful act to end their lives, particularly as they personally hand-slaughtered them. The co-owner of Halal Pastures gave affectionate individualized descriptions of her chickens where some "are naughty and just don't want to go to bed," demonstrating her level of attachment. Haraway (2008) stresses the importance of "shar[ing] suffering" with animals in violent contexts as it can be a "productive ethical practice" (Green and Ginn 2014, 167) to reflect more deeply on animal suffering. Producers in the alternative halal industry "share suffering" and vulnerability with their animals through the emotional trauma of the killing process. One slaughterperson expressed their distaste for slaughter by stating, "It's horrible. I don't like doing it" (OHC, former owner). Others described their grief as they formed connections with the animals, only to have to slaughter them later. The owners of Honest Produce related how the goats on their farm originally intended for slaughter were "on hold for now" as their two youngest children had formed a bond with the animals. This reflects the often complex nature of farmer/livestock relations (Riley 2011; Wilkie 2005) where farmers interact with the animals regularly and build attachments, and must also send them to slaughter (Holloway 2001), yet weep over their dead bodies in times of mass culling (Convery et al. 2005). The owner of Halal Pastures poignantly described how she was unable to help her husband kill goats in the abattoir or even consume goat meat after an incident when "I went to help my husband with the slaughter and the goat was nibbling on my fingers." This shows that embodied practices of care can emerge in spaces of killing, where "everyday gestures of love, care and remorse . . . open up the possibility of ethical behaviour in the interstices of violence" (Govindrajan 2018, 31).

The vulnerability of slaughterers in the alternative halal movement was enhanced by the small-scale nature of the operation and the emotional bonds they have formed with the animals. This is in contrast with the techno-mediation and detachment in large abattoirs; Higgin et al. (2011, 182) observe in their visit to a large halal chicken abattoir that the chickens' "only direct contact with humans occurs . . . when they are removed from their crates and unceremoniously hung upside down. . . . Everything else is . . . detached." The fact that the animals are hand-slaughtered on a small, intimate scale in the alternative halal movement allows for less detachment from the act of killing and more ethical and emotional vulnerability reported by the slaughterers. However, those writing from Critical Animal Studies perspectives stress that this vulnerability does not make such acts ethically neutral; Holmberg (2011, 159) argues that "sharing suffering" is not sufficient if it does not also include a commitment to the "obligation to end suffering." Moreover, while this chapter has largely discussed the vulnerability of slaughterers in these small-scale, low-output spaces, it is important not to overlook the vulnerability (physical and financial as well as psychological) of those working in industrial abattoirs with high-speed assembly lines and sizeable productivity quotas, who face risks of injury, psychological distress, and job precarity (Purcell 2011).

Figures in the alternative halal meat industry invoked religious meaning in their act of killing to seek protection from their vulnerability during the slaughter process:

> The slaughter-person is also protecting themselves from the fact that they are taking a life. I do it in the name of God, so I am protecting myself from the fact that I am taking a life. (OHC former owner)

When asked what halal slaughter meant to them, many cited the belief of a higher purpose for the slaughter, and therefore the need to dedicate the killing to God, which sanctified and purified the act:

> When you take a life, whether it's a grain or a harvest or a chicken, you have to dedicate it to something. (OHC former owner)

People therefore imbued acts of animal slaughter with religious meaning as a means of providing protection from the vulnerability of the act of killing. In some ways this resonates with Haraway's (2008) argument that a "logic of sacrifice" is created to justify animal death. Similarly, Herzog (2010) emphasizes the guilt that is continually present with the act of eating animals and argues that rituals are created in order to fulfill the need to "atone" for the act, as described by Bjørkdahl and Syse in this volume. Serpell (1986, 207) likewise highlights this tendency in ancient societies, where ritual sacrifice diverted blame for animal killing, since death "was a sacred duty and therefore forgivable." Animals within the alternative British halal meat industry were killed in a physically close, tangible, and religiously imbued manner. The immediacy of the death, the close bodily and temporal interaction with the animals, and the sacred meaning attached to the act therefore seemed to create a more reflective and vulnerable slaughterer.

THE SACRED AND THE SECULAR

Motivations for this reconnection with spaces of food production and animal death are complex and refracted through multiple sacred and secular value systems. This section explores how these intersections between the sacred and the secular in the British alternative halal movement become inscribed on certain significant scales, especially the body, the slaughterhouse, and the food network. Food is a particularly important domain from which to explore religion and morality because food "often invokes anxieties about what is being ingested and what moral boundaries are being crossed" (Lever 2018, 890) and illustrates how the boundary between the sacred and the secular is highly embodied (Gökarıksel 2009).

First, at the scale of the body, anxiety over food production that is prevalent in numerous secular AFNs such as organic agriculture (Guthman 2009) is augmented in halal consumption by religious concerns. These concerns stem from faith-based notions that physical food, what is consumed and what is not consumed, has a lasting spiritual impact. Sinan, an employee of a Muslim environmental campaigning organization, stated that

> low quality food makes a massive difference to what's going to be in our bodies, both spiritually and physically.

Similarly, one Honest Produce customer, when asked why it was important to source free-range meat, answered, "Meat impacts our worship, and our spiritual wellbeing" (Customer 8). It is therefore evident that there is a spiritual significance attached to food as it becomes linked to the salvation of the soul (Van Waarden and van Dalen 2013). Therefore, the halal ethical movement is distinguished from the secular ethical due to religious preoccupations of spiritual contamination. However, it is increasingly difficult to distinguish religious foodways, where devotees pursue spiritual rewards from certain eating practices from nonreligiously motivated, or "quasi-religious," foodways. This blurring of the religious and the secular within the domain of food consumption has been widely discussed in anthropological food studies. Zeller (2014) provides an example of a quasi-religious foodway by analyzing the oral histories of vegetarians and locavores, and finds that the language used is overwhelmingly religious, with people describing their becoming vegetarian as a "conversion" and linking avoiding certain foods with cultivating a "healthy soul." According to Zeller (2014), associating diets with a wider spiritual significance is a way for adherents to alleviate their anxiety and disillusionment with the contemporary global food system. Such combinations of religious and nonreligious motivations for food "confound neat understandings of religion" (Finch 2014, xii).

Second, the space of the abattoir, an "unofficially sacred" space diverging from the traditionally sacred space of the church and the mosque (Kong 2001), becomes a site imbued with religious meaning in the alternative halal industry; it becomes a space in which religious differences over how an animal should be slaughtered are played out, showing how "what constitutes an acceptable kill" is refracted through a set of social, religious, and scientific norms (Higgin et al. 2011, 173). The use of stunning before slaughter is an issue that divided opinions among the ethical halal farmers (and indeed the global halal meat industry); the OHC employed stunning for all their animals, and Honest Produce only for their sheep. Halal Pastures avoided stunning completely, citing a desire to remain as faithful as possible to the original "God-revealed" practice of slaughter. There was also the concern that the stunning process would kill the animal before the neck cut, rendering the meat religiously impermissible to eat. Despite this divergence in opinions, representatives from all three farms stressed that the overemphasis on the last few seconds of the animal's life was misplaced, and that what was more important was how the animal was reared. One former owner of the OHC claimed that believing that "stunning has got to be the be-all and end-all" paralyzed debates about more pressing issues such as animal welfare in rearing. Through farmers and religious authorities engaging with debates about the religious permissibility of stunning, the space of the slaughterhouse becomes laden with religious meaning because close attention is paid to the nature of the rituals that take place in these sites.

Third, the scale of the AFN itself acts as a site for both alignment and conflict between the sacred and the secular. Proponents of the alternative halal movement actively sought to differentiate themselves from the mainstream halal industry, demonstrated by the fact that Honest Produce and the OHC chose not to obtain halal accreditation from the HMC or HFA, the UK's two main halal certifying bodies. This is due to an aversion to the animal welfare standards in HMC- and HFA-certified abattoirs. In fact, Dr. Ali from Honest Produce argued that, due to poor animal welfare, the mainstream halal industry was "not halal in the birth of the animal, not halal in the life, and not halal in the death." Similarly, Shezana from Halal Pastures described how, prior to establishing their own abattoir onsite, herself and her husband would use an HMC-certified abattoir for their animals. After driving four to five hours to this slaughterhouse, she recalled having to wait a further few hours to enter and perform the slaughter, causing the chickens to be distressed. She remembered feeling anxious on behalf of the chickens, who were "used to running around," and the frequent delays seemed to her to be evidence of a lack of "respect for the animal," contributing to her disillusionment with mainstream halal establishments. Proponents of the alternative halal movement seemed at times to identify more with secular organic standards than with fellow religious establishments. This is illustrated by the fact that Honest Produce's packaging for their chicken is labeled "free range" and omits the "halal" descriptor. In fact, Dr. Ali expressed the opinion that the religious factor for mainstream halal was essentially symbolic, and that the ritualistic Arabic words meaning "In the name of God, God is great" uttered at the time of slaughter were not sufficient to make the meat halal. He furthermore added,

> What distinguishes us is not religion alone. If you want a matrix on which to divide things, don't do it by religion, but by good practice and bad practice.

Despite this promotion of secular organic standards, the alternative halal movement was not completely accepted within that sphere. The OHC practiced stunning before slaughter for all of their animals, and highly valued their organic certification as an "auditable, legal entity" that gave concrete assurance of standards. Halal Pastures and Honest Produce were however unable to obtain organic certification for their meat as they practiced non-stun slaughter, which contravenes organic regulations. Therefore, despite, as Shezana from Halal Pastures claimed, going "above and beyond" the requirements for animal treatment in the organic certification guidelines (with their chickens being slaughtered at 84 days, beyond the minimum organic requirement of 81 days), Halal Pastures' produce could not be labeled "organic." For the same reason, Honest Produce's packaging for their un-stunned chicken is labeled "free range," as opposed to "organic." In the secularized realm of food, authority for quality standards is provided by formal certifications, whereas halal quality standards are determined by religious and scriptural authority (Van Waarden and van Dalen 2013). This demonstrates how moral guidelines set by religion can conflict with secular codes of morality codified in formal certifications such as organic.

Across each of the scales—the body, the slaughterhouse, and the AFN—it is evident that it is not so easy to separate out secular organic standards and religious motivations, as proponents saw the two as inextricably linked, highlighted by one farm owner defining the scriptural term *tayyib* as "how the animal is treated and raised." Shezana from Halal Pastures and Kate from the OHC gave similar opinions, arguing that Muslims should be at the forefront of the environmental movement by reconnecting with their faith. Dr. Ali from Honest Produce claimed that there was a disconnect between Islamic ideals and practice in the mainstream industry, where "people are chasing the profit-motive, rather than being motivated by the Prophet." Likewise, in Istasse's (2015) study on an ethical halal farm in Belgium, the owners attributed their high animal welfare standards to their interpretation of Islamic religious teachings, and the Taqwa Food Cooperative in Chicago was established as an attempt to bridge the disconnect between food production practices and

Islamic ideals of caring for animals (Robinson 2014). Thus, sacred and secular motivations are consistently entangled in such spaces of production and at the bodily scale.

CONCLUSIONS

This chapter has examined the alternative halal meat movement as a countercultural phenomenon attempting to resist dominant meat cultures and corresponding tendencies toward increasing consumption, intensification, and disconnection. Moments of reconnection were shaped by processes of building trust, quelling anxiety, and evoking mixed feelings of fear and hope in consumers. Access to information about the conditions in which their food was produced strengthened consumers' relations of trust with the producers and allowed for more informal networks of certification. Moreover, meat producers themselves were active in differentiating themselves from the conventional industrial halal standard through advertising and holding open days to allow customers to observe spaces of animal rearing and killing. This reconnection also involved encounters with animal death, where consumers were able to inspect spaces of killing, and where slaughterers experienced heightened vulnerability and sought divine protection through an intimate, small-scale slaughter process. Moreover, "unofficially sacred" spaces such as the farm and the abattoir were laden with religious meaning through the practices and beliefs of the slaughter-person.

The alternative halal meat movement demonstrated how complex assemblages were refracted through different ethics value systems. It also provided an interesting example of a movement at the intersection of multiple cultural changes: the growth of halal in Europe, the rise of AFNs, and the merging of the sacred and the secular. Religion was a meaningful motivator for ethical practice; all the pioneers of the alternative halal farms cited religious duty as their primary motivation for engaging in ethical farming. At the interface of the sacred and the secular, religious and secular agents of morality did conflict at times, such as in the example of organic certification, yet for the most part were complementary, and in fact not always easily distinguishable from each other, especially when the concept of *tayyib* was invoked, which involved focusing on the process of giving the animal "a good life" as well as "a good death." Further research could delve more thoroughly into how competing agents of secular and religious morality play out on a larger scale in the mainstream British halal meat industry. Conflicting secular and religious concerns could also be explored beyond the realm of halal, in kosher slaughter. As kosher standards expressly forbid stunning before slaughter (whereas with halal standards there is some disagreement), studying the interface between alternative ethical kosher movements and secular organic certification bodies would provide an insight into dialogues between religious and secular authority.

NOTE

1. One of these farms has since ceased selling products to the public due to their concern about feeding rising demand and overconsumption of meat. They have decided to focus instead on consumer education campaigns to promote less but better meat consumption.

REFERENCES

Almas, Reidar.1999. "Food Trust, Ethics and Safety in Risk Society." *Sociological Research Online* 4, no. 3: 1–7.

Barclay, Christopher. 2011. "Religious Slaughter, House of Commons Library." Accessed March 23, 2021. https://humanism.org.uk/wp-content/uploads/sn01314 .pdf

Bartkowski, John P., and W. Scott Swearingen. 1997. "God Meets Gaia in Austin, Texas: A Case Study of Environmentalism as Implicit Religion." *Review of Religious Research* 38, no. 4: 308–324.

BBC. 2020. "EU Court Backs Ban on Animal Slaughter Without Stunning." Accessed March 24, 2021. https://www.bbc.co.uk/news/world-europe-55344971

Bekoff, Marc. 2002. *Minding Animals: Awareness, Emotions and Heart.* New York: Oxford University Press.

Bell, David and Gill Valentine. 1997. *Consuming Geographies: We Are Where We Eat.* London: Routledge.

Bergeaud-Blackler, Florence. 2007. "New Challenges for Islamic Ritual Slaughter: A European Perspective." *Journal of Ethnic and Migration Studies* 33, no. 6: 965–980.

Bergeaud-Blackler, Florence. 2015. "The Halal Certification Market in Europe and the World: A First Panorama." In *Halal Matters: Islam, Politics and Markets in Global Perspective*, edited by Florence Bergeaud-Blackler, Johan Fischer and John Lever, 105–126. London: Routledge.

Blay-Palmer, Alison and Betsy Donald. 2008. "Manufacturing Fear: The Role of Food Processors and Retailers in Contrasting Alternative Food Geographies in Toronto, Canada." In *Alternative Food Geographies: Representation and Practices*, edited by Damian Maye, Lewis Holloway Moya Kneafsey, 273–288. Oxford: Elsevier.

Blecha, Jennifer, and Adam Davis. 2014. "Distance, Proximity, and Freedom: Identifying Conflicting Priorities regarding Urban Backyard Livestock Slaughter." *Geoforum* 57, no. C: 67–77.

Burt, Jonathan. 2006. "Conflicts around Slaughter in Modernity". In *Killing Animals*, edited by The Animal Studies Group, 120–144. Chicago, IL: University of Illinois Press.

Convery, Ian, Cathy Bailey, Maggie Mort, and Josephine Baxter. 2005. "Death in the Wrong Place? Emotional Geographies of the UK 2001 Foot and Mouth Disease Epidemic." *Journal of Rural Studies* 21, no. 1: 99–109.

Cook, Ian. et al. 2004. "Follow the Thing: Papaya." *Antipode* 36, no. 4: 642–664.

Downing, E. 2015. "Religious Slaughter of Animals." Accessed May 31, 2021. http://researchbriefings.files.parliament.uk/documents/SN07108/SN07108.pdf

Dwyer, Claire. 2000. "Negotiating Diasporic Identities: Young British South Asian Muslim Women." *Women's Studies International Forum* 23, no. 4: 475–486.

EBLEX. 2013. "The Halal Meat Market: Specialist Supply Chain Structures and Consumption Purchase and Consumption Profiles in England." Accessed May 31, 2021. https://issuu.com/ahdb1/docs/the_halal_meat_market

Eden, Sally, Christopher Bear, and Gordon Walker. 2008. "Mucky Carrots and Other Proxies: Problematising the Knowledge-fix for Sustainable and Ethical Consumption." *Geoforum* 39, no. 2: 1044–1057.

Farm Animal Welfare Council. 2003. "Report on the Welfare of Farmed Animals at Slaughter or Killing Part 1: Red Meat Animals." Accessed May 31, 2021. https://assets.publishing.service.gov.uk/government/uploads/system/uploads/attachment_data/file/325241/FAWC_report_on_the_welfare_of_farmed_animals_at_slaughter_or_killing_part_one_red_meat_animals.pdf

Finch, Martha. 2014. "Foreword." In *Religion, Food and Eating in North America,* edited by Benjamin Zeller, Marie Dallam, Reid Neilson and Nora Rubel, xi–xiv. New York: Columbia University Press.

Fischer, Johan. 2011. *The Halal Frontier: Muslim Communities in a Globalized Market.* New York: Palgrave Macmillan.

Fitzgerald, Amy. 2010. "A Social History of the Slaughterhouse: From Inception to Contemporary Implications." *Human Ecology Review* 17, no. 1: 58–69.

Food Standards Agency. 2015. "Results of the 2013 Animal Welfare Survey in Great Britain." Accessed March 24, 2021. https://old.food.gov.uk/sites/default/files/2013-animal-welfare-survey.pdf

Food Standards Agency. 2019. "Results of the 2018 FSA Survey into Slaughter Methods in England and Wales." Accessed March 24, 2021. https://assets.publishing.service.gov.uk/government/uploads/system/uploads/attachment_data/file/778588/slaughter-method-survey-2018.pdf

Frazer, Jenni. 2015. "UK Debate on Ritual Slaughter Mobilizes Muslims and Jews." *The Times of Israel*, February 24, 2015. http://www.timesofisrael.com/uk-debate-on-ritual-slaughter-mobilizes-muslims-and-jews/

Gibson, Troy, Craig Johnson, Joanna Murrell, C. M. Hulls, S. L. Mitchinson, Kevin Stafford, A. C. Johnstone and David Mellor. 2009. "Electroencephalographic Responses of Halothane Anesthetized Calves to Slaughter by Ventral-Neck Incision Without Prior Stunning." *New Zealand Veterinary Journal* 57, no. 2: 77–83.

Gillespie, Kathryn. 2011. "Killing with Kindness? Institutionalized Violence in 'Humane' Slaughter." In *Nonkilling Geographies*, edited by James Tyner and Joshua Inwood, 149–160. Honolulu: Center for Global Nonkilling.

Gillespie, Kathryn and Patricia Lopez. 2015. "Introducing Economies of Death." In *Economies of Death: Economic Logics of Killable Life and Grievable Death*, edited by Kathryn Gillespie and Patricia Lopez, 1–13. New York: Routledge.

Gökarıksel, Banu. 2009. "Beyond the Officially Sacred: Religion, Secularism, and the Body in the Production of Subjectivity." *Social & Cultural Geography* 10, no. 6: 657–674.

Goodman, David and Michael Goodman. 2008. "Localism, Livelihoods and the 'Post-Organic': Changing Perspectives on Alternative Food Networks in the United States." In *Alternative Food Geographies: Representation and Practices*, edited by Damian Maye, Lewis Holloway, and Moya Kneafsey, 23–38. London: Elsevier.

Govindrajan, Radhika. 2018. *Animal Intimacies: Interspecies Relatedness in India's Central Himalayas*. Chicago: University of Chicago Press.

Grandin, Temple and Catherine Johnson. 2005. *Animals in Translation: Using the Mysteries of Autism to Decode Animal Behavior*. New York: Scribner.

Green, Kelsey, and Franklin Ginn. 2014. "The Smell of Selfless Love: Sharing Vulnerability with Bees in Alternative Apiculture." *Environmental Humanities* 4, no. 1: 149–170.

Grumett, David. 2015. "Animal Welfare, Morals and Faith in the 'Religious Slaughter' Debate." In *Moral Regulation*, edited by Mark Smith, 211–219. Bristol: Policy Press.

Guthman, Julie. 2004. "Back to the Land: The Paradox of Organic Food Standards." *Environment & Planning A* 36, no. 3: 511–528.

Guthman, Julie. 2009. "Food." In *The Dictionary of Human Geography*, edited by Derek Gregory, Ron Johnston, Geraldine Pratt, Michael Watts, and Sarah Whatmore, 258–260. Oxford: Wiley-Blackwell.

Guthman, J. 2011. ""If They Only Knew": The Unbearable Whiteness of Alternative Food." In *Cultivating Food Justice: Race, Class, and Sustainability*, edited by Alison Alkon and Julian Agyeman, 263–281. Cambridge: MIT Press.

Haraway, Donna. 2008. *When Species Meet*. Minneapolis: University of Minnesota Press.

Harvey, David. 1990. "Between Space and Time: Reflections on the Geographical Imagination 1." *Annals of the Association of American Geographers* 80, no. 3: 418–434.

Harvey, Ramon. 2010. "Certification of Halal Meat in the UK." Accessed May 31, 2021. http://halalfocus.net/wp-content/uploads/2013/02/Report_-_Certification_of_Halal_Meat_in_the_UK.pdf

Hayes-Conroy, Jessica, and Allison Hayes-Conroy. 2013. "Veggies and Visceralities: A Political Ecology of Food and Feeling." *Emotion, Space and Society* 6, no. 1: 81–90.

Heelas, Paul. 1998. "Introduction: On Differentiation and Dedifferentiation." In *Religion, Modernity and Postmodernity*, edited by Paul Heelas, 1–18. Oxford: Blackwell.

Herzog, Hal. 2010. *Some We Love, Some We Hate, Some We Eat: Why it's So Hard to Think Straight About Animals.* New York: HarperCollins Publisher.

Higgin, Marc, Adrian Evans and Mara Miele. 2011. "A Good Kill: Socio-Technical Organisations of Farm Animal Slaughter." In *Human and Other Animals: Critical Perspectives*, edited by Bob Carter and Nickie Charles, 173–194. Basingstoke: Palgrave Macmillan.

Hopkins, Peter. 2007. "Global Events, National Politics, Local Lives: Young Muslim Men in Scotland." *Environment & Planning A* 39, no. 5: 1119–1133.

Holloway, Lewis. 2001. "Pets and Protein: Placing Domestic Livestock on Hobby-farms in England and Wales." *Journal of Rural Studies* 17, no. 3: 293–307.

Holmberg, Tora, Celia Roberts, and Myra J. Hird. 2011. "Mortal Love: Care Practices in Animal Experimentation." *Feminist Theory* 12, no. 2: 147–163.

Hughes, A. 2000. "Retailers, Knowledges and Changing Commodity Networks: The Case of the Cut Flower Trade." *Geoforum* 31, no. 2: 175–190.

Isakjee, Arshad. 2016. "Dissonant Belongings: The Evolving Spatial Identities of Young Muslim Men in the UK." *Environment & Planning A* 48, no. 7: 1337–1353.

Isakjee, Arshad, and Brídín Carroll. 2021. "Blood, Body and Belonging: The Geographies of Halal Food Consumption in the UK." *Social & Cultural Geography* 22, no. 4: 581–602.

Istasse, Manon. 2015. "Green Halal: How Does Halal Production Face Animal Suffering?" In *Halal Matters: Islam, Politics and Markets in Global Perspective*, edited by Florence Bergeaud-Blackler, Johan Fischer and John Lever, 127–142. London: Routledge.

Ivakhiv, Adrian. 2003. "Seeing Red and Hearing Voices in Red Rock Country." In *Deterritorialisations: Revisioning Landscapes and Politics*, edited by Mark Dorian, and Gillian Rose, 296–308. London: Black Dog Publishing.

Ivakhiv, Adrian. 2006. "Toward a Geography of 'Religion': Mapping the Distribution of an Unstable Signifier." *Annals of the Association of American Geographers* 96, no. 1: 169–175.

Kneen, Brewster. 1993. *From Land to Mouth: Understanding the Food System.* Toronto: New Canada Publications.

Kong, Lily. 2001. "Mapping 'New' Geographies of Religion: Politics and Poetics in Modernity." *Progress in Human Geography* 25, no. 2: 211–233.

Kong, Lily. 2010. "Global Shifts, Theoretical Shifts: Changing Geographies of Religion." *Progress in Human Geography* 34, no. 6: 755–776.

Kunst, Jonas R., and Christian Andrés Palacios Haugestad. 2018. "The Effects of Dissociation on Willingness to Eat Meat Are Moderated by Exposure to Unprocessed Meat: A Cross-cultural Demonstration." *Appetite* 120: 356–366.

Lever, John. 2019. "Halal Meat and Religious Slaughter: From Spatial Concealment to Social Controversy – Breaching the Boundaries of the Permissible?" *Environment and Planning C: Politics and Space* 37, no. 5: 889–907.

Lever, John. 2020. "Understanding Halal Food Production and Consumption in 'the West'. Beyond Dominant Narratives." *Cambio* 9, no. 19: 89.

Lever, John, Maria Puig, Mara Miele and Marc Higgin. 2010. "From the Slaughterhouse to the Consumer: Transparency and Information in the Distribution of Halal and Kosher Meat." Accessed May 31, 2021. https://orca.cf.ac.uk/20492/1/Dialrel_report_43.pdf

Lind, David, and Elizabeth Barham. 2004. "The Social Life of the Tortilla: Food, Cultural Politics, and Contested Commodification." *Agriculture and Human Values* 21, no. 1: 47–60.

Lorimer, Jamie, Timothy Hodgetts, and Maan Barua. 2019. "Animals' Atmospheres." *Progress In Human Geography* 43, no. 1: 26–45.

Maddrell, Avril. "A Place for Grief and Belief: The Witness Cairn, Isle of Whithorn, Galloway, Scotland." *Social & Cultural Geography* 10, no. 6: 675–693.

Masri, Basheer. 1989. *Animals in Islam*. Petersfield: Athene Trust.

Miele, Mara. 2011. "The Taste of Happiness: Free-Range Chicken." *Environment & Planning A* 43, no. 9: 2076–2090.

Miele, Mara. 2013. "Religious Slaughter: Promoting a Dialogue about the Welfare of Animals at Time of Killing." *Society & Animals* 21, no. 5: 421–424.

Miele, Mara. 2016. "Killing Animals for Food: How Science, Religion and Technologies Affect the Public Debate About Religious Slaughter." *Food Ethics* 1, no. 1: 47–60.

Mukherjee, Romi. 2014. "Global Halal: Meat, Money, and Religion." *Religions* 5, no. 1: 22–75.

Muslim Council of Britain. 2015. "British Muslims in Numbers." Accessed March 23, 2021. http://www.mcb.org.uk/wp-content/uploads/2015/02/MCBCensusReport_2015.pdf

Parry, Jovian. 2009. "Oryx and Crake and the New Nostalgia for Meat." *Society & Animals* 17, no. 3: 241–256.

Parry, Jovian, and Annie Potts. 2010. "Gender and Slaughter in Popular Gastronomy." *Feminism & Psychology* 20, no. 3: 381–396.

Philo, C. 1998. "Animals, Geography, and the City: Notes on Inclusions and Exclusions." In *Animal Geographies: Place, Politics & Identity in the Nature-Culture Borderlands*, edited by Jennifer Wolch and Jody Emel, 51–71. London: Verso.

Pollan, M. 2006. *The Omnivore's Dilemma: A Natural History of Four Meals*. New York: Penguin Press.

Purcell, Natalie. 2011. "Cruel Intimacies and Risky Relationships: Accounting for Suffering in Industrial Livestock Production." *Society & Animals* 19, no. 1: 59–81.

Ramírez, Margaret Marietta. 2015. "The Elusive Inclusive: Black Food Geographies and Racialized Food Spaces." *Antipode* 47, no. 3: 748–769.

Riley, Mark. 2011. "'Letting Them Go' – Agricultural Retirement and Human – Livestock Relations." *Geoforum* 42, no. 1: 16–27.

Robinson, Sarah. 2014. "Refreshing the Concept of Halal Meat: Resistance and Religiosity in Chicago's Taqwa Eco-Food Cooperative." In *Religion, Food and Eating in North America*, edited by Benjamin Zeller, Marie Dallam, Reid Neilson and Nora Rubel, 274–293. New York: Columbia University Press.

Serpell, James. 1986. *In the Company of Animals: A Study of Human-Animal Relationships*. New York: Cambridge University Press.

Smith, Mick. 2002. "The 'Ethical' Space of the Abattoir: On the (In)human(e) Slaughter of Other Animals." *Human Ecology Forum* 9, no. 2: 49–58.

Sommers, Jack. 2014. "Halal Hysteria: Tesco, M&S, Morrison's and Waitrose Accused of Selling New Zealand Lamb Without Labelling It Halal." *Huffington Post*, May 8, 2014. https://www.huffingtonpost.co.uk/2014/05/08/halal-meat-hysteria-new-zealand-lamb_n_5285905.html

Stannard, Susie and Hannah Clarke. 2020. "Consumer Insights: Demand for Halal Meat." Accessed March 23, 2021. https://ahdb.org.uk/knowledge-library/consumer-insights-demand-for-halal-meat

Stassart, Pierre, and Sarah Whatmore. 2003. "Metabolising Risk: Food Scares and the Un/Re-Making of Belgian Beef." *Environment & Planning A* 35, no. 3: 449–462.

Stewart, Kate and Matthew Cole. 2009. "The Conceptual Separation of Food and Animals in Childhood." *Food, Culture & Society* 12, no. 4: 457–476.

Syse, Karen. 2017. "Looking the Beast in the Eye: Re-animation of Meat Eating in Nordic and British Food Culture." In *Animalities: Literary and Cultural Studies Beyond the Human*, edited by Michael Lundblad. 168–189 Edinburgh: Edinburgh University Press.

Syse, Karen and Kristian Bjørkdahl. 2021. "The Animal that Therefore was Removed From View." In *Denialism in Environmental and Animal Abuse: Averting Our Gaze,* edited by Tomaž Grušovnik, Karen Syse and Reingard Spannring, 127–141. Lanham: Lexington.

Van Waarden, F. and R. van Dalen. 2013. "Halal and the Moral Construction of Quality: How Religious Norms Turn into a Mass Production into a Singularity." In *Constructing Quality: The Classification of Goods in Markets*, edited by Jens Beckert and Christine Musselin, 197–222. Oxford: Oxford University Press.

Watts, M., 2004. "Are Hogs Like Chickens? Enclosure and Mechanization in Two 'White Meat' Fillieres." In *Geographies of Commodity Chains*, edited by Alex Hughes and Suzanne Reimer, 39–62. London: Routledge.

Whatmore, Sarah, Pierre Stassart, and Henk Renting. 2003. "What's Alternative about Alternative Food Networks?" *Environment & Planning A* 35, no. 3: 389–391.

Zeller, E. 2014. "Quasi-religious American Foodways: The Cases of Vegetarianism and Locavorism." In *Religion, Food and Eating in North America*, edited by Benjamin Zeller, Marie Dallam, Reid Neilson and Nora Rubel, 294–318. New York: Columbia University Press.

Chapter 9

Meat We Don't Greet

How 'Sausages' Can Free Pigs or How Effacing Livestock Makes Room for Emancipation[1]

Sophia Efstathiou

INTRODUCTION

One of my recent culinary fascinations comes in the form of Beyond Sausage®—a sausage made of plants. With a caped super-cow as its logo, Beyond Meat® claim:

> We started with simple questions. Why do you need an animal to create meat? Why can't you build meat directly from plants? That's our company's mission. We hope our plant-based meats allow you and your family to eat more, not less, of the traditional dishes you love. Together, we can truly bring exciting change to the plate—and beyond. GO BEYOND! (As seen on Beyond Sausage® packaging, and on the company website)

I have been studying how new scientific concepts emerge from everyday ones. I have proposed this happens by what I call "finding" and "founding" everyday concepts into scientific contexts and practices thereby producing new "founded" concepts that often keep their everyday names but can work as scientific (Efstathiou 2009, 2012, 2016; Efstathiou et al. 2019). This type of creative meaning-making is arguably also happening with ideas of meat (and milk, mince, etc.) within food science and technology. Companies like Impossible Burger®, Beyond Meat®, or, cultured meat company, Just Meat® are founding everyday ideas of meat into novel food biotechnology contexts, by activities ranging from imitating the molecular properties of

165

(animal-based) meat or growing tissue in a lab, to vision statements and marketing. Though the result here is not found science but found food.

As exciting and relevant as these innovation contexts are I begin this story one step back. Before looking at how meat concepts get found and founded into food biotech, I explore how they might get loose from animals: *How do current practices of meat production leave room to think of meat as independent from animals?*

I propose that the intensification of meat production is ironically what makes meat concepts available to be populated by plants. I argue that what I call "technologies of effacement" facilitate the intensification of animal farming and slaughter by blocking face-to-face encounters between animals and people (Levinas 1969; Efstathiou 2018, 2019). My previous ethnographic work on animal research identifies technologies of effacement as including (a) architectures and the built environment, (b) entry and exit rules, (c) special garments, (d) naming and labeling procedures, and (e) protocols for handling animals (Efstathiou 2018, 2019). Building on ethnographic research by Dawn Coppin (2003) and Nöellie Vialles (1994), in the United States and France respectively, I propose that (a) Concentrated Animal Feeding Operation (CAFO) buildings, gestation, and farrowing crates; (b) rules for entering and exiting the slaughterhouse; (c) white slaughterhouse garments; (d) unique identification systems; and (e) "trapping" animals before stunning can all operate as technologies of effacement. Though developed to serve other manifest aims, like hygiene, expediency, or safety, these technologies operate to sustain routine, inviting one to look at animals as tokens of a known type while blocking encounters between humans and animals (and also among animals) as radically different, morally significant Others (Efstathiou 2018, 2019).

The abundance of meat and animal products in global Western and Northern contexts thus relies on blocking face-to-face encounters, generating what I call an "original ignorance," perhaps a willful one, about "whom" meat comes from. Others have problematized the disappearance of the animal during intensified meat production (Vialles 1994) and provision (Bjørkdahl and Syse 2016; Syse 2017; Syse and Bjørkdahl 2021)—a reality that is likely implicated in what psychologists have identified as "the meat paradox," that is, wanting to eat, but not wanting to hurt, animals (Loughnan et al. 2010; Volden and Wethal, this volume). In this analysis "original ignorance," the ignorance (willful or not) of the origins of (often technologically) produced artifacts, is seen as an opportunity: for escape, if not for revolt.

As Linsey McGoey argues, ignorance and ambiguity can challenge the dogmatic impositions of others leaving room for emancipation (2012, 2019). Leaving the animals and the humans working to turn them into food out of the public eye offers up a chance to escape: to dislocate, along with joints, the meaning of meat from the very animals whose flesh, blood, and organs are supposed to make it up.

Inventions like the 'sausage' thus offer a conceptual opening for industrialized food processing and provision to get out of the business of slaughtering animals, and to move back, or beyond, to plants. And with the effacement of the slaughtered and the slaughterer, this makes all the more sense as ethical.

This chapter has two main sections: "Technological Intensification and Effacement" and "Ignorance and Emancipation." Though structured in sequence to tell a story these processes are overlapping and incomplete. Effacement is never total and neither is ignorance, while emancipation is still more aspiration than reality. Still, I think that intensification, effacement, ignorance, and emancipation all feature in the story that takes us from the grass to the meat, and from the meat we don't greet to its lab-based alternative.

TECHNOLOGICAL INTENSIFICATION AND EFFACEMENT

First Encounters and Separation

I first met a cow in the summer of 2020. I grew up in Athens in the 1980s—a period of high urban consumerism, pre-financial crisis. I was a meat eater, my sister and I riding our bikes round and round our apartment block, until we got home and ordered pizza with "everything" or just "ham and cheese" from the pizzeria downstairs. Meeting this cow then, several decades later, in Inderøy, a rural part of Norway, while researching meat and climate change was quite a journey. This cow was an "alpha" cow—and I was scared of her. She was huge. An imposing animal, whose head when I put my hand on her could have definitely pushed me over. But I had to step in because she left her group, instead resting, or feeding their calves under a shade, to come forward and check out my dog. My heart skipped a beat. Poor Pavlo, he cowered down in the grass making himself small so she could sniff him and decide he was harmless. Both he and I were out of our league. I was thankful, and proud, to receive her approval.

How could it be that I, a chubby urban kid, was consuming the flesh of an animal like her for decades without lifting a finger—let alone skipping a heartbeat? That is an achievement of modern animal agriculture.

The domestication of animals for food originated independently in different parts of the world, most likely by herding wild animals and selectively breeding them into more manageable herds. Some of the earliest evidence of such activities is found in the Middle East, dating between 14,500 and 12,000 years ago. Fast forward to the current landscape of what geographer

Tony Weis calls "islands of concentrated livestock within seas of grain and oilseed monocultures" (Weis 2013, 8): A lot has changed. However what Nöellie Vialles flags as a key shift in modern animal agriculture is separating slaughter—in space—from towns, and—in language—from killing.

Vialles's ethnography, *Animal to Edible* (1994), is a seminal study of slaughterhouses in the 1980s, in the French region of Adour. Because of the moment it captures of increasing intensification, with mechanization substituting skills, and because of its evocative theoretical insights, this book informs a lot of my analysis.

Slaughterhouses move away from town centers starting in the late eighteenth century (Vialles 1994, 20–21). Private slaughter is prohibited in the early nineteenth century in France, "clearing" the butcher—and the street where he works—from the blood of the animals and the sight of violence (Vialles 1994, 17). By the mid-nineteenth century this separation becomes definitive of the *abattoir*. The very first edition of Émile Littré's dictionary of French in 1863 defines it as "place set aside for the slaughter of animals such as bullocks, calves, sheep, etc. that are used for human consumption. Abattoirs are located outside the surrounding walls of towns" (quoted in Vialles 1994, 15).

The word "abattoir" dates from 1806, derived from the verb *abattre* meaning to bring down something standing, and used originally to describe felling trees before applied to "putting down" army horses, and then other animals (Vialles 1994, 22–23). The places originally called *tueries* [*tuer* = to murder] or *écorcheries* [*écorcher* = to flay] get thus named abattoirs: set apart, and transforming animals from standing to recumbent. This cut, between the killing of the animal and its butchering, is one of the first big "scissions" that modern practices make to distance animals' death from the table:

> From this point on, slaughtering was required to be industrial, that is large scale and anonymous; it must be non-violent (ideally: painless); and it must be invisible (ideally: non-existent). (Vialles 1994, 22)

This evocative conclusion drawn by Vialles resonates with my proposal. Meat replacements promise to fulfill this ideal future of meat coming from painless and nonexistent slaughter. Perhaps one could stop here. Already in Vialles's analysis the "logic" of the intensified meat industry dissolving itself is visible.

However this is not the case until and unless meat replacements and/or alternative ways of making meat succeed. And alternatives arise also with a wish to relate to animals differently.[2]

What follows explores how intensified animal farming and slaughter block human-animal encounters, feeding into a loss of meaning and "original ignorance" that meat replacements come to fill in. But first, let us consider how and why encountering another being can be argued to be morally significant.

Levinas and the Ethics of the Face

Emmanuel Levinas (*b.* 1906–1995) was a French philosopher of Jewish Lithuanian origin. During World War II, Levinas was a prisoner of war, held in a forced labor camp in Germany. During that period, Levinas and his fellow prisoners made a friend: a dog they named Bobby. Levinas writes about how the gaze of "so-called free" German guards or citizens "stripped" them of their "human skin" reducing them to "a gang of apes" (1990, 152–153). Instead, Bobby came to meet the prisoners every morning and greeted them jumping happily every time they returned to the camp, recognizing them as (his) people (Levinas 1990, 153).

For Levinas, ethics is not premised on similarity, a shared family, nation, or species. Rather what binds us morally is a radical alterity, the "inner being," or "secrecy," we hold for each other (1969, 57–58). This secrecy escapes explanation. Being is not a matter of epistemology, but ethics. And ethics becomes accomplished when one pauses one's spontaneity to respond to the Other:

> The strangeness of the Other, his irreducibility to the I, to my thoughts and my possessions, is precisely accomplished as a calling into question of my spontaneity, as ethics. (Levinas 1969, 43)

Ethics is a pause or a questioning of one's spontaneity. This happens in encountering the Other through their "face":

> The way in which the other presents himself, exceeding *the idea of the other in me*, we here name face. This *mode* does not consist in figuring as a theme under my gaze, in spreading itself forth as a set of qualities forming an image. The face of the Other at each moment destroys and overflows the plastic image it leaves me, the idea existing to my own measure and to the measure of its *ideatum*—the adequate idea. It does not manifest itself by these qualities, but *kath'auto* [i.e., in person, per se]. It expresses itself. (Levinas 1969, 50–51. Emphasis in original)

The face is peculiar: on the one hand it is "superficial." It leaves a plastic image to sense or look at. Yet it is boundless. The face overflows any image it leaves, opening a window into the inner life of the Other, which though remains secret. The face acts as *a mode*, a way, or potential, for encountering the Other *according to themselves*, per se. This is the opposite of how social theorist Erving Goffman defines a "personal front" (Goffman 1990, 34): the face is not a sign vehicle for others to interpret or expect, but what destroys expectations.

I follow the work in Atterton and Wright (2019) in extending Levinasian ethics to nonhumans. Levinas emphasizes the importance of the eyes and the body in expressing as the face: "The eyes break through the mask—the language of the eyes, impossible to dissemble. The eye does not shine; it speaks" (Levinas 1969, 66). And further: "And the whole body—a hand or a curve of the shoulder—can express as the face" (Levinas 1969, 262). I thus here define animals' "face" as the modes through which an animal exudes their "inner being" or "secrecy" that may be expressed in the body, eyes, movements, or other sensescapes (voice, touch, smell, etc.) but that is not reducible to these.

Further, having a 'face' is not sufficient for facing (cf. Efstathiou 2019). As we see in the example of Levinas and his Nazi guards, humans who could face him, do not. It is then important to attend to what conditions facing or—reversely—effacing the Other: blocking, erasing, or otherwise negating their face. By blocking face-to-face encounters and speeding up work, I suggest that "technologies of effacement" facilitate and shape the ethos of intensified industrial labor—perhaps generally—but especially in intensified meat production.

Technologies of Effacement in Intensive Animal Farming and Slaughtering

I have analyzed the normative challenges that researchers face in experimenting with other animals, as partly accounted for by the operation of *technologies of effacement* in the lab (Efstathiou 2018, 2019). These are techniques, tools, or procedures developed to "rationalize" engagements with others, while at the same time blocking a direct experience of the Other through their face, for example, by modifying sensory-symbolic, visual, olfactory, tactile, sonic, or other features the Other presents with. These technologies often script encounters between humans and animals, as encounters with what is already known as opposed to secret (Efstathiou 2019, 150). Five types of technology of effacement operate to structure human-animal encounters in the lab and seem to also operate in intensified farming and slaughter: (a) built environments and architecture, (b) entry and exit procedures and special garments;, (c) animal handling protocols, (d) naming and identification techniques (Efstathiou 2019, 150). I here discuss meat production not provision, as I focus on encountering a living Other, though arguably a dead other also has a face.

Architectures and Built Environments

Architecture and the built environment is one of the key ways to manage encounters between animals and people. I survey here CAFO building plans, as well as animal confinement technologies within CAFOs.

CAFO Buildings

Besides slaughter, farming too has become invisible. One of the telltale signs of intensified animal farming is the absence of animals outside. The transition from "extensive" to "intensive" farming is marked by the development of large and technologically sophisticated built enclosures characterized—depending on their animal population and their density—as CAFOs. Capital-intensive CAFO buildings are designed to keep livestock inside year round, providing artificial light, air ventilation, and temperature-controlled conditions with no outside access and no windows for outsiders looking in. These usually unmarked and secured spaces make it almost impossible to physically encounter livestock animals if one is not part of the operation. But also for humans employed in a CAFO human-animal encounters become rare as the proportion of animals to humans increases, and the occasions for interaction diminish, taken over by automatic systems for feeding and watering animals, cameras for monitoring them, and dispensing medications. The CAFO building itself then secludes a general public from meeting animals, while minimizing human-animal encounters also within the farm. To illustrate these points I consider mega-hog farm development in the United States, following Dawn Coppin (2003).

Up to approximately the 1970s in the United States, most hogs lived in open farmland or dirt lots, with little protection from the weather. Farmers in the 1950s might have sent them to "finishing" facilities owned by companies like Cargill,[3] to get fattened up before sale. There, animals would be more confined but still have access to an open laying facility and open air (Coppin 2003, 599). This all changed in the 1970s and 1980s with the development of new technologies for total confinement, medication, reproduction, nutrition, and waste management (Coppin 2003, 599). Architectural innovations coevolved with pig breeding and consumer preferences. Pigs in industrial farming were bred to go down from 1.5 inches of back fat—which kept them warm during winters outside—to just a third of an inch, to match consumer demand for leaner meat (Coppin 2003, 603). Also lighter skin breeds, initially bred to distinguish domesticated pigs from their wild relatives, were sensitive to sunburn making sun exposure without shelter also problematic.

Confinement was coupled with concentration, small pig farms getting replaced by ones housing thousands of pigs. In 1967 the United States had over one million pig farms, that are now down to about 60,000 farms, while the number of hogs per farm increased more than fivefold (Coppin 2003, 601).[4] At the same time, family-owned farms got contracted by bigger now global conglomerates (Chemnitz and Becheva 2014, 12–13).

This sheer increase in the proportion of animals to humans per CAFO makes it hard for human-animal encounters to happen—let alone to offer occasions for humans and animals to face each other, as morally significant Others. But of further import are built enclosures that further script whom the human encounters if such encounters do take place.

The "assembling" of the pig, from fetus to a slaughter weight, takes place in purpose-built spaces. After pigs are inseminated (most commonly artificially), the pregnant sow will be kept in an individual "gestation" crate for almost four months, and then a few days before she is due to give birth moved to another individual "farrowing" crate where she will stay for another two weeks suckling her piglets. The piglets will then be moved to a "nursery" for a month, then to a "growing" building, and then to a "finishing" one, where they will stay until they are five or six months old, when they will be loaded off to slaughter (Coppin 2003, 600).

Encountering an individual pig in a farm happens through architected pathways. The human gaze gets ordered by spatial enclosures to meet individuals of an animal type, or even a meat preparation stage—instead of facing radically different Others. Instead of allowing pigs to mix in a herd, achieving different relations to each other, but mandating the human carer to encounter animals individually and negotiate their social dynamics, spatial enclosures and specialized monitoring technology automatically deliver the care that each animal group is assumed to need, expediting work at the same time as blocking face-to-face encounters. Especially relevant here are confinement technologies that at once rationalize work and restrict a pig's body and face.

Confinement Crates

The individual "gestation" crates sows are kept in in the United States are standardly 2 meters long by 60 centimeters wide, providing no option for the pig to turn around. The sow will be kept there throughout her pregnancy—estimated at three months, three weeks, and three days. The farrowing crate is slightly wider, giving her some space to lie down but again not turn around, for fear of either turning away from her piglets, or crushing them. In some cases sows are strapped down to the crate floor to make them continuously available for piglets suckle, but that seems to reduce their milk production

(Coppin 2003, 604—see image on p. 606). The crates are not an environment that the sows prefer. Crates have plastic flooring with slits, through which sows' excrement is collected underneath in a "lagoon" and the floor is kept bare so that the excrement can fall through despite pigs' preference for solid flooring and for so-called environmental "enrichment" materials—"rich" only by comparison to bare human architectures: hay or toys. Sows will give on average 5 to 8 litters in their farm lifetime, and 2.5 litters a year. Thus for about 10 months a year, the sow will be confined in a space above her excrement, where she cannot move freely, let alone express species-specific behaviors like digging, playing, bathing, or nesting.

These confinement stalls prima facie provide individual care for the sow and her piglets. Gestation crates' manifest function is to immobilize a sow and to ensure that she is getting enough nutrition, vitamins, medicine, and water, with no competition from other pen mates while pregnant. Similarly farrowing crates manifestly provide for the mother and allow for breastfeeding, with the added function of ensuring that the sow's body does not crush any piglets with its substantial weight. Confinement technologies pay each sow individual attention. However, attention is not paid to her as a "secret" animal Other, but rather to her as a meat-maker. The crated sow is encountered as a piglet grower and a milk-dispenser: the gestation crate holds her womb in place, so the future piglet—and future meat—is not miscarried, and the farrowing crate makes her teats available to the piglets—in cases of restraint, continuously.

By blocking animals' bodies from full expression confinement technologies block their face. Yet, effacement is never total. The eyes still speak, the sow has a voice, and she bites the bars of her crate. Still, facing her becomes hard. The crates and automated systems for monitoring them expedite meat-growing, minimizing the chance that a human will come face-to-face with a sow, bar in an emergency. Note also that confinement crates also block animals from encountering each other. The crated sow then gets doubly effaced, from humans, and from others in her social group, including her piglets.[5]

Entry and Exit Procedures and Special Garments

During my work in an animal lab in Norway, I observed that procedures for entering and exiting the lab, and specifically the taking off of one's clothes (cute shirts, favorite jewellery, or other personal items) and rituals like washing of one's hands, before one dons the uniform and personal protective equipment of the lab, were important stages in blocking the face, and coming to assume the position, or professional "front" (Goffman 1990, 34), of the laboratory researcher. These rituals and garments operated as technologies of effacement by separating performances in the lab from "everyday" ones while also physically modifying people's faces and body: protective caps collecting hair and semi-covering ears, face masks muffling voices, protective goggles shielding eyes, rubber gloves sheathing hands. These preparations provided new surfaces with which humans and animals encountered each other, in and for research.

Vialles mentions the "standard whites" used in the slaughterhouse, consisting of "rubber boots, cotton jacket and trousers, plastic apron and disposable cap" (1994, 101). Besides providing a uniform that symbolizes the special role one assumes as a slaughterer, white has a distinct symbolic and practical function. White fits a logic of hygiene. Though it looks like the color that can get dirtiest fastest, white is ironically most resistant to dirt as it can be washed at high temperatures and bleached. As a color that is no color it cannot get lost. White also fits a logic of innocence: medical doctors, high clergy, and brides are all known to dress in white. White complements the imagined red of blood. Following Vialles, white garments also operate to negate the blood of death also in the slaughterhouse: "The colour of blood has been everywhere ousted by white: white walls, white accessories, white clothing, from head to foot" (1994, 66). White uniforms thus work to erase encounters with the bleeding Other, practically and symbolically by evoking the clean and innocent.[6]

Entry and exit procedures are also crucial for slaughterhouse work. Consider the strict division between the "clean sector" in the "front" of the building and the "dirty sector" in the "back" (Vialles 1994, 35–36). The front of the slaughterhouse or the clean entrance is where people encounter meat. Instead, animals are off-loaded in the back of the building through the dirty entrance to the dirty sector, where also renderers' vans are loaded with what are considered waste products from the slaughtering process. Things in the "back" happen first, but by calling the front the "front," one assumes the gaze of someone meeting the meat first, never greeting the animal. Instead the animal gets "brought in" through the back door, symbolically and literally. Clean and dirty sectors are never to meet. The vans that service them never cross the middle (Vialles 1994, 36). In between the slaughter hall provides an ambiguous middle, where the animal exists and doesn't, a space of transfiguration that also performs this literal and symbolic cut between the animal and the meat, the dirty past, and the future animal-free meat one wishes to encounter.

Already the cut made in language between animals as carriers of dirt and pollution, yet of their own flesh as clean raises a paradox: removing the "animal" from the meat is what makes it clean—and yet the animal must, as part of itself, as its own meat, already be clean. These conflicts in how to encounter animals in these spaces are aggravated with technological intensification. Founding the animal as edible is a process effacing the animal. It involves immobilizing, stunning, suspending, and bleeding a living animal, then flaying him, cutting off his "extremities" (head, legs, sometimes tail), and cutting into (or punching through for sheep) the body to separate it from its skin (or scalded and de-haired in the case of pigs), eviscerating or gutting the animal and washing his insides, sometimes splitting his carcass in two (for pigs and large bovines), and weighing it, all to get to the meat (Vialles 1994, 41). This is what Vialles calls "de-animalising" the animal (1994, 49, 71): what I see as transfigurations needed to found an animal as food, and what also involves effacing him. These processes erase the animal's "face," literally by chopping off his head, almost immobilizing his body (movements will still occur when the animal is suspended and bleeding), and progressively silencing him, preventing an encounter with the animal as an Other, beyond the properties of his fascia. Taking the ground off one's feet is a key symbolic transformation of the animal to the edible, found, picked up, and on its way to meet a butcher (French: *boucher*) and a mouth (French: *bouche*).

Importantly, the division of clean and dirty sectors is a division of labor which blocks workers from facing animals, and from facing killing. A person working in either sector is not going to meet the same animal alive and as meat. Rather, one is stationed at, working and met with a stage in an animal's processing into a sellable carcass. This is important, because even when working to slaughter animals, one may be shielded from facing them, and from the full impact of one's actions.

Animal Handling Protocols

The introduction of technologies and built structures for guiding animals in a single file through a "race" to immobilize them before stunning contributed immensely to speeding up slaughter, resulting in fewer injuries and more intact carcasses, faster. Refining these technologies means livestock are slaughtered in the thousands every second, and billions annually making meat appear in the plenty.[7] I will focus on the stunning pen or "trap" (*piege*) in French. Stunning is a standard protocol and guaranteed encounter between a living animal and a human. The trap I argue is a key technology of effacement, blocking facing the moment before killing, promising its "painlessness."

Trapping a docile animal is analyzed by Vialles as the opposite of hunting a wild one: the hunted animal is often recognized for its individuality and skills, its plans or priorities, it may even be given a name by the hunter (1994, 113). Like in the instance of making the animal a pet, hunting recognizes an equal footing between the human and the animal (Vialles 1994, 113). Already hunting animals by trapping is designed to efface the individual animal (and human), designed with a certain species, environment, and hunter in mind.

Traps operate as technologies of effacement also in the slaughterhouse. In the absence of traps, and in the case of large bovines, humans would have to throw their bodies onto the animal, pulling to restrain it by a rope around his horns or neck, or tying this to a hook in the floor, while someone drives a poleax to the bovine's forehead—now replaced by a captive bolt gun (Vialles 1994, 121). The trap is instead placed in the animal's path. Tricking the animal to walk into it, the animal gets immobilized before an encounter with a human, so that the slaughterer can shoot the bolt gun at a better stabilized target.

Even in this encounter one could face the animal in question, perhaps witness their surprise or struggle and pause or be moved by it. But in come the speed and "rationalization" of the work. Following guidelines, and with struggle removed, the human eyes will locate the right point to shoot on the animal's forehead versus meet his eyes (EC 2018b). As Vialles notes, in private slaughter, "a contract" might be made between the animal and human for the first to provide their flesh for the latter to eat in exchange for food, shelter, and protection, while the slaughter itself would be an activity celebrated with others, as the killing of the animal. Industrialized slaughtering challenges the terms of that contract, as the person killing the animal has no connection to it:

"I tell people I'm a hired killer," slaughterers will say jokingly "I'm paid to kill." If there is still a contract here it is of a quite different kind, involving the animal purely as an object, just like the victim of a criminal "contract." (Vialles 1994, 119)

Here the lack of connection to the animal and the peculiarity of killing someone one does not know are negotiated by the slaughterers by joking.[8] Effacement works both ways: by killing someone one doesn't wish to kill one becomes a "hired" or "contracted" killer, masking their "face" vis-à-vis the Other, behind their professional front.

Effacement becomes especially morally problematic at the point of murder. Levinas says discussing murder,

The alterity that is expressed in the face provides the unique "matter" possible for total negation. I can wish to kill only an existent absolutely independent, which exceeds my powers infinitely, and therefore does not oppose them but paralyzes the very power of power. The Other is the sole being I can wish to kill. (1969, 198)

The effacement of animals as morally significant Others creates a problem. If, following Levinas, the Other is the sole being one can wish to kill, then the killing of these faceless animals becomes something one cannot wish to do.

No slaughterer can wish to kill these animals—and no consumer. And yet we do kill animals and allow them to be killed.

People who do not want to kill, kill animals who do not want to die, for people who do not want to hurt anyone, but who want to eat a lot of meat cheaply.

I consider one more technology of effacement before discussing the possible unintended benefits of effacing.

Identification and Labeling Techniques

Current systems for identifying animals can also contribute to efface them. Consider, for example, the Trade Control and Expert System (TRACES) developed by the EU. TRACES tracks the locations and movements of European livestock using unique identification numbers issued to them on birth, replicated as barcodes on their ear tags, and as passport numbers stored in national and international digital registries. TRACES aims to record information on animal travel to enable tracing the sources and pathways of possible disease or infection outbreaks among livestock.

These tools individuate an animal. Yet, they also typify them. Animal identification numbers are unique, but they are also the same: all numbers. Previous systems for identification on the bodies of animals, for example, by systems of cuts on animals' ears or branding, would at least beg one to look at the animal body—even if these signs are diagrammatic and operating in a similar manner as numbers to pinpoint individuals in a sequence. As a result, individuation tools such as identification tools and labeling techniques script human and animal encounters away from facing, and toward counting and measuring the Other, as one of the same.

Added Faces

Often the loss or blocking of the animal and human face will be supplemented by imagery that adds a face to it. Consider the cartoon animation produced to communicate the TRACES livestock identification system (European Commission, undated). The video playfully names one bull "Chuck" and one cow "Anna" showing them travel the world with their unique passports, until they meet and heart bubbles emerge. The personification of the animal is here working as what I call an "added face" (Efstathiou 2019, 156–157).

Added faces hope to work as faces, creating the sense of individuality that one might expect from a face. They are encountered with all kinds of technology of effacement. One can see them as animal images in institutional walls, "personalized" uniforms or—once it comes to food provision—as animal depictions on product boxes. A typical image is one of animals grazing freely, with a farmer on their side, or the image I saw recently on the side of the Norwegian milk company Tine®'s bus, inscribed with "Maybe the world's finest milk—on its way to you—Tussi, Turi and Tina," picturing three goats, two of them blurred in the background, but one featured with a close-up on her face. Added faces make faceless or effaced produce and labor possible to encounter again under some guise of "normality."

Added faces may be found in practices contrasting intensified farming and slaughter, what Bjørkdahl and Syse call "meat nostalgia" in consumption and marketing (2016). Consider, for example, Norwegian Michelin star awarded restaurant Credo. Customers of that restaurant are presented with an image of the named animal whose milk or flesh they are about to consume. This approach attempts to connect to the animal and recognize the work involved to get a meal to the table, a trend that Syse identifies with other young—predominantly—male chefs (Syse 2017). These changes may be pointing to alternative ways of making meat, though arguably in these encounters the animals are already found as food, rather than encountered as radically different Others who pause one's spontaneity.

Does Effacement Matter?

I have so far proposed that human-animal encounters in intensified animal farming and slaughter rely on technologies of effacement, blocking encounters between humans and animals as Others with a face. In the void of the ethics of the encounter, springs up industrial work ethos—so-called hired killing (Vialles 1994, 119). Another way to think of this transformation is that ethics gets taken over by epistemology: instead of facing radically different individuals one uses them as already known and knowable types (for profit).

But are such technologies of effacement really that important? Isn't de-animalizing already embedded in our language? After all, what is the point of intermediary concepts of animal products like "meat," "beef," "pork," "milk," "egg whites" if not to already provide a way to avoid explicitly referring to the animals they would have originated from? These are not "animal flesh," not "cow flesh," not "pig flesh," not "a mother cow's breast secretions," not "secretions from a chicken's ovum." Perhaps these terms fulfill the transformation needed in order to consume—respectfully—a living Other (Bjørkdahl and Syse 2016). Though note that no such distancing is afforded to chicken or to fish who we are allowed to eat as they come, despite the popular chicken "nuggets" and fish "fingers."

Arguably these concepts have functioned to shield the eater from the fact of choosing to kill and consume a—usually—healthy, young, living animal, its babies, or its babies' food. Perhaps they shield consumers of the so-called meat paradox: loving animals and loving meat (Loughnan et al. 2010; Volden and Wethal, this volume). But an important element in the intensification of agriculture is that these terms come to stand in completely for animals, who come to disappear from sight, literally, through the confined and secured spaces of the CAFO and the slaughterhouse, but also in and through the sped-up temporalities and reduced room that (human and nonhuman) animals' expressive bodies and relationships are allowed to take. Blocking the face amounts to blocking pauses, enforcing routine and speeding up production that will make more and more animals disappear and more and more meat appear, faster, closer, and more cheaply.[9]

The effacement of humans and animals within intensified production systems thus contributes causally to the omnipresence of animal products. The forms and textures and tastes that animal flesh and animal secretions come to take become what many humans in the global West and North are first familiar with, and love. Indeed with some more work and technology and some more ignorance these forms might prove sufficient to take animals out of the equation completely.

IGNORANCE AND EMANCIPATION

One of the important points Vialles raises, and which is also argued in Coppin (2003), is the transformation of slaughtering practices from public and celebrated to private and shameful:

> Nowadays, slaughtering has become an invisible, exiled, almost clandestine activity. We know it goes on, of course, but it is an abstract kind of knowledge. We have no wish to eat corpses (we are carnivores, not carrion-eaters), so animals have to be slaughtered. But we demand an ellipsis between animal and meat. (1994, 5)

In this ellipsis (what means "lack," in Greek) there is a space for some emancipative thinking to flourish.

I here propose that, ironically, ignorance offers a key for moving away from—at least—intensified modes of making meat from animals. Blocking humans from facing animals keeps animal-based products familiar and their origin ambiguous. And here also comes, ironically, a possible way out: the possibility that we keep our "traditions" and keep cooking with meat, and products "we love," just substituting their ingredients with plant-based materials, and adding a face to *them*. After all, wouldn't plant-based products be better fronted by happy animals? Enter the Beyond Meat® "super-cow"[10] (figure 9.1).

The super-cow of Beyond Meat® symbolizes a power that livestock have lost: staying alive. By putting an ellipsis between the animal and the

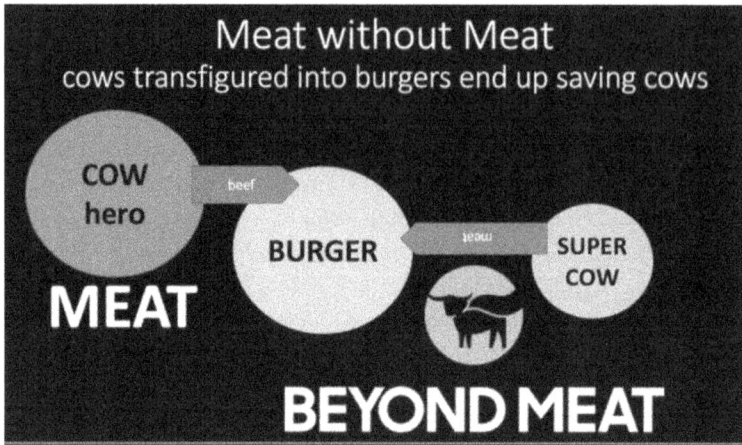

Figure 9.1   Meat Without Meat.

food product, concepts like the "burger," or "sausage," or "milk" operate as bridging concepts, helping hold their animal origins ambiguous, but familiar enough for other "super-materials" to enter the picture. And yet the burger in its current meaning would not have been possible without cows dying. Picture here the billions of animals that throughout the development of intensified agriculture and slaughter have been "sacrificed" and transfigured into more and more processed food products with increasing speed and dropping prices, coming to spread and populate "traditional dishes" everywhere: taking on a life of their own, while the animal disappears. 'Burgers,' 'sausages,' 'nuggets,' 'scallops,' 'pulled pork,' and 'milk' as concepts and forms come to save their animal mothers and fathers by making them redundant. It would sound like science fiction, if it weren't true.

This phenomenon of becoming and being more familiar with the outcome of a causal process, as opposed to its original causes or sources, is common in industrialized worlds. One way to identify it is as an "original ignorance" playing on the concept of an "original sin"—embodied in the Christian tradition by biting into the forbidden fruit of the tree of knowledge. Original ignorance is a lack of knowledge of things' origins or their history. This captures the experience of knowing burgers a lot more and better than cows, but it is a general phenomenon. For example, I encountered a "stile" (a constructed gate for humans—and not animals—to enter and exit fields) after years of going through "turnstiles" (on the train, subway, etc.), even though the latter surely derived from the first. Similarly, I remember visiting the botanical gardens of the Huntington Library only to suddenly smell my childhood soap: I looked down and saw a strange little flower. Being more at home with the derivatives of often industrial or technical processes whose "original" sources become strange is what I propose to call "original ignorance." Perhaps original ignorance is also a sin. But perhaps it leaves room for reinvention or even atonement.

Linsey McGoey's work inspires me here (2012, 2019). Following feminist philosopher Eve Sedgwick, she notes that deliberate ambiguity and ignorance can act as a "rebuke" of oppressive and inadequate classificatory ordering systems (McGoey 2012, 6–7). Similarly, the ambiguity of meat concepts and the original ignorance of consumers make space for meat to resist its animal origins. By holding a space of deliberate ambiguity concepts like "meat," "sausage," or "burger" rebuke their expected classification as animal-based. Combined, effacement, original ignorance, and ambiguity bend the proverbial crate bars for animals to escape their meat identities—and meat its (dirty) animal past.[11]

CONCLUSION

A lot of writing on the ethics of animal agriculture starts from a position of authority, or privilege, assumed to be had by humans. Instead I draw attention to human-animal encounters as occasions for radically different Others to meet and face each other. These encounters will all be unique. Yet I proposed that what I dub "technologies of effacement" are a significant part of intensified farming and slaughtering practices, operating to shape such encounters into encounters between meat professionals and livestock.

I started with the following question: *How do current practices of meat production leave room to think of meat as independent from animals?*

To an analysis of the de-animalization of the animal provided by Vialles (1994), I added his "effacement." I proposed that technologies of effacement are intimately involved in intensifying animal rearing and slaughter, making it faster and streamlined, while removing opportunities for humans and animals to pause their spontaneities and face each other, as morally significant Others. I identified CAFO architectures and confinement crates, slaughterhouse garments and entry and exit rules, protocols for stunning and identification and labeling as functioning to block the "face" of animals and humans.

Is 'facing' a moral solution to animal agriculture? There is no ethics recipe here for *how* to respond to the Other. What I offer are some ways to explore what conditions encounters as ethics, and why intensification may ironically dissolve itself.

The deliberate ambiguity of intermediary terms like "sausage," "milk," or "burger" coupled with an original ignorance of the animal and familiarity with animal products offers a space for emancipative action. Thus sausages, made plentiful and familiar in part by effacing the pig, come "back" as plant-based superheroes, breaking free their pen-mates from the hog farm.

As McGoey suggests: "Presumptions of equality demand not outrage at inequality but constant verifications of equality itself, as a practice rather than a reward or goal" (2012, 10). Maybe, like Carol Adams does (2018), this could mean introducing vegan burgers to meat eaters, or city kids to cows.

NOTES

1. I use single quotes to denote 'concepts', double quotes for "terms", and no quotes for things themselves.

2. Bjørkdahl and Syse analyze this shift in sensibilities and ethics about animals as a move from anthropocentrism to "biocentrism" (2016, 222–228).

3. Cargill founded in 1865 is the third biggest meat industry globally in sales, with a reported 114.6 billion USD revenues in the first quarter of 2020. https://www.forbes.com/companies/cargill/.

4. The largest pig farm is currently constructed in China, using vertical housing similar to apartment buildings to house 84,000 sows and their offspring, producing over two million pigs per year (https://www.reuters.com/article/us-china-swinefever-muyuanfoods-change-s-idUSKBN28H0MU). For an estimate of pig farms in the United States see https://www.porkcares.org/americas-pig-farmers/our-farms/.

5. Organizations concerned with animal welfare want to ban gestation and farrowing crates. This is the case for gestation crates in some regions, like Sweden, the UK, and nine U.S. states, but not for farrowing crates.

6. Note that recent EU recommendations advise personnel tasked with stunning to wear dark clothes (EC 2018a). Perhaps this soothes the animals, matching clothing used in livestock facilities that animals are familiar with.

7. Watch the seconds pass on this evocative Animal Kill Clock measuring the thousands of animals killed in the United States every second. https://animalclock.org.

8. Humor offers a way to express difficult emotions or tension in a manner that generates camaraderie more easily than anger or sadness. It is easier to laugh than to cry together.

9. Current meat pricing schemes exclude the environmental costs of intensified enterprises.

10. The iconography might be depicting a bull, a masculinized superhero, but it should be a cow, as the meat and dairy industry relies on primarily females' reproductive labor.

11. Note also the evocative claim in Van der Weele and Driessen (2019) that "normal" meat becomes further ambiguous, generating moral ambivalence, with the continued innovation of new meats.

REFERENCES

Adams, Carol. 2018. "There is Nothing More All American than the Veggie Burger." *New York Times*, Opinion, June 30, 2018. Available Online.

Atterton, Peter, and Tamra Wright, eds. 2019. *Face to Face with Animals: Levinas and the Animal Question*. SUNY Press.

Bjørkdahl, Kristian and Karen Lykke Syse. 2016. "Death and Meateriality." In *Taming Time, Timing Death*, edited by Rane Willerslev and Dorthe Refslund Christensen, 213–230. Routledge.

Chemnitz, Christina and Stanka Becheva, eds. 2014. *Meat atlas: Facts and Figures About the Animals We Eat*. Heinrich Böll Stiftung and Friends of the Earth Europe. Available online.

Coppin, Dawn. 2003. "Foucauldian Hog Futures: The Birth of Mega-Hog Farms." *Sociological Quarterly* 44 (4): 597–616.

Efstathiou, Sophia. 2009. *The Use of 'Race' as a Variable in Biomedical Research*. PhD diss. University of California, San Diego.

Efstathiou, Sophia. 2012. "How Ordinary Race Concepts Get to be Usable in Biomedical Science: An Account of Founded Race Concepts." *Philosophy of Science* 79 (5): 701–713.

Efstathiou, Sophia. 2016. "Is It Possible to Give Scientific Solutions to Grand Challenges? On the Idea of Grand Challenges for Life Science Research." *Studies in History and Philosophy of Science Part C: Studies in History and Philosophy of Biological and Biomedical Sciences* 56: 48–61.

Efstathiou, Sophia. 2018. "Im angesicht der gesichter: Technologien des Gesichtsverlusts in der tierforschung". In *Philosophie der Tierforschung*, edited by Wunsch Matthias Böhnert Martin and Kristian Köchy. Volume 3: Milieus und Akteure, 9–53. Verlag Karl Alber.

Efstathiou, Sophia. 2019. "Facing Animal Research: Levinas and Technologies of Effacement." In *Face-to-Face with Animals: Levinas and the Animal Question*, edited by Atterton Peter and Wright Tamra, 139–163. New York: SUNY Press. Available online.

Efstathiou, Sophia, with Rune Nydal, Astrid Laegreid, and Martin Kuiper. 2019. "Scientific Knowledge in the Age of Computation: Explicated, Computable and Manageable?" *Theoria. Revista de Teoría, Historia y Fundamentos de la Ciencia* 34 (2): 213–236.

European Commission, undated. "TRACES—Animal Traceability." Film Available online. https://audiovisual.ec.europa.eu/en/video/I-107984 https://www.youtube .com/watch?v=k5eeVyN9rDE

European Commission. 2018a. *How to Handle and Restrain Cattle, Sheep and Goats*. Luxembourg: Publications of the European Union. Available online. https://ec .europa.eu/food/animals/animal-welfare/animal-welfare-practice/slaughter-stun- ning/2018-factsheets_en

European Commission. 2018b. *How to Stun Cattle (Penetrative Captive Bolt)*. Luxembourg: Publications of the European Union. Available online. https://ec .europa.eu/food/animals/animal-welfare/animal-welfare-practice/slaughter-stun- ning/2018-factsheets_en

Goffman, Erving. 1990 [1959]. *The Presentation of Self in Everyday Life*. Penguin Books.

Levinas, Emmanuel. 1969 [1961]. *Totality and Infinity*. Trans. A. Lingis. Pittsburgh, PA: Duquesne University Press.

Levinas, Emmanuel. 1990. *Difficult Freedom: Essays on Judaism*. Trans. S. Hand. Baltimore: Johns Hopkins.

Loughnan, Steve, Nick Haslam, and Brock Bastian. 2010. "The Role of Meat Consumption in the Denial of Moral Status and Mind to Meat Animals.» *Appetite* 55, no. 1: 156–159.

McGoey, Linsey. 2012. "Strategic Unknowns: Towards a Sociology of Ignorance." *Economy and Society* 41 (1): 1–16.

McGoey, Linsey. 2019. *The Unknowers: How Strategic Ignorance Rules the World*. Zed Books Ltd.

Syse, Karen Lykke. 2017. "Looking the Beast in the Eye: Re-animation of Meat Eating in Food Prose". In *Animalities: Literary and Cultural Studies Beyond the Human*, edited by Michael Lundblad, 168–187. Edinburgh University Press.

Syse, Karen Lykke and Kristian Bjørkdahl. 2021. "The Animal that Therefore was Kept Out of View." In *Denialism in Environmental and Animal Abuse: Averting Our Gaze*, edited by Grušovnik Tomaž, Karen Lykke Syse and Reingard Spannring, 127–144. Lexington Books: Rowman & Littlefield.

Van Der Weele, Cor, and Clemens Driessen. 2019. "How Normal Meat Becomes Stranger as Cultured Meat Becomes More Normal; Ambivalence and Ambiguity Below the Surface of Behavior." *Frontiers in Sustainable Food Systems* 3: 69.

Vialles, Nöellie. 1994. *Animal to Edible*. Trans. J. A. Underwood. Cambridge: Cambridge.

Weis, Tony. 2013. *The Ecological Hoofprint: The Global Burden of Industrial Livestock*. Zed Books Ltd.

Chapter 10

What Happens When Cultured Meat Meets Meat Culture?

(Un)naturalness and (Un)familiarity in the Meat of Today and Tomorrow

Johannes Volden and Ulrikke Wethal

INTRODUCTION

The fifth of August 2013 would become a landmark date in the history of cultured meat. Mark Post, a leading scientist in the field, served the world's first hamburger grown directly from animal cells to a panel of judges. They were pleasantly surprised, noting that it "tasted close to meat."[1] Eight years later, this novel meat—commonly referred to as "cultured meat"[2]—is about to take the leap from laboratory bioreactors onto consumers' dinner plates. In what has been described as a "watershed moment," Singapore became the first country in the world to grant regulatory approval for a cultured meat product in December 2020 (Huling 2020). As a real step toward making cultured meat an accessible alternative for consumers, this development is indeed significant. Nevertheless, while proponents of cultured meat underscore its promise to radically transform our food system, we are in many ways "locked-in" to unsustainable agricultural practices and meat-intense diets (Joy 2009; McMichael 2009). As such, there may be many bumps in the road for such a transition—not least the issue of harnessing interest among consumers (Bryant and Barnett 2020).

In this chapter, we unpack consumers' response to cultured meat. We begin by introducing the phenomenon and history of cultured meat, before reviewing current literature on relations between cultured meat and sustainability. We devote our main discussion to the role of perceived (un)naturalness and (un)familiarity in mediating consumer skepticism toward cultured meat, and how consumer responses are imbued in contemporary "meat cultures." The concept of "meat culture" here refers to "shared beliefs about, perspectives on, and experiences of meat," developed through "representations and discourses, practices and behaviours, diets and tastes" (Potts 2016, 20). While meat cultures (and systems) do vary across geographies and social groups, we focus primarily on contemporary Western meat cultures characterized by industrial, "post-domestic" meat production.[3] We ultimately argue that deeply entrenched systems and cultures existing around meat pose barriers for consumer acceptance of such a "technotopian" alternative to conventional meat.

ON THE ROAD TO SUSTAINABLE (CULTURED) MEAT

There is little controversy in stating that contemporary food production is deeply unsustainable. The global food system requires vast amounts of energy, land, and water, and is responsible for at least 25 percent of global greenhouse gas (GHG) emissions (Ritchie and Roser 2020). Moreover, half a decade of rapidly industrialized and intensified agricultural practices has led to rapid deforestation, biodiversity loss, soil loss, and natural resource depletion (Ericksen 2008).

Neither is it controversial to point to *meat* as a culprit for this unsustainability. Globally, meat production has more than quadrupled since the 1960s, and consumer demand is expected to increase further in the next decades (Bhat et al. 2019). This growing rate of meat production and consumption poses extensive risks for the environment and global health (González et al. 2020). Therefore, perhaps *the* greatest challenge of transforming the food system, and indeed to ensure a sustainable future, will be to facilitate sustainable protein production (Fresco 2009). How to go about such a transition, however, is certainly a more controversial topic.

Most consumers seem unwilling to reduce meat intake despite being increasingly concerned about both animal welfare and sustainability (Loughnan et al. 2010). In the critical meat consumption literature, this conundrum is commonly referred to as the "meat paradox," pointing to the fact that we continue to eat large amounts of meat without having resources to adequately justify that we breed and kill animals for food. To deal with the cognitive dissonance arising from this, consumers engage in twin processes of *denial* and *rationalization* (Joy 2009; Syse and Bjørkdahl 2021)—both, as we shall see, influencing the dynamics in consumers' perceptions of (cultured) meat. As consumers are inclined toward consuming meat both structurally *and* culturally, a "second nutrition transition"—this time toward reduced meat intake—is unlikely to occur at a meaningful scale any time soon (Cole and McCoskey 2013). If we consider ourselves "locked-in" to meat consumption, we need to rethink how we produce our meat in the first place. Enter cultured meat.

Cultured Meat: From Science-Fiction to Reality

In simple terms, cultured meat is meat grown from animal stem cells, cultivated outside the animal.[4] There are two main ways to produce cultured meat: through culturing cells or through fermenting bacteria (see, for example, Burton 2019, 35). To date, most focus has been on cell-culturing. The process can be simplified as such: once "starter" cells are collected, they are "fed" glucose and amino acids and grown into proteins in a bioreactor (Kadim et al. 2015; Post et al. 2020). The only involvement of the animal is through the donation of a suitable cell.[5] Hence, several tonnes of meat can be produced from just a few cells. In theory, shifting to cultured meat production could allow bypassing conventional animal agriculture altogether, while also increasing food security and human well-being, reducing animal suffering, and mitigating some of the most pressing environmental ramifications connected to meat production and consumption (Sharma et al. 2015; Gasteratos 2019).

Neither the idea, nor the process, of cultivating meat from cells can be considered wholly new. Winston Churchill's early prediction of "synthetic foods" has become almost clichéd point of reference when considering the history of cultured meat, where he famously wrote that "we shall escape the absurdity of growing a whole chicken in order to eat the breast or wing, by growing these parts separately under a suitable medium" (Churchill and Spurrier 1931). Prior to that, the French surgeon and biologist Alexis Carrel had been able to keep embryonic chicken heart tissue cultures alive and dividing for 34 years, from 1912 to 1946 (Jiang 2012). Going back even further, the idea of cultured meat can be found in utopian fiction novels from the 1800s (McHugh 2010). The U.S. Food and Drug Administration's approval of production of cultured meat in 1995 marked an important step for the technology (Bhat et al. 2019). Since then, major actors in cultured meat development have been NASA, funding research for the purpose of feeding astronauts in the early 2000s; the Dutch government, funding research at Utrecht University between 2004 and 2009; and several private sector actors (Chiles 2013). In 2008, the first cultured meat symposium was held in Norway (Kadim et al. 2015), and then Post's 2013 burger signified that cultivating meat was not only possible but that it could become commercially viable (Stephens et al. 2019).

With technological advancement and economies of scale, cultured meat production has become much cheaper and more efficient. With a hefty cost of 335,000 USD, Post's burger was quickly dubbed "the most expensive burger in the world" (Jah 2013). This price has been brought down to only a fraction since then, however, and some expect production costs to become competitive with that of conventional meat eventually (Mattick and Allenby 2013). There are currently numerous start-ups around the world working on cultured meat, in addition to other cell-based products such as milk, eggs, and leather (Stephens et al. 2019). While some companies have near market-ready products, commercialization has been impeded by regulatory procedures (Fernández 2020). Given the rapid technological advancement, cost reduction, and scaling of production, some have pointed to the similarities between today's cellular agriculture and the Internet in its infancy (Shigeta 2020). As Mark Post once stated in an interview, "There is no future for traditional meat. . . . Eventually, I think, we will completely dissociate meat from its traditional form."[6]

The Promises of Cultured Meat: Can We Have Our Cake and Eat It Too?

The belief in cultured meat's ability to disrupt the current meat system rests on the premise that cultured meat would benefit the environment, human health, and animal welfare. In terms of environmental footprint, provisional life cycle analyses indicate that cultured meat production will contribute to less emissions, and will use far less land and water, than conventional meat production (Tuomisto et al. 2014). While environmental impact will depend on how cells are grown and nurtured, new plant-based cell-culture media and feeds are being developed to promote sustainability (see Post et al. 2020). However, cultured meat production is more energy intensive than conventional animal farming, and renewable energy resources are required to make upscaling sustainable (Mattick et al. 2015). Unlike conventional meat production, cultured meat only produces CO_2 and no other GHG emissions, meaning that all direct emissions can in theory be mitigated by future renewables (Jiang et al. 2020).

Cultured meat may help solve many of the health risks tied to conventional meat consumption. For instance, transitioning to cultured meat could significantly reduce the risks of food contamination, the spreading of animal diseases and zoonoses, and antibiotic resistance associated with industrial livestock production (Landers et al. 2012; Sharma et al. 2015; Post et al. 2020). Because cell-cultivation occurs in a sterile production environment, cultured meat may offer a higher level of food safety than conventional meat in general (Welin and Van der Weele 2012). Finally, while meat-heavy consumer diets lead to harmful health conditions and lifestyle illnesses such as obesity, diabetes, and hypertension (Sharma et al. 2015), cell-culturing technology might be able to alter the nutritional profile of meat and engineer meats with reduced health risk (Hopkins and Dacey 2008; Bhat et al. 2015).

Cultured meat opens the possibility to not only reduce environmental impact of food production and consumption, but also imagine new ways of cultivating land and managing natural resources. Much of the 77 percent of agricultural land currently used for livestock or livestock feed (Ritchie and Roser 2019) could instead be used to grow crops for human consumption and thus help increase global food security (Tuomisto 2010). Allegedly, land used for livestock production could be repurposed, and grazing land "rewilded" to reproduce new habitats for wild plant and animal species while ensuring a higher carbon uptake from photosynthesis. Transitioning to cultured meat production would drastically reduce the demand for livestock, freeing up space for those remaining (Sharma et al. 2015). This could in turn allow for maintaining a more humane livestock sector alongside cultured meat. Hence, in theory, cultured meat could make the production process even more efficient, while at the same time improve animal welfare. In the spirit of techno-optimism, the "promissory" discourse on cultured meat (Jönsson 2016, 2020; Helliwell and Burton 2021) tells us that we can have our cake and eat it too.

The Pitfalls of Cultured Meat: Too Late for Change?

However, there are still many challenges and uncertainties to cultured meat production. While production seems feasible, challenges are related to commercialization and upscaling of cell-based proteins while making them safe, affordable, and desirable for consumers (Stephens et al. 2018). While animal proteins are relatively straightforward, mimicking fat cells, nerves, blood, and meat "scaffolding" is far more difficult, and this will be a determining factor for the overall success of the industry (Jiang et al. 2020): Will it in fact look and taste like meat? As with increasingly meat-like plant-based analogues, implementing such a novel food into our current regulatory and policy framework may also prove challenging, and different interest groups are already contesting the rights to the "meat" label (Stephens et al. 2018). Moreover, researchers have pointed out the need for more high-quality, peer-reviewed life cycle analyzes to assess potential climate effects (Lynch and Pierrehumbert 2019). Several studies have become more modest in their claims about climate benefits than what was previously proclaimed (Mattick et al. 2015; Tuomisto 2019), as this will depend on the specific environmental footprints and use of decarbonized energy in production (Lynch and Pierrehumbert 2019).

While most accounts point to these as challenges *to be overcome*, cultured meat can also be criticized on more fundamental terms. Jönsson (2016) problematizes the positive hype, arguing that cultured meat agriculture is not unlike other "technotopian" visions for future developments. Drawing on lessons learned from previous technology-driven major disruptions in other industries, Burton (2019, 43) further stresses the importance of considering pitfalls and limitations: "Visions of radically different food futures . . . are formed when optimism for the new technology is high and understanding of the limitations low." Some have argued that cultured meat represents a potentially problematic continuation of the development of more technology-intensive production systems globally and an increasing dependence on technology in society (Bhat et al. 2015) and creates new forms of socioeconomic inequality, as well as new "winners" and "losers" within the food system (Stephens et al. 2018; Helliwell and Burton 2021).

A Final Hurdle: Are Consumers Ready?

Cultured meat clearly does not belong to the universe of science fiction any longer. But, gaining *consumer accept* has been framed as "perhaps the most significant challenge" for realizing cultured meat (Bryant and Barnett 2019, 104). Cultured meat might be considered advantageous for consumers: unlike most other meat alternatives, it could simply replace the meat components already figuring in established meat practices and cultures. Seemingly trivial aspects of "doing food," such as acquiring relevant cooking skills, currently represent barriers for reducing meat consumption (Twine 2017; Mylan 2018). With cultured meat, the focus is put on changing systems rather than meat consumption *practices* per se. According to many of its proponents, cultured meat therefore has the potential to reinvent contemporary meat *systems*, without necessarily intervening with stubborn meat *cultures*. Such a "shallow" reading of contemporary meat cultures, however, fails to acknowledge that meat cultures result from a dynamic interplay between the forces of consumption and production (Horowitz 2006). As pointed out by Rollin et al. (2011, 100), if benefits are not perceived to be important enough, "the majority of people [will] question the need for, and usefulness of, novel food technologies." Moreover, as cultured meat is presented as a meat substitute, it is by default also compared directly to conventional meat, and consumer acceptance must be understood in light of established dynamics of production and consumption. Through the lens of complex meat cultures, inevitable success for the transition to cultured meat seems less obvious.

It does not matter how efficient, sustainable, or cost-effective the technology is, if consumers do not want the final product. While the industry is optimistic, and consumer accept seems to be increasing (Bryant and Barnett 2020), consumers are still skeptical. The idea of cultured meat seems to initiate a "yuck"-response in consumers, who perceive it to be "unnatural," "fake," "unhealthy," and "disgusting" (ibid). The perception of cultured meat as *unnatural* is particularly interesting considering how relations between people, nature, and technology have evolved over time in modern food systems (Potts 2016). While there is lots of variance in production methods, we here take versions of "factory farms" as point of reference when referring to conventional meat production. Factory farming, which constitutes 74 percent of all farming globally,[7] is defined as "corporations that confine, breed, fatten, and slaughter nonhuman animals using modern industrial methods" (Glenn 2004, 64). When taking into account that both the technology-intensity of food production and the distance between consumers and processes that turn animals into food have increased fundamentally over the past 50 years (Bjørkdahl and Syse 2019), a transition toward cultured meat arguably seems like a less radical development. Still, the naturalness aspect remains at the heart of consumers' attitudes. Leaning on scholars such as Siegrist et al. (2018, 214), we understand perceived naturalness as a "heuristic attribute that consumers use as a positive indicator of food quality." Moreover, in the context of cultured meat, we understand perceptions of naturalness to be entwined with emotions of disgust (Wilks, Hornsey, and Bloom 2020) and co-shaped by processes within the mentioned "meat paradox."

In 1994, bioethicist Arthur Caplan coined "the yuck factor" to describe various instinctive and negative responses to new food technologies (Schmidt 2008). The term has become widely used in relation to cultured meat. "Yuck" is rooted in disgust, which evolutionary psychologists argue stem from our ancestors having to protect themselves from foreign threats—such as contamination with poisons, pathogens, and parasites—in the process of expanding food supplies (Russell and Lux 2009; Egolf et al. 2019; Thiele 2019). However, while disgust is understood as a physical reaction to threats, it is not necessarily an innate emotion (Russell and Lux 2009). Rather, it has played an important role in regulating social interaction through moral codes and group membership, developed through social learning processes, and mediated through social norms (Kelly and Morar 2014; Thiele 2019).

This is also how disgust can be connected to a broader scholarship on meat-eating rationalization. Here, Melanie Joy (2009) has been particularly influential in explaining how people become socialized into believing that meat eating is natural, grounded in our biology, and needed to live healthy lives. Joy coined the three "Ns"—*natural, normal,* and *necessary*—used to justify paradoxes of meat eating. In this literature, the "natural" category is often linked to human biology—eating meat is understood to be part of human nature (Dowsett et al. 2018). This form of argumentation speaks directly to biology—biological hierarchy, natural selection, human evolution, and so on—thus pointing to the inherent naturalness of eating meat; the argument being that our bodies biologically both need and crave meat. Further linked to survival, strength, development, and health (Piazza et al. 2015), meat is also thought of as a *necessity*. Here, connections between meat and masculinity enter too, based on the assumption that men in particular need meat for strength and health (Rothberger 2013). The "normal" category refers to justification through social norms: it is normal to eat meat because the majority does—and have always done—so, and because meat is a routinized and unquestioned part of the everyday life (Piazza et al. 2015; Mylan 2018). Clearly, there are sliding transitions between the three categories—upheld and justified by social institutions and organizations—each of them reinforcing the others (Joy 2009). Joy's conceptualization was further developed by Piazza et al. (2015), adding a fourth "N"—*nice*—to demonstrate the importance of taste, appreciation, and enjoyment in rationalizing meat eating. Noticeably, moral virtue seems to be downplayed, as the growing distance between sites of meat production and practices of meat consumption facilitates consumer denial of the processes that bring animal flesh onto dinner plates (Syse and Bjørkdahl 2021). Our argument here is that some forms of rationalization co-shape what is considered potential threats to health, strength, and established social norms, and hence also contribute to shaping "yuck." We return to how this plays out when consumers are faced with the idea of cultured meat later.

(UN)NATURAL OR (UN)FAMILIAR? UNPACKING CONSUMERS' QUALMS OVER CULTURED MEAT

Consumer responses to the idea of cultured meat have been lukewarm compared to other meat alternatives on the market (Hartmann and Siegrist 2017; Jiang et al. 20). Hence, the topic of consumer acceptance has taken center stage in social studies of cultured meat. In order to understand why and how aversive responses against cultured meat occur and persist, we start by highlighting the ways in which cultured meat is framed in public debates, before discussing how emotions of disgust, perceptions of naturalness, and product familiarity in contemporary meat cultures shape how consumers perceive of cultured meat.

Technology Framings and "Yuck" Responses

As cultured meat is still, in most cases, a hypothetical product, how it is *framed* forms the basis for consumer acceptance. This makes it highly sensitive to the kind of descriptions provided (Bryant and Barnett 2020), which have centered around two main narratives. The first, endorsed by both animal activists and academics, highlights beneficial aspects in relation to animal welfare, climate change mitigation, and food security by framing cultured meat as "clean," "animal-free," or "victimless" meat (Bhat et al. 2015; PETA 2017; Animals Australia 2018). The second, dominated by industry actors (and academics), presents cultured meat as a transformative technology with the potential to radically shift how we produce and think of meat today, as well as to alter future relations between animals and humans (Painter et al. 2020). The latter has been central in media attention: primarily event driven, popular press has typically framed cultured meat as a "scientific discovery" (Bryant 2020, 2; Painter 2020), employing "imagery such as test tubes and lab coats" to illustrate this point (Bryant and Barnett 2020, 20). Commonly used names for cultured meat—"in vitro," "synthetic," "artificial," "lab-grown"— have been found to anchor cultured meat to existing food technologies, such as genetic engineering (Bryant and Barnett 2019). More speculative accounts of the game changing potentials for cultured meat have surfaced, further emphasizing the peculiarities of cultured compared to conventional meat production. For instance, the idea of "hybrid meats"—blending different species to create new taste and nutritional profiles—has emerged. More controversial are the ideas of decoupling meat products from existing animal species, or to cultivate meat from exotic animals and extinct species (Bhat et al. 2015). Even the prospect of "ethical" or "victimless" cannibalism (Milburn 2016) has sparked sensationalist headlines.[8] Online commentaries and blogs have referenced dystopic visions from mid- to late 1900s scientific and fictional narratives of cultured meat as a consumer capitalist "frankenfood" developed to the extreme (Chiles 2013). While the technological framing has taken center stage, it is important to note that both framings focus on production process, rather than consumption, and stress how cultured meat *differ* from conventional meat.

As noted, the idea that scientists are cultivating meat from animal cells in laboratories seems to trigger a "yuck" reaction in consumers, who consider it to be "freakish," "weird," and "fake" (Verbeke et al. 2015; Laestadius and Caldwell 2015; Bekker et al. 2017), with perceived unnaturalness emerging as a major concern (Wilks et al. 2020). "Yuck" is understood as an intuitive moral judgment, with roots in disgust (Kelly and Morar 2014). Connected to selective advantage, Charles Darwin described the disgust emotion as "excited by anything unusual in the appearance, odour, or nature of our food" (cited in Miller 1998, 1). While some forms of repugnance seem to be universal (Rozin and Fallon 1987), disgust perceptions also differ widely between countries and communities, and have changed throughout history (Scmidt 2008). Hence, disgust can be understood to be socially learned and culturally mediated (Russell and Lux 2009)—in other words requiring "enculturation" (Thiele 2019, 4).

While technology in many ways has "reduced the evolutionary impact of natural predators and ecological adversity" (Thiele 2019, 3), it also evokes concerns around "tampering with nature" and "playing god" (Rollin et al. 2011). Egolf et al. (2019) suggest that risk assessments are unconsciously performed through the "disgust system," where *new* food technologies are perceived as unnatural and thus riskier, illustrating how perceptions of risk and the natural intersect. Moreover, while consumers tend to perceive "natural" (or pure) products as healthier and less risky (Rozin 2005; Siegrist et al. 2017), there seems to be little agreement of what naturalness entails in practice. Rather, perception of naturalness develops through established practices and learning processes, co-shaped by social norms and specific cultural contexts. On these grounds, disgust—and, by extension, naturalness—can be considered a "moving target" (Thiele 2019, 4).

Having been particularly pronounced in consumers' aversive reactions to technologies such as cloning, nanotechnology, and genetically modified crops (Kulinowski 2004; Russell and Lux 2009), perceived unnaturalness is now also emerging as a key barrier for consumer acceptance of cultured meat (Hartmann and Siegrist 2017; Siegrist and Sütterlin 2017; Bryant and Barnett 2020; Jiang et al. 2020). Given consumers' established sensitivity toward technological mediation in foods, lofty and technical representations of production processes seem to prevent consumers from embracing this novel food. Siegrist et al. (2018) examined consumers' willingness to taste cultured meat by using technical versus nontechnical phrasing for its descriptions and found that acceptance can be increased by providing a nontechnical description. The authors suggested that if descriptions and information highlight similarities with conventional meat, perceived unnaturalness and disgust likely decrease and consumers are more willing to eat it. This is a paradox for an industry that emphasizes differences and disruptive potential over similarities with conventional meat. Moreover, it underscores the need to understand how consumers compare conventional and cultured meat, as it seems to rest on a dichotomy—constructed in consumers' minds—between conventional meat as *natural* and cultured meat as *unnatural* (Siegrist and Sütterlin 2017).

Studies have, for instance, found that consumers understand the domestication of animals to be less unnatural than, for instance, genetic engineering (Rozin 2005; Siegrist et al. 2017). Scholars have considered this surprising given that genetic engineering produces minimal change to genotype and phenotype through the insertion of one single gene, while domestication represents an intrusion to wildlife, producing major and irreversible changes in the genotype and phenotype of wild species (Rozin 2005). Indeed, according to Potts (2016, 13), we have witnessed an "artificial evolution" of certain species of wild animals into hordes of livestock, far outnumbering their wild counterparts. This has been enabled by industrial farming practices, in which "technological changes have enabled the selective breeding, intensive farming, speedy killing, dismembering and packaging of nonhuman species" (Potts 2016, 18). Meanwhile, standardization and mechanization remove agriculture away from traditional conditions (Potts 2016). Whether we talk about conventional or cultured meat production, the bottom line is that "naturalness" is a poor evaluation metric. Nevertheless, it is telling of what qualities consumers do and do not expect from a "natural" foodstuff today: if the argument is that any inherent naturalness declines along with increased human and/or technological intervention (Rozin 2005), we must acknowledge that such intervention is more easily perceived by consumers when new technologies are added to the equation. Crucial in this context are the findings of Wilks et al. (2020), that analytical reasoning of systemic benefits for people, nature, and animals is not necessarily central to peoples' perception of naturalness. Rather, these are affective responses based on disgust and safety concerns, which again are understood as socially contingent.

In extension, information about (unfamiliar) production processes in general affects consumers' perceptions of naturalness (Rozin 2005; Siegrist 2016). Naturalness perceptions are often balanced off against closeness to what is considered traditional production modes (e.g., handmade, local, etc.), whereas machine contact and processing tend to decrease perceptions of naturalness (Abouab and Gomez 2015). Additionally, chemical transformation can have a stronger effect on peoples' naturalness perception than physical transformation, and the extent to which a product has been in contact with what is considered unnatural entities also negatively affects naturalness perceptions (Rozin 2005). Granted, imaginaries of meat grown in petri dishes driven by large chemical reactors are quite far away from the familiar, the traditional, what is encultured into being normal—both in terms of meat consumption and production. Moreover, Tenbult et al. (2005) have found that those products consumers understand to be necessary for people's diets are immediately conceived to be more natural than less necessary products. As previously noted, the common belief in meat's importance for strength and good health is at the heart of rationalizing meat eating (Joy 2009). The firm establishment of meat in diets and cultures across the world is thus significant for understanding how perceptions of disgust, the natural and existing worldviews entwine. Acceptance, then, would ultimately depend on consumers' efforts to actively evaluate the benefits of cultured meat, as presented by its promoters, against conventional meat.

Confronting the (Cultured) "Meat Paradox"

As we have noted, when cultured meat is presented to consumers, the production process—and how it differs from that of conventional meat—is foregrounded. To understand consumers' reluctance to adopt cultured meat, then, we must not only understand aversions to cultured meat but also acceptance of conventional meat. We turn to these dynamics in light of the "meat paradox."

The meat paradox is considered a result of spatial, social, and cultural processes of alienation between consumers and the animals we eat (Bjørkdahl and Syse 2019; Syse and Bjørkdahl 2021). For most of agricultural history, humans have lived in proximity to, and developed close relationships with, their animals (Leroy and Praet 2015). However, in many contemporary ("post-domestic") societies, farm animals have become increasingly concentrated and isolated, their identities reduced to that of livestock (Joy 2009) or machines in a factory. After decades of streamlining and industrializing production methods, both the physical and cognitive distance between consumers and animals have increased, and the production processes connecting them are rendered out of sight and out of mind (Syse and Bjørkdahl 2021). This way, most consumers have become removed from resources and rituals previously used to justify and make sense of animal killing and, thus also, meat eating. Consequently, the share of people possessing knowledge of the work and skills involved in meat production has decreased (Ibid). As meat eating is abundant and meat production largely outsourced, the once intimate connection between humans and the animals we eat is challenged (Leroy and Praet 2017). Rather, contemporary meat cultures in consumer societies revolve primarily around the *consumption*, not production, of meat. Therefore, while the starting point for production—the animal itself—remains tangible, the remaining production and provisioning processes have increasingly become a "black box" for consumers. In comparison, these processes are what is brought to the forefront when consumers are confronted with cultured meat.

In contemporary meat cultures, meat has become a very convenient foodstuff (Leroy and Degreef 2015). With industrial production and streamlined provision systems—aided by supermarkets, refrigerators, freezers, and new meat packaging technology—meat sales became more efficient, accessible, and standardized (Syse and Bjørkdahl 2021). Attributes which tie the final product to its origin are increasingly removed, and different techniques and technologies are used to alter shape, form, texture, taste, and color of meat products as not to resemble the animal (Leroy and Degreef 2015). As Hopkins and Dacey (2008, 580) write,

> The way meat is presented to consumers avoids triggering horror or sympathy by being sterile and distancing—it appears in neat and nicely wrapped packages under bright lighting in the supermarket; fresh, clean and detached from its source, sometimes ground or covered in spices, and largely cut in such a way that we cannot even tell by looking which part of the animal the tissue comes from.

Through advertising and packaging designs, meat industries have been able to construct a discourse around production that emphasizes animal welfare, but which arguably misrepresents actual production conditions (Bjørkdahl and Syse 2021). This evolution has rendered meat an "ingredient," further abstracted from the animals it derives from, so that people simply see "food" (Joy 2009, 5). Moreover, as the interlinkages between production practices and consumption have been removed from the social consciousness in many Western countries, "food simply 'comes from the supermarket' and little thought is given to how it got there" (Hoogland et al. 2005, 16).

Keeping the meat paradox in mind, then, it is not surprising that consumers often react negatively when presented with foods—and descriptions of foods—that are reminiscent of their animal origin compared to when this is not the case (Kunst and Hohle 2016; Syse and Bjørkdahl 2021). In fact, conventional meat production and provision are steeped in processes that might be unsettling for the consumer and ignite disgust, and even those who are comfortable with their meat consumption tend to experience discomfort if confronted with the process of industrial meat production (Hopkins and Dacey 2008). Given the largely hidden production processes, consumers must seldom face these issues in direct relation to their own meat consumption. Rather, people find ways to "forget, neglect, ignore, overlook, cover up, and marginalize that meat comes from a sentient creature" (Syse and Bjørkdahl 2021, 131). Hence, even consumers who have moral qualms with consuming animals are allowed to continue eating meat, by opting for "meal preparations where meat and especially its animal origin are less prominent, for example due to higher forms of processing" (Grunert 2006, 156–157). This enables *denial* among meat eaters. Indeed, "savvy marketers and good advertising people know how to appeal to emotion, gut rationality, and visceral fears. That's what they're selling—the manipulation of 'yuck'" (Caplan, cited in Schmidt 2008, 525).

This established convenience is arguably disturbed as consumers are directly confronted with role of the animal in cultured meat processing. To highlight the revolutionary potential of cultured meat, the industry has sought to emphasize the production process and how it diverges from conventional meat. Thus, cultured meat, it seems, unsettles unquestioned processes, and ignites new evaluation processes, for consumers. Paradoxically then, consumers seem to become more concerned with (the role of) the animal in relation to cultured meat consumption than in relation to conventional meat consumption.

Practicing animal slaughter at an astonishing rate and scale is fundamental for the conventional meat industry, yet this is not necessarily evident to the consumer due to the ways in which meat is consumed today. Even though this paradigm would be rendered obsolete by cultivating meat from cells instead of harnessing it from slaughtered animals, consumers are unavoidably reminded of the animal origin of their food when presented with cultured meat. The strong focus on production processes makes the connection between animals and meat eating inevitable—and seemingly uncomfortable—for consumers.

Clearly, harnessing acceptance for a product that does not yet exist on the market is challenging. While consumers' assessments of conventional meat are tied to the consumption of meat as a food ingredient, their assessments of cultured meat can only be based on available information. As we have argued, dominant framings of cultured meat emphasize its radical divergence from conventional meat. While surfacing as naturalness, then, it seems that consumer accept may be more contingent on *familiarity*—an argument which is also supported by empirical data (Wilks et al. 2020). While the promise of cultured meat rests on its ability to easily replace meat as a food ingredient, thus allowing consumers to uphold familiar food routines and practices, it undeniably also appears to be something altogether different from regular meat, thus being *unfamiliar* to consumers. As such, we see the contours of a "cultured meat paradox": although cultured meat could, in theory, solve the meat paradox, the meat paradox could also be a barrier for its success in the first place. The experiences that could forge similar emotions and practices in relation to cultured meat, as those of conventional meat, are not (yet) possible or available to consumers. This lack of familiarity is arguably central to aversions against cultured meat, as how we perceive and understand food depends on the material, tangible food product itself as well as the discourses attached to it.

Future Scenarios for (Cultured) Meat: Changing Human-Animal Connections?

Returning to modes of production, proponents hold that cultured meat has the potential to disrupt a highly problematic meat industry while reducing the social and environmental harms associated with livestock farming. Today, the developments in the field are shared between numerous small actors in the form of start-ups across the world, in all continents. This may not be the case in the future, once larger actors start gaining interest. Given the significant role that information source plays on disgust responses (Siegrist et al. 2018; Bryant and Barnett 2020), the issue of trust in who and what is promoting new food technologies becomes central (Egolf et al. 2019). In the context of cultured meat, some of the most prominent voices and academics in the field also have stakes in the success of the industry (Painter et al. 2020). Jönsson (2016, 729) refers to such actors as "sociotechnicians"—"actors simultaneously working on technological projects and defining their goals and questions." Such blurring of interests could make people more skeptical to the technology and question its promissory discourse. Moreover, while technology is propelled forward by the influx of industrial giants, such as Tyson

Foods and Cargill, investing in cultured meat development (Wilks et al. 2020), this trend may also lead to worries of monopolizing and how it could affect people, animals, and the environment. In a more "dystopian" scenario, then, cultured meat could become another mega industry serving the interest of large corporations and not consumers, fostering further (social, cultural, spatial) alienation (Jönsson 2016).

Yet some have envisioned new ways to forge stronger human-animal connections through cultured meat. For instance, Van der Weele and Driessen (2019, 2) sketch out a "pig in the backyard" scenario, "in which new technology [is] mingled with traditional cultural ideals, the hope of guilt-free meat-eating and intimate relations with genuinely happy animals and the values of local production." Through small-scale, de-centralized meat production in "animal-friendly (urban) farms," a handful of well-treated animals in a small cultivation farm could supply the local community with meat (Van der Weele and Tramper 2014, 294). Next to these cell-donor animals, a comparatively small quantity of high-quality free-range animals could be reared for conventional slaughter and sold as premium meats. While this would not solve the "cultured meat paradox" discussed earlier—and still demand a radical shift in how consumers perceived the relations between animals, production, and consumption of (cultured) meat—such localized, "village-scale" production (ibid: 296) could, in theory, give local communities ownership of their food resources, while allowing full traceability and transparency from "farm to fork." In such a scenario, shorter food chains could free up resources from transport. Would consumers find such a system less natural than today's factory farms and "(dis)assembly line" slaughterhouses? Though a worthwhile thought experiment, however, such a neighborhood scale production is unlikely to become the norm so long as the cultured meat industry seeks to outcompete conventional agriculture, as exemplified by current startups' plans for upscaling (Helliwell and Burton 2021, 185; see also Jönsson 2021).

CONCLUSION

Despite the current meat system's stubbornness, recent developments in alternative meats, and particularly the advent of cultured meat, indicate a potential for disruptive change in how we produce and consume meat. In this chapter, we have illuminated the promises and potential pitfalls of cultured meat, particularly emphasizing the role of consumers in rejecting or embracing this novel meat technology. We have argued that, somewhat paradoxically, the cognitive and physical distance between humans and animals that has been facilitated by ever-industrialized animal agriculture may lead consumers to reject cultured meat, given the renewed focus on the *production process* as opposed to the final product or meat ingredient. This underscores the challenges of rapidly developing technologies in disrupting deeply embedded meat systems and cultures manifesting over centuries.

To reduce emissions from unsustainable protein production, change in consumer demand is essential (Fresco 2009). In this regard, cultured meat offers a "technotopian" solution to the "meat paradox," promising continued meat consumption while reducing meat's impacts on the environment, animals, and potentially human health. Despite these promises, many consumers remain unconvinced. Harnessing enthusiasm among consumers would arguably require them to be either highly critical toward their own meat intake or genuinely open to and excited about new food technologies. As we, together with others, have argued, however, neither is the case. Consumers seem relatively comfortable in their meat-eating habits. Not only do consumers rationalize their own meat consumption (Joy 2009), but industry actors aid this by facilitating a widespread denial of the connection between animal killing and meat eating (Syse and Bjørkdahl 2021). Moreover, the balance between "wow" and "yuck" when confronted with food technology is delicate, as previously demonstrated by, for instance, consumers' rejection of GMO foods (Kulinowski 2004). Equally sensational, technology-heavy framings of cultured meat fuel consumers' "yuck" responses, often on the grounds of it breaking with what is perceived as natural.

While it is difficult to predict the future of food technologies, the rapid development of cultured meat and upscaling of the industry suggests that it can become a key component of meat systems and cultures in the coming years and decades. What a future with cultured meat will look like is highly uncertain. Still very much framed as a scientific discovery, the question is what cultured meat will be once it properly escapes the laboratories and reaches a wider market, if at all. To answer this question, we will need to collectively imagine broader (cultured) "meat futures"—to chart out and imagine the possibilities and challenges for both cultured and conventional meat in the times to come. How meat cultures evolve along with cultured meat, and how this will affect consumers' relations to animals and food, remain to be seen.

NOTES

1. https://www.bbc.com/news/science-environment-23576143 (accessed December 8, 2020).

2. Other names include "in vitro," "cell-based," "clean," and "cultivated" meat. While the general practice of producing agricultural products directly from cells was

officially dubbed "cellular agriculture" in 2016, there is no official name for cell-based animal muscle tissue yet (Bryant and Barnett 2019).

3. Bulliet (2005) describes contemporary Western societies as "post-domestic," referring to the psychological and physical decoupling of humans and animals achieved, for example, through increased industrialization.

4. For more in-depth technical descriptions, see, for example, Kadim et al. (2015) and Sharma et al (2015).

5. Until completely animal-free cell-culture media are in use, the "feed" for the cells may also contain animal ingredients (see, for example, Post et al. 2020).

6. https://bistro-invitro.com/en/mark-post/ (accessed May 21, 2021).

7. The Sentience Institute has calculated that 90 percent of global farm animals live in factory farms. This includes 74 percent farmed vertebrate land animals and practically all farmed fish. Source: https://www.sentienceinstitute.org/global-animal-farming-estimates#ftnt1 (accessed December 9, 2020).

8. In 2020, another art installation consisting of meat produced by its artists' own cells sparked controversy: https://www.nytimes.com/2020/12/07/arts/design/Ouroboros-Steak-design-museum.html (accessed April 29, 2021).

REFERENCES

Abouab, Nathalie, and Pierrick Gomez. 2015. "Human Contact Imagined during the Production Process Increases Food Naturalness Perceptions." *Appetite* 91 (August): 273–277. https://doi.org/10.1016/j.appet.2015.04.002.

Animals Australia. 2018. "Soon You'll Be Able to Eat Meat without Hurting Animals!," February 20, 2018. https://www.animalsaustralia.org/features/real-meat-without-hurting-animals.php.

Bekker, Gerben A., Hilde Tobi, and Arnout R. H. Fischer. 2017. "Meet Meat: An Explorative Study on Meat and Cultured Meat as Seen by Chinese, Ethiopians and Dutch." *Appetite* 114 (July): 82–92. https://doi.org/10.1016/j.appet.2017.03.009.

Bhat, Zuhaib Fayaz, Sunil Kumar, and Hina Fayaz. 2015. "In Vitro Meat Production: Challenges and Benefits over Conventional Meat Production." *Journal of Integrative Agriculture* 14 (2): 241–248. https://doi.org/10.1016/S2095-3119(14)60887-X.

Bhat, Zuhaib F., James D. Morton, Susan L. Mason, Alaa El-Din A. Bekhit, and Hina F. Bhat. 2019. "Technological, Regulatory, and Ethical Aspects of In Vitro Meat: A Future Slaughter-Free Harvest." *Comprehensive Reviews in Food Science and Food Safety* 18 (4): 1192–1208. https://doi.org/10.1111/1541-4337.12473.

Bjørkdahl, Kristian, and Karen Lykke Syse. 2019. "Kjøtt, Fremmedgjøring Og Fornektelse." *Nytt Norsk Tidsskrift* 36 (03): 255–267.

Bjørkdahl, Kristian, and Karen Lykke Syse. 2021. "Welfare Washing: Disseminating Disinformation in Meat Marketing." *Society & Animals*, 1–19. https://doi.org/10.1163/15685306-BJA10032.

Bryant, Christopher J. 2020. "Culture, Meat, and Cultured Meat." *Journal of Animal Science* 98 (8). https://doi.org/10.1093/jas/skaa172.

Bryant, Christopher J., and Julie C. Barnett. 2019. "What's in a Name? Consumer Perceptions of in Vitro Meat under Different Names." *Appetite* 137 (June): 104–113. https://doi.org/10.1016/j.appet.2019.02.021.

Bryant, Christopher, and Julie Barnett. 2020. "Consumer Acceptance of Cultured Meat: An Updated Review (2018–2020)." *Applied Sciences* 10 (15): 5201.

Bulliet, Richard W. 2005. *Hunters, Herders, and Hamburgers: The Past and Future of Human-Animal Relationships.* Columbia University Press.

Burton, Rob J. F. 2019. "The Potential Impact of Synthetic Animal Protein on Livestock Production: The New 'War against Agriculture'?" *Journal of Rural Studies* 68: 33–45.

Cassuto, David N. 2007. "Bred Meat: The Cultural Foundation of the Factory Farm." *Law and Contemporary Problems* 70 (1): 59–87.

Chiles, Robert Magneson. 2013. "If They Come, We Will Build It: In Vitro Meat and the Discursive Struggle over Future Agrofood Expectations." *Agriculture and Human Values* 30 (4): 511–523.

Churchill, Winston. 1931. "Fifty Years Hence." *Originally Published in Strand Magazine.*

Cole, Jennifer Rivers, and Suzanne McCoskey. 2013. "Does Global Meat Consumption Follow an Environmental Kuznets Curve?" *Sustainability: Science, Practice and Policy* 9 (2): 26–36.

Dowsett, Elisha, Carolyn Semmler, Heather Bray, Rachel A Ankeny, and Anna Chur-Hansen. 2018. "Neutralising the Meat Paradox: Cognitive Dissonance, Gender, and Eating Animals." *Appetite* 123: 280–288.

Egolf, Aisha, Christina Hartmann, and Michael Siegrist. 2019. "When Evolution Works against the Future: Disgust's Contributions to the Acceptance of New Food Technologies." *Risk Analysis* 39 (7): 1546–1559.

Ericksen, Polly J. 2008. "Conceptualizing Food Systems for Global Environmental Change Research." *Global Environmental Change* 18 (1): 234–245.

Fernández, Clara Rodgríguez. 2020. "You Will Be Eating Cultured Meat Soon: Here's What You Need to Know." *Labiotec.Eu*, April 2, 2020. https://www.labiotech.eu/in-depth/cultured-meat-industry/.

Fresco, Louise O. 2009. "Challenges for Food System Adaptation Today and Tomorrow." *Environmental Science & Policy* 12 (4): 378–385.

Gasteratos, Kristopher. 2019. "90 Reasons to Consider Cellular Agriculture." FAS Student Papers. DASH Harvard. http://nrs.harvard.edu/urn-3:HUL.InstRepos:38573490.

Glenn, Cathy B. 2004. "Constructing Consumables and Consent: A Critical Analysis of Factory Farm Industry Discourse." *Journal of Communication Inquiry* 28 (1): 63–81.

González, Neus, Montse Marquès, Martí Nadal, and José L Domingo. 2020. "Meat Consumption: Which Are the Current Global Risks? A Review of Recent (2010–2020) Evidences." *Food Research International* 12, 109341.

Grunert, Klaus G. 2006. "Future Trends and Consumer Lifestyles with Regard to Meat Consumption." *Meat Science* 74 (1): 149–160.

Hartmann, Christina, and Michael Siegrist. 2017. "Consumer Perception and Behaviour Regarding Sustainable Protein Consumption: A Systematic Review." *Trends in Food Science & Technology* 61: 11–25.

Helliwell, Richard, and Rob J. F. Burton. 2021. "The Promised Land? Exploring the Future Visions and Narrative Silences of Cellular Agriculture in News and Industry Media." *Journal of Rural Studies* 84 (May): 180–191. https://doi.org/10.1016/j.jrurstud.2021.04.002.

Hoogland, Carolien T, Joop de Boer, and Jan J Boersema. 2005. "Transparency of the Meat Chain in the Light of Food Culture and History." *Appetite* 45 (1): 15–23.

Hopkins, Patrick D, and Austin Dacey. 2008. "Vegetarian Meat: Could Technology Save Animals and Satisfy Meat Eaters?" *Journal of Agricultural and Environmental Ethics* 21 (6): 579–596.

Horowitz, Roger. 2006. *Putting Meat on the American Table: Taste, Technology, Transformation.* JHU Press.

Huling, Ryan. 2020. "BREAKING: World's First Approval of Cultivated Meat Sales." *Food Policy Blog, Good Food Institute* (blog). January 12, 2020. https://gfi.org/blog/cultivated-meat-singapore/.

Jah, Alok. 2013. "Synthetic Meat: How the World's Costliest Burger Made It on to the Plate." *The Guardian*, May 8, 2013, sec. Food Science. https://www.theguardian.com/science/2013/aug/05/synthetic-meat-burger-stem-cells.

Jiang, Guihun, Kashif Ameer, Honggyun Kim, Eun-Jung Lee, Karna Ramachandraiah, and Geun-Pyo Hong. 2020. "Strategies for Sustainable Substitution of Livestock Meat." *Foods* 9 (9): 1227.

Jönsson, Erik. 2016. "Benevolent Technotopias and Hitherto Unimaginable Meats: Tracing the Promises of in Vitro Meat." *Social Studies of Science* 46 (5): 725–748.

Jönsson, Erik. 2020. "On Breweries and Bioreactors: Probing the 'Present Futures' of Cellular Agriculture." *Transactions of the Institute of British Geographers* 45 (4): 921–936. https://doi.org/10.1111/tran.12392.

Joy, Melanie. 2009. *Why We Love Dogs, Eat Pigs, and Wear Cows: An Introduction to Carnism.* Red Wheel.

Kadim, Isam T., Osman Mahgoub, Senan Baqir, Bernard Faye, and Roger Purchas. 2015. "Cultured Meat from Muscle Stem Cells: A Review of Challenges and Prospects." *Journal of Integrative Agriculture* 14 (2): 222–233.

Kelly, Daniel, and Nicolae Morar. 2014. "Against the Yuck Factor: On the Ideal Role of Disgust in Society." *Utilitas* 26 (2): 153.

Kulinowski, Kristen. 2004. "Nanotechnology: From 'Wow' to 'Yuck'?" *Bulletin of Science, Technology & Society* 24 (1): 13–20.

Kunst, Jonas R., and Sigrid M. Hohle. 2016. "Meat Eaters by Dissociation: How We Present, Prepare and Talk about Meat Increases Willingness to Eat Meat by Reducing Empathy and Disgust." *Appetite* 105: 758–774.

Laestadius, Linnea I., and Mark A. Caldwell. 2015. "Is the Future of Meat Palatable? Perceptions of in Vitro Meat as Evidenced by Online News Comments." *Public Health Nutrition* 18 (13): 2457–2467.

Landers, Timothy F., Bevin Cohen, Thomas E. Wittum, and Elaine L. Larson. 2012. "A Review of Antibiotic Use in Food Animals: Perspective, Policy, and Potential." *Public Health Reports* 127 (1): 4–22.

Leroy, Frédéric, and Filip Degreef. 2015. "Convenient Meat and Meat Products. Societal and Technological Issues." *Appetite* 94: 40–46.

Leroy, Frédéric, and Istvan Praet. 2015. "Meat Traditions. The Co-Evolution of Humans and Meat." *Appetite* 90: 200–211.

Leroy, Frédéric, and Istvan Praet. 2017. "Animal Killing and Postdomestic Meat Production." *Journal of Agricultural and Environmental Ethics* 30 (1): 67–86.

Loughnan, Steve, Nick Haslam, and Brock Bastian. 2010. "The Role of Meat Consumption in the Denial of Moral Status and Mind to Meat Animals." *Appetite* 55 (1): 156–159.

Lynch, John, and Raymond Pierrehumbert. 2019. "Climate Impacts of Cultured Meat and Beef Cattle." *Frontiers in Sustainable Food Systems* 3: 5.

Mattick, Carolyn, and Brad Allenby. 2013. "The Future of Meat." *Issues in Science and Technology* 30 (1): 64–70.

Mattick, Carolyn S., Amy E. Landis, Braden R. Allenby, and Nicholas J. Genovese. 2015. "Anticipatory Life Cycle Analysis of in Vitro Biomass Cultivation for Cultured Meat Production in the United States." *Environmental Science & Technology* 49 (19): 11941–11949.

McHugh, Susan. 2010. "Real Artificial: Tissue-Cultured Meat, Genetically Modified Farm Animals, and Fictions." *Configurations* 18 (1): 181–197.

McMichael, Philip. 2009. "A Food Regime Genealogy." *The Journal of Peasant Studies* 36 (1): 139–169.

Milburn, Josh. 2016. "Chewing over in Vitro Meat: Animal Ethics, Cannibalism and Social Progress." *Res Publica* 22 (3): 249–265.

Miller, William Ian. 1998. *The Anatomy of Disgust*. Harvard University Press.

Mylan, Josephine. 2018. "Sustainable Consumption in Everyday Life: A Qualitative Study of UK Consumer Experiences of Meat Reduction." *Sustainability* 10 (7): 2307.

Painter, James, J Scott Brennen, and Silje Kristiansen. 2020. "The Coverage of Cultured Meat in the US and UK Traditional Media, 2013–2019: Drivers, Sources, and Competing Narratives." *Climatic Change* 162 (4): 2379–2396.

PETA. 2017. "Yes, This Is Actual Meat, but No Animal Died for It." *PETA* (blog). March 30, 2017. https://www.peta.org/living/food/memphis-meats-debuts-lab-grown-chicken-clean-meat/.

Piazza, Jared, Matthew B. Ruby, Steve Loughnan, Mischel Luong, Juliana Kulik, Hanne M. Watkins, and Mirra Seigerman. 2015. "Rationalizing Meat Consumption. The 4Ns." *Appetite* 91: 114–128.

Post, Mark J., Shulamit Levenberg, David L. Kaplan, Nicholas Genovese, Jianan Fu, Christopher J. Bryant, Nicole Negowetti, Karin Verzijden, and Panagiota Moutsatsou. 2020. "Scientific, Sustainability and Regulatory Challenges of Cultured Meat." *Nature Food* 1 (7): 403–415.

Potts, Annie. 2016. "What Is Meat Culture?" In Potts, Annie (ed) *Meat Culture*, Human-Animal Studies series, vol 17, 1–30. Leiden; Boston: Brill.

Ritchie, Hannah, and Max Roser. 2019. "Meat and Dairy Production." Online Respurce. ourworldindata.org. https://ourworldindata.org/meat-production.

Ritchie, Hannah, and Max Roser. 2020. "Environmental Impacts of Food Production'." Online Resource. ourworldindata.org. https://ourworldindata.org/environmental -impacts-of-food.

Rollin, Fanny, Jean Kennedy, and Josephine Wills. 2011. "Consumers and New Food Technologies." *Trends in Food Science & Technology* 22 (2–3): 99–111.

Rothgerber, Hank. 2013. "Real Men Don't Eat (Vegetable) Quiche: Masculinity and the Justification of Meat Consumption." *Psychology of Men & Masculinity* 14 (4): 363.

Rozin, Paul. 2005. "The Meaning of 'Natural': Process More Important Than Content." *Psychological Science* 16 (8): 652–658. https://doi.org/10.1111/j.1467 -9280.2005.01589.x.

Rozin, Paul, and April E Fallon. 1987. "A Perspective on Disgust." *Psychological Review* 94 (1): 23.

Russell, Stewart, and Colleen Lux. 2009. "Getting over Yuck: Moving from Psychological to Cultural and Sociotechnical Analyses of Responses to Water Recycling." *Water Policy* 11 (1): 21–35. https://doi.org/10.2166/wp.2009.007.

Schmidt, Charles W. 2008. "The Yuck Factor: When Disgust Meets Discovery." *Environmental Health Perspectives* 116 (12): A524–A527. https://doi.org/10.1289 /ehp.116-a524.

Sharma, Shruti, Sukhcharanjit Singh Thind, and Amarjeet Kaur. 2015. "In Vitro Meat Production System: Why and How?" *Journal of Food Science and Technology* 52 (12): 7599–7607. https://doi.org/10.1007/s13197-015-1972-3.

Shigeta, Ron. 2020. "Lab-Grown Meat Is Scaling Like the Internet." *The Spoon* (blog). October 26, 2020. https://thespoon.tech/lab-grown-meat-is-scaling-like-the -internet/.

Siegrist, Michael, and Bernadette Sütterlin. 2017. "Importance of Perceived Naturalness for Acceptance of Food Additives and Cultured Meat." *Appetite* 113 (June): 320–326. https://doi.org/10.1016/j.appet.2017.03.019.

Siegrist, Michael, Bernadette Sütterlin, and Christina Hartmann. 2018. "Perceived Naturalness and Evoked Disgust Influence Acceptance of Cultured Meat." *Meat Science* 139 (May): 213–219. https://doi.org/10.1016/j.meatsci.2018.02.007.

Stephens, Neil, Lucy Di Silvio, Illtud Dunsford, Marianne Ellis, Abigail Glencross, and Alexandra Sexton. 2018. "Bringing Cultured Meat to Market: Technical, Socio-Political, and Regulatory Challenges in Cellular Agriculture." *Trends in Food Science & Technology* 78 (August): 155–166. https://doi.org/10.1016/j.tifs .2018.04.010.

Stephens, Neil, Alexandra E. Sexton, and Clemens Driessen. 2019. "Making Sense of Making Meat: Key Moments in the First 20 Years of Tissue Engineering Muscle to Make Food." *Frontiers in Sustainable Food Systems* 3. https://doi.org/10.3389 /fsufs.2019.00045.

Syse, Karen and Kristian Bjørkdahl. 2021. "The Animal that Therefore was Removed From View." In Tomaž Grušovnik, Karen Syse and Reingard Spannring (eds)

Denialism in Environmental and Animal Abuse: Averting Our Gaze, 127–141. Lanham: Lexington.

Tenbült, Petra, Nanne K. de Vries, Ellen Dreezens, and Carolien Martijn. 2005. "Perceived Naturalness and Acceptance of Genetically Modified Food." *Appetite* 45 (1): 47–50. https://doi.org/10.1016/j.appet.2005.03.004.

Thiele, Leslie Paul. 2019. "The Decline of Yuck: Moral Judgment in the Anthropocene." *Technology in Society* 59 (November): 101153. https://doi.org/10.1016/j.techsoc.2019.101153.

Tuomisto Hanna L. 2010. Food security and protein supply–Cultured meat a solution? Paper presented at: Delivering food security with supply chain led innovations: Understanding supply chains, providing food security, delivering choice. London, 7–9.September. Available at: https://staticmer.emol.cl/Documentos/Campo/2011/08/02/20110802122710.pdf (accessed 7 October 2021).

Tuomisto, Hanna L. 2019. "The Eco-Friendly Burger." *EMBO Reports* 20 (1): e47395. https://doi.org/10.15252/embr.201847395.

Tuomisto, Hanna L., and M. Joost Teixeira de Mattos. 2011. "Environmental Impacts of Cultured Meat Production." *Environmental Science & Technology* 45 (14): 6117–6123. https://doi.org/10.1021/es200130u.

Twine, Richard. 2017. "A Practice Theory Framework for Understanding Vegan Transition." Animal Studies Journal 6 (2): 192–224.

Verbeke, Wim, Afrodita Marcu, Pieter Rutsaert, Rui Gaspar, Beate Seibt, Dave Fletcher, and Julie Barnett. 2015. "'Would You Eat Cultured Meat?': Consumers' Reactions and Attitude Formation in Belgium, Portugal and the United Kingdom." *Meat Science* 102 (April): 49–58. https://doi.org/10.1016/j.meatsci.2014.11.013.

Weele, Cor van der, and Clemens Driessen. 2019. "How Normal Meat Becomes Stranger as Cultured Meat Becomes More Normal; Ambivalence and Ambiguity Below the Surface of Behavior." *Frontiers in Sustainable Food Systems* 3. https://doi.org/10.3389/fsufs.2019.00069.

Weele, Cor van der, and Johannes Tramper. 2014. "Cultured Meat: Every Village Its Own Factory?" *Trends in Biotechnology* 32 (6): 294–296. https://doi.org/10.1016/j.tibtech.2014.04.009.

Welin, Stellan and Cor van der Weele. 2012. "Cultured Meat: Will It Separate Us from Nature?" In Potthast, Thomas and Simon Meisch (eds) *Climate Change and Sustainable Development*, 348–351. Wageningen: Wageningen Academic Publishers

Wilks, Matti, Matthew Hornsey, and Paul Bloom. 2020. "What Does It Mean to Say That Cultured Meat Is Unnatural?" *Appetite*, September, 104960. https://doi.org/10.1016/j.appet.2020.104960.

Index

About the Authors

Dr. Arve Hansen is a researcher at the Centre for Development and the Environment, University of Oslo, Norway.

Dr. Karen Lykke Syse is an associate professor at the Centre for Development and the Environment, University of Oslo, Norway.

Dr. Kristian Bjørkdahl is a postdoctoral fellow at the Centre for Development and the Environment, University of Oslo, Norway.

Dr. Jostein Jakobsen is a researcher at the Centre for Development and the Environment, University of Oslo, Norway.

Dr. Ulrikke Wethal is a postdoctoral researcher at the Centre for Development and the Environment, University of Oslo, Norway.

Mr. Johannes Volden is a doctoral fellow at the Centre for Development and the Environment, University of Oslo.

Professor emerita Kristi Anne Stølen is a social anthropologist at the Centre for Development and the Environment, University of Oslo, Norway.

Dr. Marius Korsnes is a researcher at the Department of Interdisciplinary Studies of Culture, Norwegian University of Science and Technology, Norway.

Dr. Chen Liu is an associate professor of Cultural Geography at the School of Geography and Planning, Sun Yat-sen University, China.

Dr. Kenneth Bo Nielsen is an associate professor at the Department of Social Anthropology, University of Oslo, Norway.

Ms. Hibba Mazhary is a college geography lecturer at St Catherine's College, University of Oxford, UK.

Dr. Sophia Efstathiou is a researcher in the Programme for Applied Ethics, at the Norwegian University of Science and Technology, Norway.

www.ingramcontent.com/pod-product-compliance
Lightning Source LLC
Chambersburg PA
CBHW022312280326
41932CB00010B/1070